MULTICULTURAL
STUDENT PROGRAMS

Trees let your arms fall:
raise them not sharply in supplication . . .
This is no gallant monsoon's flash,
no dashing trade wind's blast.
The fading green of your magic
emanations shall not make pure again
these polluted skies . . . for this
is no ordinary sun

Hone Tuwhare[1]

There are only 90,000 people out there.
Who gives a damn?

Henry Kissinger, 1969[2]

DAY OF TWO SUNS

US Nuclear Testing and the Pacific Islanders

JANE DIBBLIN

NEW AMSTERDAM
New York

First published in the United States of America in 1990 by

NEW AMSTERDAM BOOKS
171 Madison Avenue
New York, NY 10016

By arrangement with Virago Press Ltd., London.

Library of Congress Cataloging-in-Publication Data

Dibblin, Jane.
  Day of two suns: US nuclear testing and the Pacific Islanders/Jane
Dibblin.
     p. cm.
  Includes bibliographical references.
  ISBN 0-941533-73-5 (alk. paper) — ISBN 0-941533-83-2 (pkb. : alk.
paper)
  1. Marshall Islands—Politics and government. 2. Marshall Islands—
Social conditions. 3. Nuclear testing victims—Marshall Islands. 4.
Nuclear testing—Marshall Islands. I. Title.
DU710.D53 1990   90 -39780
996.8'3 — dc20   CIP

ISBN 0-941533-73-5 (cloth)
ISBN 0-941533-83-2 (paper)

This book is printed on acid-free paper.

Printed in the United States of America.

Contents

This book contains a number of references to and quotations from interviews conducted in the Marshall Islands by Mr Glenn Alcalay. Mr Alcalay was a Peace Corps volunteer on Utrik atoll, Marshall Islands, between 1975 and 1977. He initiated a multi-million dollar compensation award for several 'down-wind' atolls, which was successfully attached to the annual US congressional Trust Territory appropriations Bill in 1977.

Mr Alcalay has testified before the US Congress on numerous occasions on behalf of the radiation victims in the Marshall Islands and has petitioned the Trusteeship Council, the Special Committee of Twenty-Four, and the Fourth Committee on Decolonisation of the General Assembly of the United Nations on their behalf.

As a fluent speaker of Marshallese, Mr Alcalay has made several return visits to the Marshalls and has conducted hundreds of interviews with islanders. He was aboard the *Rainbow Warrior* during the historic May 1985 evacuation of the Rongelap islanders. As a freelance writer, Mr Alcalay has been writing about the problems of the Marshall Islands, as well as the other people of Micronesia and the Pacific in general, for more than ten years.

At present Mr Alcalay is at work on his Ph.D in medical anthropology at the New School for Social Research in New York City, studying the sociocultural impact of the nuclear weapons testing programme in the Marshall Islands. In addition, he is at work on a book on the effects of the nuclear testing in the Marshall Islands. He also serves as an adviser to the municipal councils of Rongelap and Utrik atolls with regard to the ongoing problems related to the nuclear testing.

All quotations in this book from Mr Alcalay's interviews are copyrighted by Glenn Alcalay.

Preface

In the autumn of 1986 I went to the Marshall Islands in Micronesia to research this book. I had met and interviewed three women from Micronesia – Lorenza Pedro from Belau, Lijon Eknilang from the Marshall Islands and Chailang Palacios from the Marianas – when they came to London in 1985 and 1986 on speaking tours organised by Women Working for a Nuclear Free and Independent Pacific, a Greenham initiative. They wanted their story told more widely; this book emerged, in part, out of discussions with them.

The seeds of the idea had been sown, however, in 1984 when I heard Hilda Halkyard-Harawira, a Maori woman from Aotearoa/New Zealand, speak passionately and knowingly at an international conference about the nuclear assault on the Pacific. Ursula Owen at Virago provided the soil in which these seeds could grow: a publisher for the book.

This book focuses on two of the Pacific communities devastated by nuclear testing: the people of Rongelap atoll, irradiated by fallout; and the people of Kwajalein atoll, thrown off their land so that their islands and lagoon could become a dartboard for missiles launched from the west coast of the United States. The people of Rongelap have chosen to leave their still-contaminated home and to live on one of the few islands in Kwajalein atoll not taken over by the US. It was there that I went to talk to them.

The background to the testing is the domination of the Marshall Islands by colonial powers over four centuries. There are many contradictions for a white western woman writing a book about the experiences of Black women and men. I have tried to avoid aiding the process of colonialism; rather than observing and interpreting the Marshallese from the perspective of my own culture, I have attempted to describe the events and their political context, and allow the voices of Marshallese people to relate their own experiences.

Wherever I went in the Marshalls I was met with an incredibly warm welcome and a great deal of enthusiasm for this project. As well as 'talking story' – sharing their experiences and insights – people variously put me up, gave me food, interpreted for me, showed me round, inspired me, teased me and generally looked after me. I'd like to thank Abacca Anjain, Jeton Anjain, Nietok Anjain Bien, Renam Anjain, Lijon Eknilang, Katrine Jilej, Admini Koon, Darlene Keju-Johnson, Rosalie Konou, Hermy Lang, Roko Laninvelik, Kinoj Mawilong, Aisen Tima, Julian Riklon and many, many others. Emmet Aluli in Molokai, Hawai'i, was also a source of wisdom, help and encouragement.

This is not the first attempt at documenting the injustices which have been perpetrated in the name of western security in the Marshall islands. Writers to whom I am most indebted for their work and advice are Glenn Alcalay, Harold Jackson, Giff Johnson and Owen Wilkes. The Women Working for a Nuclear Free and Independent Pacific in Britain have also produced two very good booklets (see bibliography).

Writing books and articles is only one way of bringing about change: while I've been doing this, others have been writing letters, gathering petitions, organising demonstrations, conferences and benefits. A tribute is due to all those working in various parts of the globe.

The book itself is a product of many people's help in supplying information, suggesting ideas and reading drafts. For that I'd like to thank Jane Parkin, my editor at Virago, Meg Beresford, Kathy Bor, Fan Bradshaw, Frances Conelly, Martin Dace, Helen Dibblin, Jinny Dunscombe, Julia Goodwin, Jane Graham, Joan Grant, Robyn Holder, Zohl de Ishtar, Mary Kaldor, Loretta Loach, Malcolm MacIntosh, Fiona Morton, Pratibha Parmar, Sheena Phillips, Caroline Rault, Bridget Roberts, Sigrid Shayer, Joan Smith, Jenny Skempton, Manami

Suzuki, Tremor, Sue Upton, Kate Vickers, Edward Vulliamy and colleagues at the *New Statesman*. My family and friends took care of me when I returned from the Marshall Islands with hepatitis and dysentery, kept me going, made me laugh and tolerated my absences; Michele Guimarin did all of the above and she also retyped sections, did extra research, and shared the worries. Thank you.

The advance on the royalties for the first print run paid for the expenses of writing the book: travel, phone calls, photocopying, postage and so on. The royalties on any second print run will go to the nuclear-free and independent Pacific movement. Royalties from the American edition will be given to the Rongelap Resettlement Fund.

In the first edition of this book I overlooked an important acknowledgement. In chapter four, pages 68 to 70, I mentioned David Robie by name but forgot to credit his book describing the evacuation of Rongelap, *Eyes of Fire: The Last Voyage of the Rainbow Warrior* (Philadelphia, New Society Pubs., 1987). The book was also left out of the bibliography, along with Hiromitsu Toyasa's *Goodbye to Rongelap* (TsEukiji Shokan Publishing, Tokyo, 1986), which was footnoted in chapter four. My apologies to Toyasaki and Robie.

Preface to the American Edition

In July 1989, three years after first researching this book, I returned to the Marshall Islands to find Rongelap's senator, Jeton Anjain, in a surprisingly optimistic mood. Maintaining their vigil on the island of Mejato, the people of Rongelap are still waiting to return home. In 1988 an independent review of the Department of Energy data revealed that the danger of continuing to live on Rongelap was more grave than the DOE had ever admitted. The review discovered that DOE scientists had found depressed white blood-cell counts and high levels of plutonium in the urine of people living in Rongelap—but had failed to tell them.

Some months later a report by Dr. Henry Kohn announced that it was safe to return to Rongelap—but only for adults, not children, and then only to the southern islands of the atoll: the northern islands are still 'hot' and food must not be harvested on them. Amazed at the idea that they should return without their children, the people of Rongelap stayed on Mejato. Since then, though, the Kohn report has been shown to be deeply flawed, underestimating exposure levels. In the light of this criticism, it now seems as though the US will at least agree to a truly independent study of radiation levels of the Rongelap people and their atoll. For years the Rongelap people have been asking whether their atoll is safe and for a realistic prognosis of their health; Senator Anjain feels hopeful that if these questions are answered, his people might be able to make an informed choice about their future.

On the other side of Kwajalein lagoon daily life on Ebeye is now a little less brutal thanks to improvements won through the sail-in protests. But the future of this tiny, overcrowded island is still dependent on the twists and turns of international diplomacy. Despite the credibility of the Star Wars programme being severely questioned—and despite the slight easing of Cold War tension in the wake of the INF treaty and subsequent overtures by President Gorbachev—the Pentagon shows no sign of reducing its testing programme on Kwajalein. Indeed, the number of US personnel there has doubled in recent years, and four extra islands have now been turned into pin cushions for incoming missiles for the expanded Star Wars programme.

While the Marshallese people continue to wrestle with the consequences of nuclear testing two new proposals are on the table which, if they get the go-ahead, will make the islands once again a receptacle for anything too dirty for the US's own back yard. The first, proposed by Admiralty Pacific and backed by Marshallese president Amata Kabua, is to dump household waste from the USA in the islands. While this would create landfill—and the Marshalls desperately need extra land, particularly as the sea level rises due to the greenhouse effect—the proposal is seen by some Marshallese politicians and environmental groups as opportunistic and ill thought-out. Even household waste contains a high level of detergents, bleaches and other chemicals which can disturb the local ecology, particularly in tropical conditions.

The second proposal, which appears to be President Kabua's own idea, is to reap rich financial rewards for offering uninhabited atolls as dumping grounds for high-level nuclear waste. Given the international public outcry that would almost inevitably follow transportation of such waste, it is unlikely that it will happen, although the US Department of Energy is considering the Marshalls as part of its geological survey of possible sites.

Perhaps the most exciting political development in Pacific Island politics has taken place in Belau. On an unusually hot day in April 1988, after I had completed the first edition of this book, I sat in the corridors of the University of London students' union talking with a most remarkable Belauan woman, Bernie Keldermans.

She and a hundred other Belauan machas (women elders) had just filed a motion to reopen their lawsuit challenging the waiving of voting regulations in the August 1987 referenda which had allowed Belau's nuclear-free constitution to be overturned.

Their original lawsuit had been withdrawn after severe intimidation: Keldermans' father had been assassinated and the houses of women elders firebombed. Their decision to reopen their case required substantial courage; I was struck by Keldermans' faith that they would succeed in preserving Belau's nuclear-free status and preventing the Pentagon from using Belau as a Trident submarine base. Indeed, on 21 April, in a dramatic turn-round of events in Belau, the court did rule in the women's favour.

But Belau's political scene remains turbulent. In August 1988 a New York court found Belau liable for the $4.5 million loan financed in 1983 to pay for the IPSECO power plant, which never produced a single watt of electricity. Shortly afterwards Belau's president, Lazarus Salii, committed suicide.

Salii was facing tremendous political pressure: he had gambled his country's future on an expensive and superfluous power plant and had banked on paying for it with US financial aid, promised in return for Belau's accepting the Compact of Free Association with the US, which would give the US military access to the country's land and airports. The court victory of the women elders meant Salii could not complete his part of the deal; the Compact remains unsigned. But the Bush Administration is still lobbying hard for its ratification —and has a well-placed friend in Salii's successor, President Ngiratkel Etpison.

The women's success lifted the spirits of the anti-nuclear lobby in Belau and in other parts of the Pacific. Small but significant shifts have also taken place in Tahiti and in the South Pacific, where space for debate around the French nuclear testing and around the possibilities for independence has tentatively opened up.

A pro-independence, indigenous Tahitian, Jacqui Drollet,

has been appointed minister for health, the environment, and scientific research in a new coalition government, while a recently launched pressure group, Tomite Te Ra'i Hau, has brought together churches, trade unions, political parties and individuals concerned about the effects of nuclear testing. Its first conference, on peace and development, resulted in a variety of demands, including an independent medical research institute and radiological monitoring. It's not the first time in Tahiti's history that such demands have surfaced, although this time they have a sympathiser in Drollet, who may be able to use heightened public concern over the tests to bring pressure for change.

As this edition goes to press in August 1989 the Polynesian Assembly is debating the nuclear question for the first time in its history. Opposition groups are calling for a popular consultation over the continuation of the testing. According to the French constitution this would have have no legal status but Polynesian politicians believe that a 'no' vote would embarrass the French. But meanwhile a controversial report by Jacques Cousteau, which played down any danger to health from the testing, has served to strengthen the hand of the French government in the international arena.

As the Pacific Island nations look to the end of the century, they are facing a challenge which may prove the most serious in their chequered history. The waves of the Pacific Ocean are, quite literally, threatening to submerge the low-lying atolls and to wash away the coastal infrastructure of the more mountainous islands. Scientists predict that if global warming—the greenhouse effect—continues at present rates the seas will rise by a meter in the next 60 years. And atolls like the Marshall Islands are less than a meter above sea level. If the Pacific Islands are rendered uninhabitable then their 5 million people will be forced to flee—and whole cultures, languages and histories will be lost to the world. As an international conference in Majuro in July 1990 concluded, it is the industrialised nations of the world which have caused the greenhouse effect and only they can attempt to avert this catastrophe.

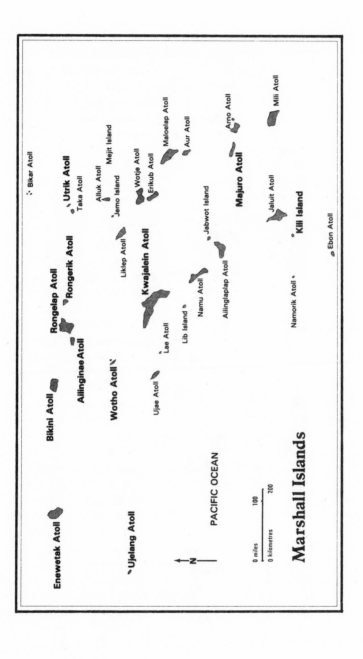

Marshall Islands

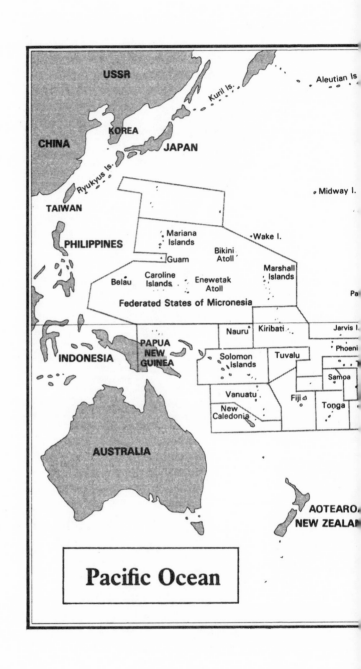

Pacific Ocean

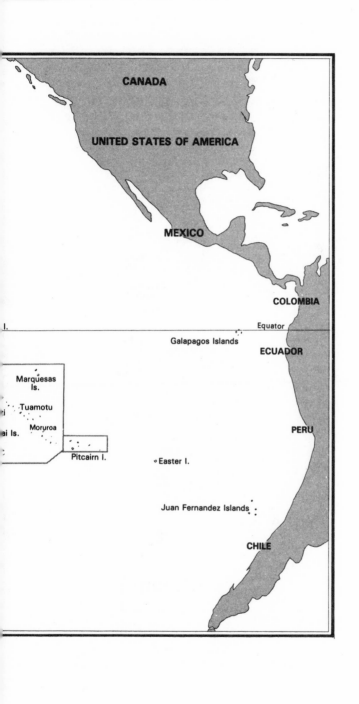

PART ONE

Testing:
The Marshall
Islanders' Experience

1

Introduction

Katrine Jilej has lived for the past three years on Mejato, a low-lying coral island, its white beaches fringed with palms, in the turquoise waters of the North Pacific. It may sound like paradise, but for Jilej and her people it's more like purgatory. They are waiting for the day when they can go home.

Home is Rongelap atoll, 100 miles to the north. Like Mejato, it is part of the Marshall Islands, in Micronesia, 2,100 atolls and islands scattered across the ocean between Hawai'i and the Philippines.

At the end of the Second World War, Micronesia was made a United Nations Trust Territory under the wing of the US. Micronesia also includes the Mariana Islands (now a US Commonwealth), the Republic of Belau and the Federated States of Micronesia, made up of the Kosrae, Yap and Pohnpei islands. Guam is also geographically part of Micronesia but is politically separate, being a US territory.

In 1954 the US exploded a 17-megaton bomb, 1,300 times the destructive force of the bombs dropped on Hiroshima and Nagasaki, on the island of Bikini. 'Bravo', as it was codenamed, was one of 66 tests conducted in the Marshalls by the Americans between 1946 and 1958, a crucial stepping-stone in the Cold War race for nuclear superiority. The island of Rongelap was directly in the path of Bravo's fallout. Since then, the Rongelap people have been plagued by ill-health – most commonly, thyroid tumours, cataracts and babies so deformed they could not live. Chapter Three of this book looks in detail at this first generation of testing and asks why Bravo was detonated when the US military was aware that the wind was blowing towards Rongelap. Were the Marshallese used as guinea pigs for radiation experiments, as they claim?

The Rongelap people have recently been forced to abandon their homes. A US study released in 1982 showed their islands were still 'hot' and warned them – 28 years after the event – not to eat food from the northern part of the atoll. After repeated pleas for help in moving were refused by the US Congress, they eventually turned to the international environmental organisation, Greenpeace, and were moved by the *Rainbow Warrior* in 1985, immediately before it was blown up in Auckland Harbour, Aotearoa/New Zealand, by the French secret services.

They now live on Mejato, a tiny island on temporary loan to them. It was one of the very few uninhabited islands in the Marshalls, where land is scarce – and essential to survival. But there were good reasons why no one had been living there previously: it is sub-fertile and the wild coconut and pandanus trees bear little fruit; unlike Rongelap, Mejato does not afford plentiful fishing in a calm lagoon.

Once economically independent, living off the land and the sea and a small income from the sale of copra (dried coconut), the people are now reduced to sitting around waiting for the US Direct Aid ship to come past with their new diet of white rice, sugar, flour, tinned peaches and tuna – caught in Pacific waters and shipped back to them in cans. When the ship doesn't come, they dip into their small fund from supporters around the world and send someone to make the 130-mile round trip to buy supplies. From November to March they are virtually cut off, prisoners of the sudden tropical storms and huge waves.

Meanwhile the Rongelap people are still waiting for an independent survey of the damage done to their atoll and to their health to assess whether it is possible to clean up the islands. In Chapter Four, Rongelapese talk of their painful decision to leave their homeland and the slow task of rebuilding a new community.

Testing in the Marshall Islands did not end with the halting of atmospheric nuclear explosions. Bowing to public pressure, President Eisenhower announced he would sign the Partial Test Ban Treaty in 1958, but the respite for the Marshall Islands lasted one brief year. In 1959 they were chosen as the perfect site for the next generation of testing. This time it was missiles which were to be tested, for accuracy and speed. Launched in California, they would crash into the islands and lagoon of Kwajalein atoll, 4,800 miles away.

A US navy base had been established on the biggest island in the atoll immediately after the Second World War. Its population was dumped on to the tiny neighbouring island of Ebeye. Already an overcrowded labour camp, Ebeye's problems were to worsen dramatically as more and more people were cleared from the necklace of islands which make up Kwajalein atoll. There are now over 9,500 people living on Ebeye, on 66 acres or one-tenth of a square mile of land. Britain would have to accommodate twice the world population to achieve the same density.[1]

MX , Minuteman . . . all the US long-range missiles have been tested there. In recent years the Pentagon has been more than ever anxious to hang on to Kwajalein as the nuclear arms race went into a new gear. For in 1984 a missile fired from Vandenberg Air Base in California was intercepted by one fired from Kwajalein: SDI, or Star Wars, was declared possible. Since then, Kwajalein has been the test site for Star Wars components.

Military researcher Owen Wilkes has written: 'If we could shut down the Pacific Missile Range, we could cut off half the momentum of the nuclear arms race.'[2] Kwajalein itself has been called 'one of America's most strategic sites in the world' and 'the cornerstone of President Reagan's Strategic Defense Initiative'.[3] The Pentagon regards it as essential to the development of new US weapons:

> All of our high-tech strategic systems have some relationship to the Kwajalein facility. If we didn't have Kwajalein we wouldn't be able to test such long-range stuff over open, largely uninhabited areas of the earth's surface.[4]

If the INF deal signed by President Reagan and General Secretary Gorbachev in December 1987 heralds an end to the Cold War, SDI may be negotiated away. But although most observers are sceptical whether SDI will ever work, there is little reason to hope that the Kwajalein Missile Range will soon become redundant. Richard Falk, Professor of International Law at Princeton, pointed out, 'Often before, arms control steps have accompanied, rather than inhibited, escalations in the qualitative arms race.'[5] INF, he says, may perhaps be in part 'a matter of gaining the protective colouring of arms control to enable an all-out push on Star Wars'. Kwajalein is earmarked as a major test site for SDI components and there are no indications that this will not continue.

This, then, is an account of how the drive to prepare for nuclear war has already uprooted whole communities in its path. It is a story of displacement, of a people robbed of their ancient ties with land they had tended and cared for, and which had sustained them for centuries. It is also a story of the resilience and courage of Marshall Islanders still fighting to reclaim their land and their self-sufficiency, and of the determination and loyalty of their supporters around the world.

The people of Rongelap and others whose land and health have been contaminated by fallout are still demanding justice in US courts. As well as bringing law-suits and lobbying Congress, the people of Ebeye have organised imaginative and creative direct actions, sailing back to their islands in fleets of small boats and occupying them for months at a time. They describe their protests – the successes and the ensuing backlashes – in Chapter Five.

6

It is a story in which Marshallese women figure prominently. Radiation spares no one with its cancers, cataracts and assault on the immune system; it wreaks havoc on the reproductive systems of both men and women. But it is Marshallese women who have borne the pain and confusion of repeated miscarriages and mutated babies. Life is hard for every displaced person on Ebeye, but when poverty renders domestic life brutal; when water has to be fetched and carried and carefully shared between drinking, cooking and washing; when food is scarce and must be stretched; when the family's nerves are shattered from overcrowding, it is invariably women who have to hold the home together. As Chapter Six shows, women's role outside the home is also ruptured by the proximity of a military base which fractures local social and economic structures and pushes some women into prostitution.

But for all the battering of their culture, their health and their self-respect, Marshallese women are still finding a way to survive and to try to regain control of their lives; the sail-ins were undertaken and sustained largely by women, taking their children or grandchildren with them. In Chapter Seven women talk about the impact of westernisation on their lives and how they cope with the conflicting demands of different cultures.

There is very little written material documenting life in the Marshall Islands before the arrival of the Europeans. Some clues exist in the traditions which remain, but of course these have been gradually modified as the people have adapted to the different social systems of colonising nations. A description of some aspects of the present-day political structure and organisation of Marshallese society appears as Appendix II.

The second part of this book asks how the US has been able to treat the Marshall Islands as a convenient testing ground. It argues that the systematic encouragement of economic dependency is part of a pattern found elsewhere in the Pacific.

The third part looks at how people are trying to shape their future: Pacific initiatives – and setbacks – and the possibilities of solidarity work in the west.

Throughout this book I've tried to use the names of countries chosen by the people who live there: so, Belau, not Palau, as it is sometimes called; Moruroa, not Mururoa; Vanuatu, not the New Hebrides. When there are two claims on the name of a country, by the indigenous people and the settlers, I have shown them both: hence, Aotearoa/New Zealand and Kanaky/New Caledonia.

Finally, the part of the world normally referred to as the Third World I have called the First World given, as June Jordan points out, 'that they were first to exist on the planet and currently make up the majority'.[6]

2

Invaders: 'Missionaries and Soldiers – Hand in Hand'

The Marshall Islands were formed, millions of years ago, by volcanic eruptions on the sea bed. Around the edges of the volcanic peaks – islands above the ocean's surface – coral began to grow. As the volcanoes slowly sank back into the sea bed, live coral – colonies of tiny animals – continued to grow on the skeletons of dead colonies. A coral reef was in the making. Broken coral collected on the shallow reef, forming a necklace of small, flat islands around a central lagoon where the volcanic peak had once been.

The higher islands of Micronesia to the west of the Marshalls – Guam, Yap and Belau – were first settled in perhaps 3000 or 2000 BC by travellers who arrived by canoe from the Philippines or Indonesia. Around 1000 BC another wave of travellers arrived in the North Pacific, this time from the south, perhaps from Vanuatu (from 1906 to 1980, known as the New Hebrides). They settled what were later called the Marshall and Gilbert chains in the east of Micronesia and spread out westward through the Caroline Islands. Though the main difference in culture and language remains along an east–west split, at least ten distinct languages have been documented in Micronesia.

Four nations

Micronesia has been colonised for nearly four centuries and by four nations: Spain, Germany, Japan and the USA. Britain also tried to gain a toehold but was only partially successful.

The Spanish
The Spanish arrived in Guam in 1521, in search of spices to season and preserve their meat. The first meeting set the tone of the Pacific islands experience of these new arrivals. A flotilla of *prao*, swift dugout canoes with single outriggers and triangular sails, put out from shore to greet the raggedy remains of Magellan's fleet. When the islanders boarded his ships and began inspecting the Europeans and their equipment, Magellan panicked and ordered his sailors to disperse them with cross-bows. The following morning he set out with a band of 40 sailors armed with swords and burning torches and attacked the first village he came across. Seven islanders were killed; the rest fled as their homes were razed by fire.

For the next 40 years Micronesians continued to be called on by Spanish explorers and traders who used the islands as a stepping stone to the Moluccas, or Spice Islands, off the coast of Indonesia. At times Micronesians were captured and taken as navigators or as slaves. Then in 1565 Spain laid claim to the Philippines, providing itself with a doorway to China: junks had long since brought Chinese merchandise to be traded with the Filipinos. Paradoxically, the new Spanish conquest relieved the eastern islands of Micronesia from sporadic invasions by outsiders, for the Spanish ships sailed well to the north of the Marshalls and Carolines, avoiding their treacherous reefs. The western islands, however, and especially the bigger atolls of Guam and Ulithi and the Marianas, became the focus of Jesuit missionary fervour. The Chamorros, the indigenous people of the Marianas, resisted enforced baptism and other missionary activities by burning churches; they defended themselves against Spanish guns with sling shots and spears. It was only when a priest was killed by islanders in the eighteenth century that the missionaries withdrew from Micronesia for 50 years.

The legacy of Spanish rule remains vivid even now. Chailang Palacios, a Chamorro woman from Saipan, in the Marianas Islands, says in *Why Haven't You Known? Pacific Women Speak*:

> When the Spanish soldiers came, so did the missionaries. Hand in hand. They landed in Guam and spread out over the Marianas, then all over Micronesia. The missionaries together with the soldiers began to 'Christianise' our ancestors. They were very scared and ran away – they hadn't seen a white person before. It was very hard for us to embrace Christianity. The Spanish missionaries were blessing all the soldiers while the soldiers were . . . killing our men, raping our women.
>
> When they arrived we were about 40,000. And we ended up just 4,000 because they killed everyone that didn't want to embrace Christianity – the Catholic faith. The Spanish stayed over 100 years. They came to do good work. And they did it very well because today we are 97 per cent Catholic.[1]

The British and the North Americans

By the end of the eighteenth century the British had arrived in Australia and were anxious to explore northwards, where there lay potentially lucrative trade routes to China. In 1788, two captains, Thomas Gilbert and William Marshall, arrived in the island groups in eastern Micronesia which still carry their names. The Gilbert Islands became part of the British Empire, gaining independence in 1975. They now form part of Kiribati. Belau, to the west, became a major stopover port. Spanish ships resumed their trade and soon galleons of both Britain and Spain were stopping off in Micronesian islands to collect tortoise shells, shark fins and bêche-de-mer, sea slugs which are a gourmet dish for wealthy Chinese.

By the turn of the century, North American ships had joined

11

the sea path to China. Their initial cargoes of ginseng glutted the market: later, both North Americans and Europeans slaughtered seals and otters in the USA to trade for Chinese silks, tea and spices. By 1820 the fur trade was halted by the virtual extinction of the hunted animals, so the ships began increasingly to stop in the Pacific islands where they added to their plunder sandalwood, mother-of-pearl and edible birds' nests. Cheap iron pots and pans, muskets and alcohol, calico and gingham for dressing (now that missionaries had taught shame of bodies) were brought from Liverpool and Boston to trade with the Micronesians.

The next callers were North American whalers and Protestant missionaries. 'The missionary is the merchant's pioneer,' observed a Sydney editorial in 1829,[2] and for the Marshall Islands that was certainly to be the case. Until the mid-nineteenth century traders skirted the Marshall Islands, warned off by stories of the unwelcoming reception given to those from the outside world. Then, North American missionaries decided to try their luck: once they'd made inroads, traders followed. The island centres became more and more commercialised and geared specifically to the needs of westerners: Koror, in Belau, had a constructed port and provisions for sailors. Jaluit became the commercial capital of the Marshalls – its port resembled a western town of the time – although other more remote islands continued virtually unscathed.

Still in search of lucrative business, the traders hit on the idea of the coconut: its oil had long been used by the islanders for cooking, and for hair and body beauty, but it was only when westerners perfected techniques for making it into soap and candles that they saw it as a profit-maker. From then on, land was seized for plantations which were worked by the islanders. Copra became the basis of the island economy.

'Blackbirders' – slave ships come to collect a human cargo – started to crawl their waters, bound for cotton plantations in Fiji and Samoa, sugar plantations in Hawai'i, coffee plantations in Central America and copper mines in Peru. Many thousands of Pacific people died in slavery, of overwork, cruel treatment and homesickness. In 1882 sugar planters in Hawai'i called on their government to allow the wholesale immigration of Japanese labourers to replace Marshall and Gilbert Islanders who were dying in slavery.

The Germans

As the United States' influence as a sea power grew, the old European colonial nations began to worry. Fearful lest the Pacific fall into US hands, Britain and Germany hatched a secret plot in 1875 to divide the Pacific up into their respective spheres of influence. Britain took the South Pacific, Germany the North, buying the Marshall Islands from Spain in 1885 and the rest of Micronesia in 1899.

North American missionaries were joined by strict German Protestants, and dancing and body painting were banned.

> The Germans brought their own missionaries, who tried to teach us the Protestant religion. And this started making us, the indigenous group, fight amongst ourselves over who was more Protestant and who was more Catholic. That is always the way: when white nations come to conquer us, to colonise us, they divide us. And it is still happening.[3]

Church taxes were collected in the form of copra, much to the annoyance of the traders who were greedy for coconut oil. By 1910 islanders had to pay a poll tax, and those who failed to pay were forced to work on road gangs. The first year the tax was levied a group of Pohnpeians staged an uprising, killing the governor and other German officials. In retaliation, the Germans sent soldiers to crush the rebellion. Public education was instituted to train the population in the ways of a plantation-based cash economy. 'They must be trained to work; they must be encouraged to earn and save money,' stated a government education report.[4] German economic plans for the islands was undermined by local resistance. Nevertheless, by 1885 Micronesia was worth $500,000 a year in trade – half of it the profits from copra, the rest profits from imported goods.[5]

Many poor white men had lost their lives on ships bound for

13

the Pacific. But white traders and shipowners had profited handsomely from contact with the area. The Pacific island population, meanwhile, had been decimated. Some died in skirmishes, some in slavery. Most were wiped out by white men's diseases, particularly syphilis and smallpox. In 1820, Pohnpei still had 10,000 inhabitants; by 1885 that number was halved. Belau lost half its people in the same time, and Kosrae's population plummeted from 3,000 to just 300.

The Japanese

Early in the German Administration the Japanese began to show interest in Micronesia, firstly in the opportunities for trade and later in the possibilities of expansion. By the turn of the century, Germany began to lose economic control of the islands to the Japanese and in 1914 Japan sent her navy in support of Japanese traders in the islands, causing most of the Germans to flee. Japan stepped neatly into the ensuing political vacuum and its interests in the North Pacific were given a stamp of legitimacy after the First World War, when a League of Nations mandate awarded Micronesia to Japan.

Some older Micronesians have clear memories of Japanese rule and still speak the language. (In families with a great-grandparent, each successive generation speaks a different second language after their own: German, Japanese and now English.) Hermos Jilej now lives on Mejato and is a retired schoolteacher:

> I remember the Japanese as being very strict in school. Even outside when walking along the road if a Japanese official came past you had to bow and show respect. I think it's been very confusing for my people to have to learn German ways, then Japanese and now American. But at least under the Japanese our economy was in better shape than now under the US.

Economic expansion was only one of Japan's goals in the islands. According to Marshallese senator Carl Heine,[6] the

Japanese Administration also set out to use the islands to relieve overpopulation in Japan, to spread the Japanese culture and later to establish military, naval and airforce bases throughout the islands in the build-up to the Second World War – illegal under the League of Nations mandate.

Japanese emigration to Micronesia was slow at first but rapidly increased from 1930, so that by 1940 Japanese outnumbered the local population. By that time Japanese military personnel had joined the civilians. The Marshall Islands, however, were not a popular destination: 680 Japanese lived there in 1940 while in the Marianas there were 45,922 Japanese settlers.[7] Even more than the Spanish or Germans, the Japanese were keen to assimilate Micronesians with an organised educational programme teaching Japanese language and cultural values. Annual subsidised tours of Japan were even offered to build loyalty to Japan and its Emperor.

The copra and fishing industries, initiated in the late nineteenth century, were expanded, and Japan's South Sea Development Company invested 3 million yen in sugar plantations in the Marianas. Phosphate was mined in some islands: in Belau, for example, 60,000 tons were mined annually.[8] To support its industries, the Japanese Administration built a network of roads, and installed electricity, docks, running water, lighthouses, airfields, telephones and telegraphs in its centres of industry. More accurately, the Micronesians built them for the Japanese, for the Japanese workers took most of the skilled jobs and the Micronesians did the labouring. Often this was done in return for only three meals a day and a very paltry wage. According to one Japanese writer, this suited the Administration perfectly, as it meant the workers were fed and so kept up their strength for hard labour and it was a way of nudging the islanders towards a cash economy.[9]

In 1935 the League of Nations requested to be allowed to send inspectors to assess the military build-up in Micronesia. Japan refused, withdrew from the League but hung on to the islands. They became a closed military area, out-of-bounds to foreigners and, by 1942, under military administration. Free speech, freedom of assembly and worship were all tightly controlled.

On mountainous islands some families took to the hills to hide, but on the low-lying coral atolls of the Marshalls there was nowhere to run to. Neither the nearby island chain of Truk nor the Marshalls could provide enough food for the sudden influx of soldiers and so food was requisitioned from the islanders, who had then to resort to stealing from the farming areas at night.

Chailang Palacios describes what her people remembered of Japanese rule:

> And then there is this nation just like an octopus. The octopus that goes slowly, very slowly and suddenly it gets you. That is like the Japanese. They wanted us to join their religion, Buddhism. They liked our islands so much they stayed. They took our lands for sugar plantations, for pineapple plantations. They again made my ancestors their slaves, together with the Korean and Okinawa people, paying them five cents for the whole day . . .
>
> After stripping them of their culture, their language, their land, the Japanese forced my ancestors up into the mountains. They made us dig a hole just in case the Americans and the Japanese fought. We would be safe in that hole. It was a Sunday morning when the war came. Everyone was far away from their holes, visiting grandparents, relatives, friends. All of a sudden – bombs from the sky and the ocean. The people were crushed 50 to 100 in one hole because there was no way they could get back to their own place to hide. There was no water for those people. It was so hot, so dark, bombs all over. A lot of people died. Children died because their mothers' breasts dried up – no food.[10]

The USA – again

After nearly 30 years of jealous Japanese rule, the Marshall Islands have been opened up under entirely new management!

16

Uncle Sam has now taken charge. The opening began on D-Day, January 31 1944, when our forces unleashed a superbly co-ordinated amphibious attack against Kwajalein Atoll, centre of the Marshall Islands area . . .[11]

The US took Micronesia from the Japanese in the autumn of 1944 after more than two years of what are widely described as some of the bloodiest battles witnessed in the Pacific during the Second World War. Some 6,288 US soldiers and 70,000 Japanese soldiers were killed, and thousands more wounded. Five thousand Micronesians died, 10 per cent of an estimated population of 50,000. In the battle for Kwajalein alone, says a US Army public relations manual for Kwajalein,[12] American losses totalled 142 killed, 845 wounded and two 'missing in action'; 4,938 Japanese were killed and over 200 taken prisoner – of these, 127 were actually Korean labourers. The author fails to mention Micronesian casualties.

US Army pictures taken after they captured Kwajalein show scenes of the most awful destruction: buildings flattened to firewood kindling; the few remaining palms with their tops lopped off, huge charred trunks standing alone and decapitated in the rubble. Not one tree or shrub remained alive after the islands of Kwajalein had been pounded by 100 pounds per square foot of shells and bombs – the physical equivalent of 20,000 tons of TNT.[13] 'The entire island looked as if it had been picked up to 20,000 feet and then dropped,' said one Army observer.[14]

Lorenza Pedro, who grew up on Belau, remembers her feelings at being caught up in somebody else's war.

I remember hiding for several years during the war in the forests while the bombs dropped around us. We ate raw foods – we couldn't cook because planes might see the smoke rising above the trees and think it was the enemy and bomb us. It was terrifying. Much of our island was destroyed and many people killed. That experience has not been forgotten. We are now anxious to avoid being caught up in another war we have nothing to do with.

The Belauans now have a saying: 'When soldiers come, war comes.'

After the American takeover, Micronesians were used to help build US military bases on Peleliu, Angaur, Saipan, Tinian and Kwajalein. Tinian became the world's largest airfield, with 200,000 military personnel stationed there. From Tinian the US launched 29,000 B-29 bomber attacks on Japan. Then on 6 August 1945 a new kind of bomb was loaded on to the B-29 *Enola Gay*. Three days later, while Hiroshima's citizens were still being pulled out of the debris suffering horrific radiation burns, another Tinian-based B-29 dropped a second H-bomb, this time on Nagasaki.

At the end of the war, the newcomers in Micronesia tore down what the fighting hadn't already destroyed of the Japanese infrastructure. Where the Japanese settler economy had been most vigorous, in the west of Micronesia and in Belau, in particular, United States forces systematically wiped out evidence of the Japanese presence. In his book *Micronesia: Trust Betrayed*, former US State Department official Donald F. McHenry[15] quotes a Micronesian worker who tells of a US military officer ordering Japanese buildings in Belau to be razed to the ground. 'We're going to tear this stuff down and show the Micronesians what the Americans can build,' he said. In the intervening 40-odd years, the Americans have in fact built very little of real use to the Micronesians. US military bases and US post offices are generally the biggest and best-equipped buildings on the economically dependent islands. The Micronesians, recalls Chailang Palacios, were amazed and dismayed at the systematic destruction:

I remember my parents shaking their heads and saying, 'My God, because of America and Japan we have suffered so much.' My beloved father couldn't understand the stupidity of the American soldiers when he saw his own home, completely built of stone from the ocean and with just two holes from the bombs, and the American soldiers coming with their bulldozers and destroying all the houses and all the roads. The Americans hated the Japanese so much that they had to destroy everything.[16]

After the war a battle was fought out in the US Administration over Micronesia's political future. The War Department lobbied for outright annexation of the islands, while the State Department preferred a trusteeship system. The second option won out when in 1947 the US and the Security Council of the United Nations signed a trusteeship agreement which brought Micronesia under the wing of the US with, theoretically, the international supervision of the UN – controlled, at that time, by the US. The mandate of the Trust allowed the United States to 'fortify' the islands. In return, the US promised it would protect the health of the inhabitants, guard against loss of land and resources and 'promote the economic advancement and self-sufficiency of the inhabitants and to this end shall regulate the uses of natural resources; and encourage the development of fisheries, agriculture and industries.'

In essence, the US pledged to the international community that it would help the islands towards self-government and eventual independence. Yet two years earlier, on his return from the Potsdam Conference, President Truman had made US intentions quite clear:

> Though the United States wants no territory or profit or selfish advantage out of this war, we are going to maintain the military bases necessary for the complete protection of our interests and of world peace. Bases which our military experts deemed to be essential for our protection, we will acquire. We will acquire them by arrangement consistent with the United Nations charter.[17]

In other words, the US intended to annex the islands for its military purposes – with a rubber stamp from the UN.

3

The First Generation of Testing: Radiation Clouds over Rongelap

The Commission felt that the tests should be held overseas until it could be established more definitely that continental detonations would not endanger the public health and safety.[1] The Atomic Energy Commission to Congress, 1953.

Five weeks after the end of the Second World War, the US Joint Chiefs of Staff began to plan for a series of atomic tests and to look for 'a suitable site which will permit accomplishment of the tests with *acceptable risk and minimum hazard*' (my emphasis).[2] The criteria for the site included a large sheltered area for anchoring target vessels and measuring the effects of radiation. If inhabited, the population should be small and easily re-located. Above all, it had to be away from population centres of the US: 'overseas', as the AEC told Congress,[3] and yet in an area controlled by the US.

In late January 1946 the Joint Chiefs selected Bikini, one of the northernmost atolls in the Marshalls. It was to be the site of 66 nuclear tests between 1946 and 1958. On Sunday 10 February 1946 an aeroplane arrived in Bikini carrying

Commodore Ben Wyatt, American military governor of the Marshall Islands. The Bikinians had been converted to Christianity half a century earlier by New England missionaries and were in church at the time, singing hymns made Marshallese by taking the basic tune and adding complex harmonies. As the people left church, Wyatt greeted them and, through a translator, asked them to meet with him. His timing and the speech that followed cannot have been coincidental. According to official US Navy records, Wyatt 'compared the Bikinians to the Children of Israel whom the Lord had saved from their enemy and led into the Promised land'. He described the power of the atomic bomb, 'the destruction it had wrought upon the enemy', and he told the people that American scientists 'are trying to learn how to use it for the good of mankind and to end all world wars'. Of all the places in the world, Bikini was the best for testing these new weapons.[4] When, at the climax of his speech, he asked, 'Would you be willing to sacrifice your island for the welfare of all men?', the Bikinians were given only minutes in which to confer.

Chief Juda Kessibuki reported their trusting reply: 'If the United States government and the scientists of the world want to use our island and atoll for furthering development, which with God's blessing will result in kindness and benefit to all mankind, my people will be pleased to go elsewhere.' As well as appealing to religious sentiment, Wyatt's speech made perfectly clear the power of the US and its new weapons. As Jonathan Weisgall, a US attorney who has fought cases on behalf of the Bikinians writes: 'The option of staying on Bikini and telling the United States to look elsewhere was simply not a realistic alternative.'[5]

'One hell of a good sales job'

The removal of the Bikinians was a major exercise in public relations for the US military: 'one hell of a good sales job', as one US military official quoted in *Time* magazine put it.[6] As the

Bikinians prepared to leave – they were told they would be able to return but given no definite date – the first of the 250 vessels, 150 aircraft and 42,000 military and scientific personnel involved in Operation Crossroads, as the series of tests was called, began to arrive. With them came a media show: TV cameras and press photographers. The Bikinians were asked to re-enact their last church service three times until the camera operators got good angles; when the Bikinians decorated the community centre with flowers and held a ceremony to bid farewell to their ancestors they were asked to repeat it. Even Wyatt's original speech and the assent of the Bikinians was acted out again for the cameras. Media demand was indeed such that their departure had to be postponed for a day.

The tenor of the resulting stories is exemplified by this one from the *New York Times* entitled 'The Strange People from Bikini': 'Primitive they are, but they love one another and the American visitors who took their home.'[7] Or by this US Navy press release: 'Natives are delighted about the atomic bomb, which has already brought them prosperity and a new promising future.'[8]

This idyllic future was to be enjoyed on Rongerik, one of the few uninhabited atolls in the Marshalls, where land is at a premium. It soon became obvious why it had been left empty: according to Marshallese mythology, Rongerik was inhabited by an evil spirit that contaminated the fish in the lagoon. Many did in fact prove naturally poisonous and the atoll was considerably less fertile than Bikini. Rongerik is also much smaller: its 17 islands comprise 0.63 square miles, compared to Bikini's 36 islands and 2.3 square miles, and this meant fewer islands for food gathering. And yet an Associated Press story quoted a Navy official fantasising: 'Rongerik is much more beautiful and is a richer island than Bikini [and] about three times larger . . . Coconuts here are three or four times as large as those on Bikini and food is plentiful.'[9]

The Bikinians were left on Rongerik with only a few weeks' supply of food and water. Less than two months after they were dumped there, they asked the Navy if they could return home:

permission was denied. A 1946 *New York Times* article reported: 'the United States military authorities say they can't see why they should want to [be repatriated]: Bikini and Rongerik look as alike as two Idaho potatoes.'[10]

During the winter of 1946–7 the people suffered severe food shortages and a US doctor who visited them in July 1947 reported they were 'visibly suffering from malnutrition'.[11] Six months later another medical officer reported they were starving. Finally, in March 1948 the Bikinians were moved to a temporary camp on Kwajalein – until they were moved again to the island of Kili which, like Rongerik, could not support them.

Meanwhile, in December 1947, the US Navy announced it would take over a second atoll, Enewetak, for another series of tests (see chronology). The 145 Enewetak people were hurriedly relocated to Ujelang, an uninhabited atoll with one-third the land surface of Enewetak and with a tiny lagoon of just 25 square miles, compared to the 390 square mile Enewetak lagoon. It was not the first time the Enewetak people had been summarily uprooted: the first was in July 1946 when they'd been taken to Meck Island on Kwajalein atoll for the first two atomic tests on Bikini.

On Ujelang the Enewetak people became totally dependent on the infrequent visits of the Trust Territory field ships, for the vast distances which separated Ujelang from Marshallese centres were too much for their small boats – 640 miles to Majuro, 410 miles to Kwajalein. But the supply ships did not bring them the materials needed to ensure even a minimum of self-sufficiency. Their fishing canoes fell into disrepair when, after repeated requests for materials, fishing hooks and nets, the Trust ships brought only enough sailcloth for two canoes and enamel garden furniture paint instead of marine paint for wooden hulls. 'Without the canoes we cannot get to the other islands in the lagoon to harvest coconuts. Without the fishing equipment we cannot catch fish to get enough to eat,' said one *iroij*.[12] (See Appendix II for explanation of *iroij* and other Marshallese titles.)

Bravo

At 6.45 on the morning of 1 March 1954, eight years after testing in the Marshall Islands began, the US detonated a bomb codenamed 'Bravo' on the island of Bikini. The bomb was equivalent to 17 megatons of TNT, 1,300 times the destructive force of the bomb dropped on Hiroshima, and was specifically designed to create a vast amount of lethal fallout. That morning the wind was blowing in the direction of two inhabited atolls, Rongelap and Utrik, roughly 100 and 300 miles from Bikini. During previous tests Rongelap and Utrik had been evacuated. For some reason never yet divulged, there was no attempt to evacuate them before Bravo.

The first the islanders knew of Bravo was an intense light, like a strange sun dawning in the west. Later they heard the explosion. By mid-day the fallout, a fine powder which fell from the sky, had reached Rongelap. The children had seen photos of snow, and at first the young ones played in it. This is how Lemoyo Abon, now a teacher and mother, describes her experience of the fallout:

> I was 14 at the time and my sister Roko was 12. That day our teacher had asked us – my sister and I and our two cousins – to cook rice for the other children. We got up early to do it. When we saw the bright light and heard a sound – boom – we were really scared. At that time we had no idea what it was. After noon, something powdery fell from the sky. Only later were we told it was fallout. With Roko and several cousins, I went to our village on the end of Rongelap island to gather some sprouted coconuts. One cousin climbed the coconut tree and got something in her eyes, so we sent another one up. The same thing happened to her. When we went home – ours was the main village on Rongelap – it was raining. We saw something on the leaves, something yellow. Our parents asked, 'What's happened to your hair?' It looked like we'd rubbed soap powder in it.
>
> That night we couldn't sleep, our skin itched so much. On

our feet were burns, as if from hot water. Our hair fell out. We'd look at each other and laugh – you're bald, you look like an old man. But really we were frightened and sad.

The pale powder continued to fall until late afternoon, by which time it was about one and a half inches deep. Later it emerged that it was in fact particles of lime (calcium oxide) formed when Bikini's coral reef (a formation of calcium carbonate) melted in the intense heat of the bomb and was sucked up and scattered for miles.[13] The exact dose of radiation received by the islanders was never measured, but it was estimated that people on Utrik received 14 rem (140 msv) and those on Rongelap 175 rem (1,750 msv). The International Commission on Radiological Protection (ICRP) now recommends that a maximum permissible total body dose to a member of the general public be 0.5 rem a year. (For an explanation of nuclear terms, see Glossary, Appendix III.)

John Anjain, a magistrate on Rongelap at the time, tells what happened over the next two days – and why his people sometimes refer to the event as the 'day of two suns':

On the morning of the 'bomb' I was awake and drinking coffee. I thought I saw what appeared to be the sunrise, but it was in the west. It was truly beautiful with many colours – red, green and yellow – and I was surprised. A little while later, the sun rose in the east. Then some time later something like smoke filled the entire sky and shortly after that a strong and warm wind – as in a typhoon – swept across Rongelap. Then all of the people heard the great sound of the explosion. Some people began to cry with fright. Several hours later the powder began to fall on Rongelap. We saw four planes fly overhead, and we thought perhaps the planes had dropped this powder, which covered our island and stuck to our bodies. The visibility was less than one half mile at that time, due to the haze in the sky.

The next day, early in the morning, I looked at all of the catchments with Jabwe [the health aide] and Billiet [the

25

school principal] and we noticed the water had turned to yellow. I then warned the people not to drink from these water catchments, and told them to drink only *ni* [coconut milk]. The people began to get sick with vomiting, aches all over the body, eye irritations and general weakness and fatigue. After the second day most of the people were unable to move around as usual due to their fatigue. Just a few strong young men were up and about at that time and I asked them to fetch some coconuts for the rest of us to drink. On the evening of the second day a seaplane arrived from Enewetak with two men who brought some strange machines. They stayed only about 20 minutes and they took some readings of water catchments and soil, then took off again. They really did not tell us very much.[14]

Not far from Rongelap, US Navy ships were measuring the intensity of radioactivity. They were not instructed to rescue the Rongelap people; indeed, the task force command ordered them to sail away from the area. Twenty-eight American service personnel stationed on Rongerik atoll to provide hourly weather reports were also exposed to radiation, and were not told when Bravo would be exploded. It was two days before the Navy arrived to pick up the Rongelap islanders and the US personnel – two days in which they breathed, slept and ate the fallout.

No satisfactory answer has been given as to why they were not rescued as soon as it was known that they had been in the path of the fallout. Immediate decontamination on board ship would have at least minimised some of the horrific effects of radiation sickness. Instead, belatedly, the ships took the Rongelapese to the US military base on Kwajalein island, as Etry Enos explains:

When we arrived on Kwajalein we started getting burns all over our bodies, and people were feeling dizzy and weak. At that time we did not know if we would ever return to Rongelap and we were afraid. After two days something appeared under my fingernails and then my fingernails came off and my fingers bled. We all had burns on our ears, shoulders, necks and feet, and our eyes were very sore.[15]

Billiet Edmond kept a diary at the time. In one of his entries he described the injuries then becoming apparent:

After two days on Kwajalein, a group of military doctors began their studying on the victims. Nausea, skin-burns, diarrhoea, headaches, eye pain, hair fall-out, numbness, skin discoloration were among common complaints. It had been so for quite a while. The children were more critical. My 10-year-old adopted son had severe burns in his body, feet, head, neck and ears. I cannot help remembering those sleepless nights we had to hold him down onto his bed as he would have jumped up and down, scratching, rolling, as though insane.

Although I had also some burns on my back, feet and hands, and my hair was falling off, I knew I had been the least affected and I deeply felt pity about those who suffered the most.[16]

On Kwajalein the Rongelapese were given medical treatment. It was cursory, to say the least. Film footage of that time shows lines of Marshallese people being 'inspected'. Jabwe Jojur, health aide on Rongelap, was angered by the lack of information given to the islanders about their injuries:

When we arrived in Kwajalein we immediately showered for several hours at the military base there. After some days a medical team flew out from the US, and they are still treating us today. After three days we had burns all over our bodies, and our hair began to fall out: some people actually went bald. When we asked the Atomic Energy Commission doctors to help us understand what had happened, they did not tell us, and today they do not tell us the truth about our problems.[17]

Once on Kwajalein, the Rongelap people met up with the people of Utrik, who had also been in the path of the fallout.

27

Utrik is 275 miles east of Bikini and by the time the fallout arrived there it looked more like mist than snow. The Utrik people were only taken off the island 72 hours after being exposed. Jirda Biton, living on Utrik at the time of the test, recalls the evacuation:

We all boarded the ship using rubber lifeboats. They took eight of us at a time, and because they were in such a hurry and because the waves were so big in the ocean, I fell overboard and nearly drowned. As I turned to see my island fading into the distance, it made me very sad, and I could not believe that this was happening to us. Since we got wet boarding the ship, we shivered all the way to Kwajalein.

At Kwajalein they took us to a hospital and gave us all medical examinations and took blood samples. They then took us to a camp over on Ebeye island and told us to bathe in the lagoon every morning using soap, and we did exactly as they told us. While still on Kwajalein we saw the Rongelap people who had gotten there the previous day and we learned that we had all been affected by the fallout.[18]

A Japanese tuna fishing boat, the *Lucky Dragon*, was also caught in the path of Bravo's fallout. It was 100 miles east of Bikini when the bomb was detonated. The crew members suffered headaches and nausea and by the time they reached Japan two weeks later all 23 were suffering from radiation sickness, with skin blisters and falling hair. One of the crew members, Aikichi Kuboyama, died of liver and blood damage on 23 September. The fishermen's injuries caused an international outcry and two years later the US handed over $2 million in compensation to the Japanese government.

In addition to the physical injuries and psychological trauma the Marshallese also had to contest with insulting and degrading treatment, according to Jirda Biton.

When we were on Ebeye we had a very rough time adjusting to our new home and [an American man] came dressed up in a cat's costume. When we asked him why he was dressed up as a cat, he told us that we were like cats because we ate like animals and we did not know how to think . . .[19]

Ijunan Iron from Utrik was only nine when his people were taken to the makeshift camp on Kwajalein, but he has never forgotten how degrading it was: 'When we were evacuated and taken to Kwajalein, we were put into a camp with a rope around it like animals and they even posted a policeman in order to keep us inside the area.'[20]

How far exactly did the radiation clouds from Bravo – and indeed, from the other tests – drift? Until 1982 the official US answer was that only Rongelap, Bikini, Enewetak and Utrik had been irradiated. However, a US Department of Energy study, conducted in 1978, then revealed that the fallout was more widespread than had previously been admitted.

There are eleven other atolls or single islands that received intermediate range fallout from one or more of the megaton range tests. A number of these atolls are presently inhabited while others are used for food collection.[21]

The atolls and separate islands listed are: Ailinginae, which received fallout from five different explosions; Ailuk, from one explosion; Bikar from two; Likiep from one; Taka from one; Ujelang (where the Enewetak people were resettled) from two; Rongerik (where the Bikinians lived for two years) from four; Wotho from two; Jemo from one and Mejit from one. The report acknowledges that there was only a 'limited monitoring programme' during the testing and 'there is little or no data on possible plutonium contamination outside Bikini and Ene-wetak'. It proposes a new survey using 'current aerial survey technology and instrumentation' which should give more accurate results.

Going home, and the aftermath

For three years the people of Rongelap led an uncertain and unsettled existence, shunted around different islands, first

Ebeye, then Ejit island in Majuro atoll, waiting to be told it was safe to return home. The Utrik people, estimated to have received less heavy fallout, were told it was safe to return to their island after only three months, but one Utrik woman, Bella Compoj, says they did so full of misgivings:

> When we returned to Utrik the Americans gave us things to eat and large containers of water and told us not to eat or drink from our island. When these things ran out we naturally began to eat our local foods again. I recall seeing a woman named LiBila after our return and her skin looked as if someone had poured scalding water over her body and she was in great pain until she died a few years after 'the bomb'.

The Rongelap people had a long wait before they saw their land again, but they too returned with mixed feelings. Etry Enos recalls:

> I was afraid to return to Rongelap in 1957 but they said it was safe for us. We did not understand what 'poison' [radiation] was, and if we had we would not have returned. Now we really understand that the 'poison' is dangerous and that Rongelap is contaminated. In 1957 [we were told] that we could eat anything we wanted except the coconut crab. When we ate the arrowroot it really burned our mouths. Everything we were used to eating had changed colour and we were surprised that we were allowed to eat our foods on Rongelap, even though we knew that the foods were unusual in colour.[22]

John Anjain remembers:

> At the time of our return the High Commissioner and some representatives from the United Nations Trusteeship Council came to our island. We asked them if it was safe to return to our island and they all agreed that there was still a little bit of radiation left on Rongelap and that it might injure our health, but not very much. With that slight reassurance we returned, but we had much fear then.

After the islanders returned home they were visited regularly by a large white ship: once a year in Rongelap a jeep would buzz around the atoll, collecting people for examination. Everyone who had been on Rongelap at the time of the fallout was given a green card, entitled 'Special Examination Group: Rongelap Exposed', with a number and a photograph of their face. Some 190 other Rongelapese who had been away from home when Bravo took place joined the group on their return to the still-contaminated atoll. Each of them was also given a card, only theirs was pink and stated: 'Rongelap Unexposed'. In this way the AEC defined its test groups.

For 22 years the people of Utrik were told that the dose of radiation they allegedly received, 14 rems, was too low to cause any concern. The exposed people were therefore examined only once every three years, and those not directly exposed to fallout – who nevertheless returned to the atoll and were living off irradiated food – were not examined at all. That in itself caused resentment, with the 'unexposed' group feeling they too should be monitored and both groups feeling that radiation *was* taking its toll.

In 1956 Brookhaven National Laboratory (a New York-based company which carries out development work on the civil nuclear programme for the private sector and the US government) was contracted by the US Department of Energy to conduct the yearly surveys of the Rongelap people. Brookhaven's Dr Robert Conard, in charge of the monitoring, commented in his 'Twenty Year Review':

> Unexposed Rongelap people were included in the examinations and have served as an excellent comparison population since they are blood relatives of the exposed Rongelap people, match reasonably well for age and sex, and live under the same environmental conditions.[23]

However, evidence has emerged over the years to show that the food chain on Rongelap was still highly contaminated when the islanders returned in 1957. What does that imply for the health of the so-called 'unexposed' group – and indeed for the validity of Brookhaven statistical data presented as comparisons between the 'exposed' and 'unexposed' groups? And why were the Rongelapese sent home when their atoll was still contaminated?

When the Rongelapese returned they found that half the pigs and hens which they had had to leave behind three years earlier had died. In the days after the fallout, they told a visiting Japanese peace movement delegation in 1971, many of the animals showered with fallout became 'spiritless' and died. They also found that some of the coconut trees, bushes and upper branches of other trees had withered. According to Dr Conard's 1969 report, a helicopter survey in 1956 of plants and trees growing on the islands of Naen and Gejen in the northern part of the atoll revealed a disturbing change. These islands were not inhabited by the Rongelapese but were used as a gathering ground for food. Leaves on many trees had turned grey, others had no leaves at all. On Naen island, Conard spotted a grove of about 30 dead guettarda trees and further inland a clump of four or five dead coconut trees. Early estimates that these areas received 2,000 to 2,300 rads were later changed to 3,000 rads. 600 rads is estimated to be a lethal dose.

Even after Bravo, atmospheric testing continued on Bikini and Enewetak for another four years. Although there is no evidence to suggest Rongelap was in the direct path of fallout in quite the same way it had been during Bravo, radioactive material was scattered into the atmosphere on each occasion, adding to the general contamination of the Marshall Islands.

Brookhaven reported that after the Rongelapese were returned to their islands in July 1957 their body burdens of radioactivity shot up. In just one year, the Rongelap people's *average* body levels of radioactive caesium 137 rose 60-fold; levels of strontium 90 rose 20-fold. Given that caesium 137 and strontium 90 both have a physical half-life of almost 30 years, it was only to be expected that the natural foods on Rongelap would still be contaminated with them.

The only precautions advised by the AEC were that the Rongelap people should not eat coconut crab, or arrowroot, though they were later told it was safe to resume eating them.

The coconut crab is particularly harmful because it eats its own shell after shedding it, so that instead of excreting radioactive materials it accumulates them in high concentrations in its body.

In the wake of the testing, arrowroot has either died out or shrunk to an unrecognisable size, not only on Rongelap but on many other of the Marshall Islands. Until Brookhaven research data is released and re-analysed, it's unclear whether this is a result of radiation. But as Marshallese health worker Darlene Keju-Johnson says:

> Everywhere I go people tell me stories of how the arrowroot is disappearing. And if they do grow, they are just the size of small potatoes, not the big roots they used to be.

I asked epidemiologist and radiation expert Rosalie Bertell why the arrowroot would have disappeared and what made it more vulnerable to radioactivity than other plants:

> It is possible that it has mutated. That happened to many plants after Hiroshima and Nagasaki too. In the Hiroshima museum there are onions with multiple heads. Mutated plants become sterile. After growing oddly for some years they die out. Radiation affects plants differently because they take different nutrients from the soil. Living cells are really quite phenomenal – they select some nutrients from the environment and have a barrier against other things; there are certain plants which strip the soil of nitrogens, for example. We have released 3-400 radionuclides into a very complicated eco-system.[24]

Despite the AEC's own warning against arrowroot, however, Dr Conard noted in his 1980 review that any reaction to eating arrowroot was because it was 'improperly prepared' (a strange assumption given that it is a traditional Marshallese food) and that this had 'erroneously been associated with radiation effects in the minds of the Rongelap people'.

The AEC may have warned the Rongelapese against arrow-root but they didn't make sure they had other nutritious foods to eat. When I talked to Renam Anjain she told me the

Rongelapese often resorted to eating arrowroot when other foods had run out:

> We make a powder from arrowroot and then mix it with water. The starch goes to the bottom. You let the water drain out, put the starch in a cloth and hang it up, beating it with a stick to get all the water out. Then you put it in a pot and cook it, stirring, mixing it with coconut milk. It's very sweet, like gum, and very tasty. But since the fallout, whenever I eat it my lips bleed and hurt.

Bleeding lips and gums is one symptom of radiation poisoning.

It wasn't until 1982, however, that the US Department of Energy published a study, conducted in 1978, which numbered the different islands on Rongelap according to a scale whereby one was the least amount of radioactivity and four was the highest. It showed that certain inhabited parts of Rongelap were still as 'hot' as parts of Bikini, on which it was still considered too dangerous to live. Islands on the north of the atoll used by the Rongelapese to harvest food – coconut, pandanus, breadfruit, fish, birds, and fresh water in dry times – were numbered four.

For 25 years, then, the people of Rongelap culled contaminated food from their northern islands. People who had not been present during the fallout ingested radioactive material and the others continued to add to their 'body burden'. Any Brookhaven comparisons which assume that the 'unexposed' people are the 'norm' are clearly based upon a false premise. More pertinent still, a second risk was taken with the lives of the Rongelapese. There are few clues as to why that was: this is one of them, quoted from Brookhaven's three-year report on Rongelap and Utrik:

> Even though . . . the radioactive contamination of Rongelap Island is considered perfectly safe for human habitation, the levels of activity are higher than those found in other inhabited locations in the world. *The habitation of these people on the island will afford most valuable ecological radiation data on human beings.* (my emphasis)[25]

And this is another, from the Defense Department's 'The Effects of Nuclear Weapons':

> Valuable information concerning the development and healing of beta burns has been obtained from observations of the Marshall Islanders who were exposed to fallout in 1954 . . . who did not realise [the fallout's] significance.

Future generations

How exactly did radiation affect the health of the islanders? Even before returning to Rongelap and Utrik, people began to realise that the burns, intense itching, nausea and hair loss they had experienced in the first weeks after Bravo were not the end of their problems. One of the most disturbing and terrifying effects was on women's reproductive systems and on children yet to be born. Some women who became pregnant in the years following Bravo found they suffered an unexpectedly high number of miscarriages and severely deformed babies, many of whom died. Almira Matayoshi was 17 and living on Rongelap at the time of Bravo:

> One of my babies was born in 1955 [the year after Bravo] and it did not have any bones in its body. After that I had problems with the next pregnancy and they had to rush me to Kwajelein hospital because I was bleeding. There they gave me a D and C and it caused me so much pain that I was temporarily blinded – they had to give me ten pints of blood.[26]

Mary Sampson was only seven when she was caught in the fallout on Rongelap. When she reached child-bearing age she suffered similar experiences:

> I have had very many problems with childbearing. My first baby lived for a very short time – several minutes – but it was not healthy and did not move around very much when it

was born. I was very sad and confused because I was healthy then, and then when I thought about it I remembered that I had 'poison' in my body and that is why the baby died. Later another baby was born and it too died shortly after birth. Then I had a miscarriage after four months. Now I am always afraid when I am pregnant and this fear is shared by all women on Utrik and Rongelap. Even my healthy children may someday get radiation diseases.[27]

Women on Wotje and Utrik too have had deeply traumatic births. Kathe Judo lives on Wotje and describes what the Marshallese women now call 'jellyfish babies':

I saw three different women give birth to strange things after the 'bomb'. One was like the bark of a coconut tree. One was like a watery mass that was not humanlike. Another was again like a watery mass of grapes or something like that. I believe that these things are all caused by 'the bomb'.[28]

Nelly Aplos was 19 when she heard Bravo explode from her home island of Utrik:

Now I have lots of aches and pains in my body, notably in my back, chest and under my breast. I have lost three babies after 'the bomb' – and never had any problems before. The first baby lived for two days and then the baby's skin turned blue and it died. Later when I was six months pregnant the baby died and I was very sick at the time. After that I was pregnant for two months and then I had a *jibun* [miscarriage]. I know now that I have a lot of poison in my body and I am certain that this makes the babies weak. I was never sick during any of my pregnancies (except after I lost my babies) and this never happened before the bomb. I have heard from other women in Utrik about many cases of *jibun* . . . I also have heard of some babies who do not know how to suck from their mother's breast and who eventually die of hunger.[29]

When I spent time with the Rongelap people in 1986, I met one evening with the women on Mejato. We talked about why I was there, the problems they were facing and how women's groups and peace groups in the west could work with them. Suddenly one woman who had been sitting silently in a corner spoke up. She was Katherine Jilej, the midwife and a grandmother. She spoke forcefully through her tears:

We are very angry at the US and I'll tell you why. Have you ever seen a jellyfish baby born looking like a bunch of grapes, so the only reason we knew it was a baby was because we could see the brain? We've had these babies – they died soon after they were born.

Later she told me about her own baby:

Our first baby was born in October 1960, after the bomb, when we'd returned to Rongelap. He was born with a big lump on his head and died very, very young. All the food we were eating was irradiated but we didn't know. I wasn't even on Rongelap the day the test happened but I went back there in 1957 and I was irradiated from eating the food. I think that's why my son died.

The testimonies of women who have given birth to an unformed fetus or who have suffered repeated miscarriages are too numerous to include them all here. Many women have chosen not to show the babies to their partners; some cannot bear to see them themselves, says Marshallese health worker Darlene Keju-Johnson:

When they die they are buried right away. A lot of times they don't allow the mother to see this kind of baby because she'll go crazy.[30]

Radiation can damage an unborn child in various ways. Firstly, a fetus can be damaged by being exposed to radiation while in the mother's womb. Almost a quarter of pregnant women exposed within a mile and a quarter of the explosion in Hiroshima lost their pregnancies through miscarriages or stillbirths. Of the live births, a quarter died when they were less than one year old, and a quarter of the children who survived had mental handicaps.[31] Many children suffered microcephaly: an abnormally small head circumference and severe mental handicaps.[32] Japanese *hibakusha* (radiation survivors) were mostly unable to have children during the first three years after the bombing: those who conceived often aborted unformed, unrecognisable fetuses late in the pregnancy.

Dr Alice Stewart, a British epidemiologist, played a pioneering role in identifying the hazards of *low level* radiation to the fetus. She began when head of the Department of Preventative Medicine at Oxford University in 1955 by asking why there had been a sharp rise in the number of children who have contracted leukaemia since the Second World War. Her results, published in 1958, suggested that children whose mothers had been given X-rays when pregnant were twice as likely to develop cancer before the age of ten than those whose mothers were not. Moreover, mothers X-rayed in the first three months of pregnancy were 10 times more likely to give birth to a child who later developed cancer than those who were X-rayed later in pregnancy.

At first Stewart's work was not believed: later, it provoked major changes in guidelines for X-rays. In a follow-up to her original work, Stewart published a second study in 1970 which demonstrated a direct relationship between the dose of radiation received by the fetus and the risk of cancer. Doubling the number of X-rays doubled the risk.

The second consequence of exposure to radiation in this context is that if the germ cells – ova in women, sperm in men – of one of the parents are damaged (she or he may have been irradiated as an adult, a child or a fetus), that may produce ill effects in their children, who in turn may produce defective ova or sperm and pass the genetic 'mistake' on to succeeding generations.

The accepted evidence that radiation causes genetic damage is mostly a result of experimentation on animals[33] – in itself ethically contentious, and all the more so given that little has been done to study genetic damage to the children of workers in the nuclear industries, commercial, military or medical. This sort of damage is not immediate, but long-term and slow to manifest itself: mutations may be recessive – that is, abnormalities may not become apparent for several generations. In-depth study would require very close follow-ups with workers who have left the industry. Expensive, yes, but a fraction of the turnover of the multi-billion-pound nuclear industry.

There is no evidence of genetic damage from studies of survivors of Hiroshima and Nagasaki. Many scientists, however, argue that we cannot take this at face value. Those most sensitive to radiation died before studies were conducted; those who were included in the study were a stronger than average group who also survived the harsh winter of 1945–6, living in terrible conditions and with minimal medical care. Moreover, Japanese social observers report that *hibakusha* have suffered severe social stigma: many of those worst affected would not have had the chance to get married and have children and therefore would not have passed on any potential genetic damage.

Since then evidence has emerged which suggests that radiation which escaped into the atmosphere during a serious fire at the Windscale reprocessing plant in Cumbria in the north-west of England in 1957 may have led to a sudden cluster of cases of Down's syndrome in babies later born to women on the east coast of Ireland. Six Down's syndrome babies were born to mothers who had been teenagers at a school in Dundalk when fallout drifted over to Ireland at the same time as there was heavy rainfall in the area. Down's syndrome babies are most often born to women in their late thirties and forties, who have accumulated significant amounts of background radiation, which causes the ageing process in us all. These six women were all aged around 25.

The Marshallese culture is not traditionally a written one, reliant on reports and statistics. The Rongelapese do not, therefore, have their own figures with which to impress upon scientists what has happened to them. Instead, they trusted that Brookhaven doctors would be their advocates. I scanned the Brookhaven surveys to see if I could find figures or a collective summary of their findings on the effect of fallout on reproduction. In a rare reference to it, Dr Conard states baldly in his 1974 report:

> Psychological reaction to the fallout has been reflected at various times in fears regarding fertility . . .[34]

Later in the same report statistics are given for the rate of 'abortions, miscarriages and neonatal deaths'. (Dr Conard says he doubts whether any of the terminations were provoked because 'legal abortions are not performed in the Marshall Islands'. While his reasoning is dubious – the number of backstreet, botched and self-inflicted abortions in many countries where abortion is not legal is staggeringly high – I would agree that they were probably not provoked. Women I talked to said that on the outer islands big families were favoured and there was no shame or stigma in giving an unwanted child to another woman who had difficulty conceiving. They said that as far as they knew, abortion was not practised.) In 1954–8, immediately after Bravo, one in three – 33.3 per cent – of pregnancies of women who had been exposed to fallout resulted in fetal death, as opposed to 14 per cent in women not directly exposed to fallout. Over the next ten years, these figures started to even out, not only because women exposed to fallout began to have fewer miscarriages but also because the 'unexposed' women started to have more. By 1969–73 the figures were 21.3 per cent in the 'exposed' group and 20.7 per cent in the 'unexposed' group. What the study fails to question is whether the 'unexposed' women began to have more miscarriages as they ingested radioactive substances in food and water on Rongelap.

It seems incredible that the Brookhaven doctors make no reference to the 'jellyfish' babies. If the examinations were as rushed as they appear to have been, often with no interpreter and no woman doctor to consult on gynaecological problems, it is possible that they were never told about them. By 1960 it was widely known that radiation could produce fetal and genetic damage and the doctors should have been on the lookout for it. It is a huge omission for a survey which has purported to play a groundbreaking role in the understanding of radiation and the safety measures required from the nuclear industry.

In some areas of research and medicine, however, the prevalent attitude was – and still is – that fetal and genetic damage is in some ways an acceptable risk. In 1979, Dr R.H. Mole, a member of the International Commission on Radiological Protection (ICRP) and the British Nuclear Radiation Protection Board, wrote an article in the *British Journal of Radiology* questioning the justification for concern about the effects of radiation on a fetus – and in particular the effects of X-rays. He stated:

> The most important consideration is the generally accepted value judgement that early embryonic losses are of little personal or social concern.[35]

With regard to social concern, perhaps Dr Mole is right – in most western societies miscarriage is still a relatively taboo subject, a loss to be grieved over by individuals strictly in private: there is no ritual, no possible public mourning when a woman loses a wanted baby. It becomes a matter for social concern only in times of labour shortages or when a conventional war is fought and women are expected to produce babies for cannon fodder, neither of which is considered an imminent scenario by western leaders. But of no personal concern? Nobody who has miscarried or has been close to a woman who has miscarried a wanted baby could believe that.

In 1959 the ICRP published a report recommending occupational standards for internal radiation doses. It stated:

> A permissible genetic dose (to sperm and ovum) is that dose which if it were received yearly by each person from conception to the average age of childbearing (taken as 30 years) would result in an *acceptable burden to the whole population*.[36]

But what is an acceptable burden? If we are talking about 'mild effects' – which to begin with may manifest themselves in more women having miscarriages and stillbirths, more babies born

41

with a range of physical and mental disabilities – we're talking about 'burdens' borne by individuals, not the state. Figures can conceal the profound distress of the child who can't run around with others; the adult with a disability in a society constructed to include only those of 'standard' bodies and minds; the woman who repeatedly loses the child she is carrying. (Minimising the risks to a fetus, however, is *not* an argument for genetic engineering to rid the world of people with special needs – and often, special gifts.)

'Two-break' chromosome aberrations – further evidence that genetic damage might occur – have been noted in the Rongelap people directly exposed to fallout.[37] The Brookhaven study comments that this is consistent with other radiation survivors, and Dr Conard says that 'the possibility of genetic effects in the offspring is of serious concern to the exposed people and deserves further study'.[38] The Rongelap people, however, report that regular follow-ups have not been done on the second and third generations after Bravo. The lack of an independent investigation in the Marshall Islands means there is now the danger of the women's experiences being dismissed by doctors as anecdotal evidence, distorted by time.

Leukaemia and thyroid tumours

In 1972 the people of Rongelap were rocked by the death of a teenage boy, Lekoj Anjain. He died from leukaemia. His father, John Anjain, was with him when he died:

> In 1969 the AEC took my son Lekoj and two other children to New York for their thyroid problems. In 1972 they noticed that the white blood cell count of my son was very low. They took him to Honolulu for blood transfusions and Dr Conard told me that he would be alright. Then they notified me to go to Washington where they had taken my son. I arrived at the hospital and saw that my son was very weak. I will never forget being in Washington with my son –

42

I have never felt such sadness in all of my life. He died a few days later from leukaemia.[39]

Investigations in other parts of the world, including Britain, have since linked childhood leukaemia to radiation. Suspiciously high incidences have been found near the Windscale/Sellafield nuclear reprocessing plant in Cumbria. Many people living near the plant in Cumbria and South-West Scotland are worried about using their beaches and eating local produce: fish and chip shops carry signs assuring customers that their fish is not caught locally. In the wake of a Yorkshire TV documentary[40] and reports in the *Sunday Times*, a government inquiry was set up, chaired by Sir Douglas Black. In 1984 it reported that there were indeed high levels of childhood leukaemia in the area, but it maintained that there were *too many* to be explained by the discharges from the plant. It has since emerged that a former employee, Dr Jakeman, had compiled a report in 1956 showing that Windscale discharges of radioactivity into the sea, the ground and the air were at least 50 times larger than thought. Dr Jakeman left and his report was not made public. He has since rewritten it and another government committee (COMARE) has considered it; the committee remains guarded in its conclusions.

Most scientists now believe that exposure to radiation at an early age significantly increases a child's risk of getting leukaemia, and that thyroid problems are also often radiation related. Years after Bravo was detonated, children and adults began developing thyroid problems – benign and malignant tumours and under-active thyroids – on Rongelap, Utrik and other islands in the north of the Marshalls. Indeed, most of those who were children at the time of Bravo have since developed thyroid tumours. Reduced thyroid function can lead to stunted growth and mental handicaps in children and lethargy and depression in adults.[41] Alet Biliet, for example, was exposed when he was six weeks old. His growth stopped suddenly when he was nine and he is still only 4 ft 7 ins tall. Jilej Antak stopped growing when he was 3 ft 7 ins.

Many women who gave birth to dead or dying babies later found they had thyroid tumours themselves. Kajim Abija was on Ailinginae when Bravo was detonated. She was 32 at the time.

> After our return to Rongelap in 1957 I had a baby – just one week after it was born it turned yellow and died. [This could have been due to rhesus incompatibility and therefore unrelated to radiation.] Also, at that time, my older brother died even though he was only 34 years old . . .
>
> In 1973 I went to Cleveland to have my thyroid removed and I was really scared and thought I would never be well again. The AEC doctors keep telling us that things are alright now, yet they keep taking us to Cleveland for thyroid operations.[42]

Nelly Aplos was then 19 and living on Utrik. She was also taken to a US military hospital in Cleveland, Ohio, to have her thyroid removed. She was told by the doctors that her illness had nothing to do with exposure to radiation – but she doesn't believe them.

> The AEC doctors explained to me that a lot of people have thyroid problems which are unrelated to radiation and that my condition was unrelated. I used to believe those doctors but now I know that my sickness comes from the radiation.[43]

She also tells of others who developed symptoms of radiation sickness who were not on the atoll at the time of Bravo but have since lived there.

> I think our island has much 'poison' and know of four women (Namiko, LiMauno, Lenta and Jain) who were not here during the time of the fallout, yet all of these women have had their thyroids taken out after they lived here for some time. I also believe that many more atolls are affected from 'the bomb'.[44]

Mwendrik Kebenli, who was also on Rongelap, was not told

why her teenage son died. From her description, it could be hypothyroidism, induced by radiation:

> One of my children died at the age of 15. He went crazy, and lost the hair on his head while he was a student at RonRon in Majuro. I am sure this was caused by the poison.[45]

The Rongelapese have suffered damage to their thyroids because of the large quantities of radioactive iodine (iodine-131) produced by Bravo. The physical half-life of a radioactive substance is the time it takes for it to decompose to half its original amount. The half-life of iodine is eight days. It would normally take 10 half-lives for something to decay to an insignificant level: so for iodine-131 that means 80 days – a short time in comparison to other isotopes. However, iodine is very easily absorbed into the body, where it is concentrated in the thyroid gland. In the first few days after the fallout, the Rongelapese would have ingested large amounts of iodine-131 in rainwater, coconut milk and fruits. Babies would then take it in through their mother's milk.[46]

The only known ways to counter the ingestion of iodine-131 are to take potassium iodate tablets or eat uncontaminated foods high in iodine such as seaweed and miso in advance or within hours of the iodine-131 arriving. This will to some extent block the radioactive iodine from the thyroid. The UK now has over two million such tablets in stock in case of nuclear accidents: most are held at nuclear power stations.[47] The Marshallese, however, were not rushed potassium iodate tablets.

The maximum permissible dose of radiation to the thyroid in one week is 0.3 rems. (This is not, of course, what the body can tolerate with no harm done, but what governments and the nuclear industry estimate to be acceptable damage.) According to the AEC measurement, the exposed children under age ten on Rongelap received a dose of 500 to 1,400 rads, or 1,000 to 2,000 times more than the permissible dose. That is even more serious for children, whose thyroid glands are much smaller and therefore more vulnerable to damage.[48] Women are also more at risk than men – we get three times more thyroid cancers and the general risk of our developing radiation-induced cancer is calculated to be 1.5 times that of men.[49]

Cataracts

A remarkable number of people in the Marshalls have cataracts. Neiktemos Antak now has to wear very dark glasses all the time.

> I was born on Rongelap on 8 March 1936. I was 18 at the time of the bomb and was sitting outside drinking coffee and eating doughnuts when the fallout came. That morning I'd seen a bright flash and later heard sounds like a big rumble. I was very scared. My grandmother died in 1966 from thyroid cancer. I developed severe burns when we were in Kwajalein. Now my eyes are very weak and hurt. I may have to have an operation, I've been told, for cataracts. I'm not the only one to have this problem: quite a few of us do.

Dr Conard notes the high number of 'opacities of the lens' and cataracts but is sceptical whether they have any correlation with the nuclear tests. He notes that because of the distance involved, the fireball would not have risen over the horizon at its most intense, and he discounts radiation. Moreover, the high incidence of diabetese, which also causes cataracts, confuses the picture. A detailed study, to discern whether only older people and those with diabetese suffer from a high incidence of cataracts, does not seem to have been carried out.

Even more bizarre, according to a visiting doctor, when there was an epidemic of cataracts on Utrik, instead of examining and treating people, the US doctors simply sent two boxes of various frames and prescriptions and told them to help themselves.[50]

A second explanation for the high incidence of cataracts is given in the World Health Organisation's 1972 report which says the non-ionising radiation emitted from the huge array of missile tracking radar on Kwajalein atoll, may be in part to blame.

Diabetese

The Marshall Islands has the highest rate of diabetese in the world. This may be a result of the fallout or of the sudden change to imported junk food once local produce became contaminated – or a combination of both. As Rosalie Bertell explained:

> Some of the radionuclides tend to go to the pancreas; those stored there can destroy the cells which produce insulin. Or, if the insulin itself mutates, the person will produce lots of insulin which just isn't functioning to bring down the blood sugar levels. Unfortunately, the physician's job is not to classify its origin, just which treatment it responds to: so we don't know which kind of diabetese the Marshallese have. If you've induced a hormonal imbalance and then you bring in a radical change of diet which is very heavy in junk food and sugars, it's enough to overburden the body's capability.

General health

A whole range of other problems also began to manifest themselves after Bravo. Many people like Jailor Baktwak, who was on Wotje during the fallout, have suffered a variety of ill effects:

> In 1976 Dr Conard diagnosed the lump in my throat as a tumour and they gave me some liquid medicine. Then in 1979 Dr Conard took me to Kwajalein for two weeks and . . . from there to Honolulu, then to Brookhaven in New York for a week of tests under many bright lights. Finally I was sent to Cleveland. I was operated on and was in the hospital for three days, and they told me they were going to get rid of my thyroid but I did not know what that meant. I recall waking up and feeling very cold. Now I must take a pill every day for the rest of my life or I will die.

Today I have skin problems that come and go – like small lumps. I used to sing in the choir but after my operation I cannot sing anymore. Also, it is hard for me to become sexually stimulated, whereas this never happened before. [This is commonly associated with thyroid malfunction.] I have much fear today.

Medical examinations carried out between 1970 and 1974 on the 'exposed' and 'unexposed' population showed a startlingly high level of overall ill health in the 'exposed' group, who had a higher than average incidence of acne, anaemia, arteriosclerosis, bradycardia (very slow heart pulse), cervical erosion, prolapse of the womb, hernia, leprosy, migraine, enlarged prostate gland, rheumatic heart disease, and benign and malignant tumours. Given continuing ignorance about the effects of radiation, there is not enough evidence to rule out that these may be related to fallout.

Most people, even those who have had no specific illness, talk of feeling generally run-down and ill most of the time. Kajim Abija, quoted above, says, 'We all suffered from aches and pains and were weak with fatigue all the time.' When I stayed with Rongelap people in 1986, that was still the case; it is one aspect of radiation that is hardly talked about in medical circles, perhaps because our definition of 'health' is often confined to an absence of disease rather than a feeling of well-being.

According to Brookhaven only two deaths were related to radiation damage. One was Lekoj Anjain. The other was described by Dr Conard in his 1982 report: 'one death from cancer of the stomach in a Rongelapese man exposed to 175 rads gamma radiation may have been related to his exposure.' Yet in the same report Conard notes: 'A number of deaths in older women were thought to be due to cancer of the female genital tract, which is not reported to be radiation induced in the exposed Japanese people.' To dismiss it on the grounds of the significantly different Japanese experience rather than to allow a picture to be built up over a longer time, with more data, seems at best pre-emptive.

outlook for the Marshallese is nothing but cancer: cancer, not just of the thyroid gland, but cancer of such organs as the colon, the pancreas, the lung, cancer of the breast . . .[53]

He points out that most estimates of cancer risk are based on adults – and yet age at irradiation is crucial: the younger the more dangerous. Instead of producing an average figure, scientists should take age into account, he says, and their predictions should be long term because many cancers won't start until 30 to 40 years after the event:

> What I am saying is that every child under 15 years of age (at irradiation) at Rongelap should be destined to die of a premature cancer. And my prediction is that that will be the case, that they will die prematurely of cancer – unless they drown – and that is the one thing in a life table that does cut the number of cancers down – namely, if you die of heart disease you cannot die of cancer too . . .
>
> I am predicting a very, very bad outlook for those people.

The Brookhaven programme comes under criticism

> We all know the parable about the fox guarding the henhouse. To have the DOE judge the radiation residuals on Rongelap would be equivalent to the R. J. Reynolds Tobacco Company conducting the sole study on the relationship between cigarette smoking and lung cancer.[54]
>
> Johnsay Riklon, a Rongelapese lawyer, now living on Ebeye, to a US Congressional committee

The Rongelap people hoped that the foreign power which had 'accidentally' exposed them to radiation would do the decent thing and give them the best possible medical attention. They were to be disappointed. The whole approach of the

Brookhaven programme gradually alienated the traditionally hospitable and welcoming Marshallese.

In 1981 several people told Glenn Alcalay (a former Peace Corps volunteer to the islands, now a writer and activist on Pacific issues) what they thought of the programme. Marion Matthew, a Rongelap woman, then aged 64:

> The AEC doctors are not reliable, they never tell us honestly what our problems are and they treat us as if we were merely animals. I am not happy about the AEC programme and would like to see other doctors come out to our islands.[55]

John Anjain:

> From the beginning of the testing programme in our islands the US has treated us like animals in a scientific experiment for their studies. They come and study us like animals and think of us as 'guinea pigs'.[56]

Jirda Biton, a Utrik man who was 60 when interviewed:

> Many times I used to ask Dr Conard if we had 'poison' and he would always tell me that we did not have any poison. 'If we do not have any poison, Dr Conard, then why do you keep coming back to check us?' Since that time I have never believed Dr Conard. The people of Utrik now know that things are not alright here and we have many fears and anxieties about our health. Dr Conard has never co-operated with us here on Utrik and we believe that he just comes to study us without any compassion for us. One of the things that has bothered us over the years is the fact that the AEC doctors have never bothered to explain our problems to us – instead they treat us as if we were merely children.[57]

Western doctors are often unco-operative about showing patients their own health records. In the case of the Marshallese, the doctors on the ground didn't even keep the records, let alone show them to the Marshallese: they were kept at Brookhaven's offices in the US and a request to have a duplicate copy kept in the islands was turned down. Only in recent years, with the advent of a new health programme, has that changed. The lack of records meant the Marshallese had to keep telling the doctors the same problems year after year. This, together with the fact that many Marshallese people don't know what's wrong with them, and say the doctors didn't explain, compounds their feelings of being treated like guinea pigs.

Dr Merliss also talks of 'the basic rights of a patient' being ignored. 'I found very few Marshallese who were acquainted with the nature of their pathology. I reject firmly the thought that the people were too primitive [sic] or uneducated to absorb such information as I have found this not to be true.'[58] Indeed, the Brookhaven reports were written for other scientists and doctors. No attempt was made to publish reports for the lay person so that the Marshallese could find out about their own health or so that other interested parties – lobbyists, lawyers and the like – could understand what was happening.

Through the 1950s and 60s the Rongelap and Utrik people kept insisting that they should be given better attention. Eventually in 1973 a Brookhaven doctor was stationed in the Marshall Islands, with medical surveys being carried out four times a year on Rongelap instead of once. Utrik was still only visited once every three years.

Konrad Kotrady was the Brookhaven doctor in the Marshalls from 1975–6. When he left he wrote a controversial report, criticising the programme and suggesting changes. To the Marshallese, said Kotrady, a doctor meant, not unreasonably, someone 'giving care to all their problems and not focusing on only one small area of concern'.[59] According to Kotrady not only was the Brookhaven programme 'research oriented' instead of health oriented, as the Marshallese would have liked, but 'under closer analysis the program is even more limited in its objectives'. He went on: 'The program seems to operate in a mode of looking for those effects predicted by experts in the field of radiation medicine.' Conard's refusal to consider that radiation caused women's cancer of the uterus or jellyfish babies certainly bears that out.

By narrowing its range of questions to previously identified health problems in this relatively uncharted territory, Brookhaven badly served both the Marshallese and any long-term understanding of the health effects of radiation. It is a blinkered scientific survey which looks only for results it predicts.

The results of the Marshallese survey helped perpetrate the myth – crucial to the nuclear industry, and only recently beginning to crack open under pressure from scientists such as Alice Stewart in Britain – that low-level radiation is not harmful. And it helped to underestimate the effects of medium-level radiation. Eventually Brookhaven had to admit that the lower levels of radiation were indeed harmful:

> Within the past year (1976) it has become apparent that the theory was wrong and in reality effects attributable to radiation have been discovered at Utrik . . . there is as much thyroid cancer at Utrik as at Rongelap – three cases each. In fact, the ratio of thyroid cancer to thyroid nodules found in exposed people at both islands, is higher at Utrik than at Rongelap. In addition, a young man, son of an exposed person, was found at Utrik to have thyroid cancer and no such unexposed case has been found at Rongelap.[60]

Kotrady wondered whether, if low-level radiation hadn't been ignored in the first place, the cancers on Utrik could not have been prevented. Utrik people, like the Rongelapese, he said, could have been put on Synthroid, a drug to suppress the thyroid gland function, 'to try to prevent the development of further thyroid lesions'.

In a statement to a US House of Representatives committee[61] on 8 May 1984, Jeton Anjain, Rongelap's senator to the Marshall Islands *Nitijela*, criticised the way the study had been carried out. When the Rongelapese were taken to Kwajalein their urine samples were analysed only as a pool sample instead of individually. The food chain was also studied in such a way that it minimised the results. The Atomic Energy Commission averaged the values of radionuclides found in the land, fish and fruits eaten by the Marshallese, thus concealing the expected effect on, say, an individual living in a highly contaminated area eating a particular diet. In addition, said Anjain,

> The persons conducting the survey made certain assumptions about the diet of the people who would be living there. Their assumptions were totally inaccurate and did not reflect the customs or culinary practices of the Marshallese people. A proper survey using the actual diet of the people of Rongelap would have resulted in much greater intakes of radiation than were found in the survey . . .
>
> But even if all their methods and results were accepted, it appears strange that they would tell us to live on islands where we have *average* exposures higher than 450 millirems per year with the possibility of 2 to 5 times that much if we happen to be eating fish that have wandered over from some more contaminated islands.

Amongst the anomalies in the study was the assumption that all fish eaten would have conveniently confined themselves to the less contaminated waters. And one of the customs it overlooked was the eating of fish bones of some species: caesium-90 is lodged in bones.

In 1983 a US doctor, Karl Z. Morgan, an 'insider' to the nuclear business, also criticised the surveys for dealing only with *average* amounts of exposure: there could be variations by a factor of up to 1,000 in 'internal exposure' in individual cases due to eating habits, breathing rates, other illnesses and so on, he said.[62]

> There would be little comfort to the mother who heard from the US DOE . . . that there is nothing to worry about, the average is only 1 rem, whereas the baby may be getting a rate that is 100 to 1,000 times that . . .
>
> It is my belief that – perhaps unintentionally but certainly in reality – the data collected [by the DOE], the interpretation of the data, and the numbers they published in their papers give figures which are biased, which depreciate the risk, and certainly they come up with values far less than I have been able to come up with.[63]

US assessment of the risk of radiation to humans was further distorted, the Marshall Islands *Nitijela* noted on 11 August 1983. Its assumptions were based on a previously uncontaminated people – not a community like Rongelap, where half the people were suffering from *acute* as well as *chronic* radiation sickness.

Dr Conard notes the problem of 'the language barrier' which 'hampered communication with the people'. It seems scarcely believable that there was no interpreter, yet Kotrady confirms that in 1976 this was still the case. More shocking still, Marshallese who were sent away to Hawai'i or mainland United States for operations were often sent without an interpreter. Being taken to hospital for surgery is frightening at the best of times; how much worse to be taken to a strange country, with different customs and a different language, and where there is no one to visit you in hospital or explain what is happening. When I was with the Rongelapese on Mejato in 1986, an older woman was scheduled to go to Hawai'i to have an operation for a brain tumour. She never went. She was simply very afraid.

Other problems arose because the American doctors failed to take any account of Marshallese culture, such as their independence from the western constraints of time-keeping or their tradition that a woman should not be examined in front of male members of her family. Kotrady commented:

> The people feel they have no input into decisions about their examinations and care. The doctors always appear with a predetermined plan of what will be done, who will be seen and what will be achieved. The people are not consulted beforehand and are essentially ordered to do things the way the American doctors have established the plan. Such plans are usually formulated on American cultural guidelines and neglect the local traditions. When the people raise any hint of an objection or seek to question some point, the doctors think they are only trying to cause trouble.[64]

Kotrady gave an example of how, in March 1976, the programme directors decided to send four women, three from

Rongelap and one from Utrik, to Honolulu for detailed examinations. They were neither consulted nor asked if March was a good time, but were simply told a month previously to stop their medication. When they objected and asked for a meeting to work out a better arrangement, 'Dr Conard refused the request. Instead each lady was confronted individually such that she felt intimidated and threatened such that all she could do was accept.'

The Marshallese traditionally gather food every day. For a woman with a family, the gathering, lighting of a fire, preparing and washing up often fill much of the day. For this reason, the women asked that when the doctors visited and called them away for a half or whole day of examinations, they should be given preserved food to make life manageable. The request was repeatedly refused. The Marshallese were astonished, reported Kotrady, that such an inexpensive request be turned down when the Brookhaven programme was outfitted with such costly equipment.

If the Marshallese found their treatment by Brookhaven distressing, how did the other Brookhaven doctors regard the programme? According to Dr Conard, in his 1974 report, 'The medical surveys have been a rewarding experience for all the personnel who have participated.' Even after Kotrady's damning report in 1977 Conard published another in 1980, a year after he retired, asserting that 'the Marshallese people have basically maintained strong feelings of friendship and respect for the medical team', although he did acknowledge there were 'misunderstandings'.[65]

The success of the working relationships between the doctors and the Marshallese is not really what is at issue here, however. The questions which need to be asked are: Were the Marshallese wrong to suspect that they were treated like guinea pigs? Did they receive the best possible medical treatment? Did the US do everything possible to explain at every stage what had happened and how and what the likely effects were? Did the medical teams approach the islanders' health problems with an open mind or were they looking only for effects they already believed to be

57

associated with irradiation? Have the full facts of the extent of their illnesses been made public? If the answer to any of these is no, the next question is: why not?

In every such situation there are two possible theories: 'cock-up or conspiracy'. The truth is often a combination of the two. Until public and media concern brings such pressure to bear that there can be a thorough public inquiry, we have to assume that what has happened to the Marshallese is also a result of both.

The buck stops where?

It should be noted that no test is done without a specific purpose in mind, and at no time was the testing out of control.[66] Admiral Lewis Strauss, former director of the Atomic Energy Commission speaking about the Bravo test at a press conference in the Washington Press Club, 30 March 1954

The smokescreen of contradictory and even false statements and inaccurate studies both of the radioactivity levels and of the islanders' health problems in fact started from the time Bravo was detonated.

Ten days after the explosion, the Atomic Energy Commission made its first public statement about the incident:

During the course of a routine atomic test in the Marshall Islands, the US personnel and 236 residents were transported from neighbouring atolls to Kwajalein Island according to plan as precautionary measures. These individuals were unexpectedly exposed to some radioactivity. There were no burns. All were reported well. After the completion of the atomic tests, the natives [sic] will be returned to their homes.

It is worth analysing this statement in detail. 'There were no burns' was the message wired to newspapers around the world.

Yet, the testimonies of Marshallese people and subsequent US reports are quite clear in describing their burns: it is estimated that out of every ten people on Rongelap that day, nine suffered burns.

To say they received 'some' radioactivity is an understatement, to say the least. Official US figures estimated that the people on Rongelap at the time were exposed to 175 rems of radioactivity. (200–300 rems is expected to cause a 50 per cent mortality rate in the event of a nuclear war.)[67] The 18 Rongelapese who had canoed to Ailinginae atoll, west of Rongelap, to collect coconuts received 69 rem, and the islanders of Utrik atoll were exposed to 14 rem. In 1982 those figures were changed to 190 on Rongelap and 110 on Ailinginae, not including internal absorption doses from eating, drinking and breathing the fallout.[68] The calculations were taken in the air, three feet above the ground, about one week after the Bravo detonation, and were extrapolated back to the time and length of exposure. Finally, if the evacuation to Kwajalein was according to plan, why was it carried out *after* the Marshallese people were exposed to fallout? Or was that indeed the plan?

Bravo was an unnecessarily dirty bomb – it delivered huge quantities of fallout. That was because the size of the bomb in relation to the height of the tower used meant it detonated low off the ground and the fireball scooped up huge quantities of Bikini's coral reef. The Defense Department's publication, 'The Effects of Nuclear Weapons', states:

> Although the test of March 1, 1954, produced the worst extensive local fallout yet recorded, it should be pointed out that the phenomenon was not necessarily characteristic of (nor restricted to) thermonuclear explosions.
>
> It is very probable that if the same device had been detonated at an appreciable distance above the coral island, so that the large fireball did not touch the surface of the ground, the early fallout would have been of insignificant proportions.

That is, as in previous and subsequent tests, the US could have

59

chosen to use a higher tower, a balloon or an airburst, which would have stopped the bomb sucking up huge clouds of disintegrated coral and spewing them over inhabited islands.

A Dr Dunning described to a US Congressional sub-committee just how exposed the Rongelap and Utrik people were to the fallout:

> The Marshallese were semiclothed, had moist skin and most of them were out-of-doors during the time of the fallout. Some bathed during the two days exposure period before evacuation, but others did not, therefore there were optimal conditions in general for possible beta damages.[69]

In contrast, US personnel were better prepared. A 1956 Atomic Energy Commission report notes:

> Most of the Americans who were more aware of the danger of the fallout, took shelter in aluminium buildings, bathed and changed clothes and consequently developed very mild beta lesions.[70]

They *were* nevertheless exposed to high levels of fallout. A 1981 Defense Nuclear Agency report on Operation Castle, of which Bravo formed part, said that 31 personnel had readings of 7.8–9.6 rads on the nuclear film badges, designed to warn when 'safe' levels were being exceeded, but generally ignored. The limit which had been established for the entire operation was 3.9 rads, but so many personnel were contaminated that after Bravo 'it became necessary to issue a number of waiver authorisations permitting exposures of as much as 7.8 rads. In a limited number of cases, even this level was exceeded.' The Defense Nuclear Agency document concludes, however, on a bright note: the *average* exposure during Castle was about 1.7 rads; like the Marshallese, individual cases of high exposure were made invisible by giving an 'average' dose as the official figure. Small comfort for the many US vets – for the most part, ordinary enlisted people – who later developed radiation-linked diseases.

To this day, the Department of Energy claims its radiation of the Rongelapese was an accident. Another story is, however, now beginning to emerge.

John Anjain, magistrate of Rongelap atoll at the time of Bravo, recounts how he was told beforehand of the bomb:

> While I was in Majuro, a fellow who worked with the Atomic Energy Commission stuck out the tip of his finger – about half an inch or so – and said, 'John, your life is just about that long.' When I asked him what he meant, he explained that they were setting off a bomb on Bikini soon. I asked why they did not move people from Rongelap first [as they had done in preparation for Operation Crossroads in 1946] and he told me that they had not gotten word from Washington to evacuate the people beforehand.[71]

Senior weather technician Gene Curbow, who was on Rongerik at the time of the Bravo test, says someone must have known for days that the wind was blowing towards Rongelap, and that those in charge had ample time to cancel the test.

> The wind had been blowing straight at us for days before the test . . . it was blowing straight at us after it. The wind never shifted.[72]

An official report by the Defense Nuclear Agency, released in 1984, backs up Curbow's claim.[73] It states that the midnight weather review – six hours before Bravo was detonated – noted: 'winds at 20,000 feet were headed for Rongelap to the east . . .' The Atomic Energy Commission had plenty of time to register that the winds were blowing towards Rongelap and to postpone the test. Someone must have decided to go ahead regardless. Did those in charge go ahead because they didn't care? Did they fail to realise the risks involved? Or was the contamination of a whole population planned in advance?

Senator Ataji Balos, representative of Kwajalein in the Marshall Islands *Nitijela* and a descendant of Rongelap and Bikini, has studied the evidence and has come to the conclusion that the contamination was deliberate. He has charged the US with 'knowingly and consciously allowing the people of

Rongelap to be exposed so that the United States could use them as guinea pigs in the development of its medical capabilities to treat its citizens who might be exposed to radiation in the event of a war with an enemy country'.[74]

The US is now trying to stop lawsuits arising out of the irradiation of the Marshallese from being heard in court. The Compact of Free Association which forms the new relationship between the Marshalls and the US (see pp. 179–88), contains an 'espousal' clause, stipulating that the US has paid a lump sum for damages and from now on all responsibility must be shouldered by the Marshall Islands government – not even a sovereign nation at the time of Bravo. The Administration's anxiety to pay for silence arouses deep suspicions: is it afraid that the truth about why Bravo went ahead will emerge in the course of a court case? Is it aware that the damage done to the Marshallese will result in increasing illnesses over the coming years? Critics also question whether US officials are privately worried that a far greater number of Marshallese people are in fact harbouring radiation damage. A 1978 Department of Energy report showed that all 14 of the atolls and islands surveyed received 'intermediate range fallout from one or more of the megaton range tests'.[75] Yet the Compact provides for only four of them and there has been no survey of radiation levels on the 15 remaining atolls and single islands of the Marshalls which were not checked in 1978.

Power, control and research

Like the bombing of the Japanese cities of Hiroshima and Nagasaki in 1945, the detonation of 66 bombs in the Marshall Islands and the subsequent irradiation of the local people was a display of power and control. The Allies had already defeated Germany and Italy when the US decided to drop its nuclear bombs on Japan. The Truman Administration could have used its secret new weapon against a warship or another military target. Instead, the politicians chose to bomb two major cities.

The 'tests' – for that is, in essence, what the bombs were in

1945, too – were carried out in part to flex newly found nuclear muscles, to demonstrate to an 'ally', the Soviet Union, that the US was setting the pace for the nuclear arms race. They were also demonstrations of control. In 1945 the US conquered Japan and by the 1950s, with the Bikini tests, was treating the Pacific as its backyard, a backyard conveniently big enough to allow for dirty work to be done in a far corner, away from the master's house. The UN Trusteeship, which delivered the Marshalls into the hands of the US, was just a nice clean new name to disguise the fact that the US had, in effect, acquired a colony.

But were the tests also a macabre form of scientific research on human beings? From the minute the first nuclear bombs dropped from the belly of US planes, the suffering in Hiroshima and Nagasaki was recorded in detail. That footage has now been bought by the Japanese peace movement, which raised the money to buy back the now declassified account of their own nightmare. Likewise, the events before and after the Bravo test at Bikini were carefully filmed. The Rongelap people provided scientists with new raw data, for while people at Hiroshima and Nagasaki had suffered most from the effects of the initial blast, the Rongelapese suffered the effects of fallout, four to six hours after the bomb had been detonated. (The bombs on Japan were air bursts and so created little fallout.) US newspapers have since reported that the Pentagon used US citizens in its experiments to gauge the effects of radiation: healthy prisoners whose testicles were irradiated and poor people, mostly Blacks, who were told they were receiving medical treatment. Dr Eugene Saenger, who performed the experiments on Black people, is quoted as defending his work thus:

The most important field of investigation today is that of attempting to understand and mitigate the possible effects of nuclear warfare upon human beings. I am a person who takes the defense of this country very seriously. I think it is important to find out the kinds of things [effects of radiation on humans] we are learning from this study.[76]

Does it matter whether the irradiation was premeditated, when those who have died cannot be brought back and when children of today already carry the seeds of cancer? It matters very much to the Marshall Islanders' current fight for some kind of justice – and indeed to those military personnel also exposed at the time. It matters also because the world is desperately in need of a new social and economic order based on co-operation and co-existence, on justice and equality and mutual respect. We need to know the truth about the past and present; we need to know because we cannot build a future of hope on the rubble of secrecy and lies.

4

Leaving Rongelap

Even before the 1978 study confirmed their suspicions that the atoll was still contaminated, fear drove some people to leave Rongelap. They settled on Ebeye or Majuro, where there are hospitals, or with family on other atolls. As people started drifting away, however, concern arose that the community would lose some of its strength in its fight for justice. Renam Anjain told me:

> Most people from Rongelap want us to stick together to create a future. It's no good going to Ebeye to work for the Americans. On Rongelap, if a person is poor, we're all poor. We look after each other. And we need each other even more now.

Thus, in 1982, after much heart-searching and discussion, the people of Rongelap came to the conclusion that they would all have to leave their atoll until it was properly cleaned up. It was a difficult and deeply distressing decision. Older Rongelapese had already spent three years in exile after Bravo and dreaded being shunted around from island to island again. Besides, the ties of the Marshallese to their land are fundamental to their existence. But they had little choice. Lemeyo Abon, a school teacher, recalled:

> When we learned from the 1982 report that our atoll was still highly contaminated, after all they had told us about it being safe, we were angry. We also lost our appetite for food. Really, it just confirmed what we already knew. We knew because most of the time we'd lived there after Bravo we felt something was wrong with our bodies. When we ate local foods we'd often get stomach ache. And when we moved around, something would hurt in our stomachs, like an electric shock. We couldn't go on living there. We were terribly afraid for ourselves and our children.

Boas Jellen:

> I'm old now and I just think about the future generations. I feel so sorry for the young children. We didn't want to leave our homeland – we did it for the children.

Once resolved that they had no option but to move, the Rongelapese faced major practical problems. Where would they move to? How? Where would they get the funds to pay for the move, to lease other land, to build new houses and to feed themselves if they left their carefully tended fruit trees and bountiful lagoon?

When outsiders look at a map of the Pacific it seems there are hundreds of scattered atolls and single islands – surely there must be lots of free land, given the size of the population? In fact, land is precious – virtually priceless, as Jeton Anjain was to tell a US Congressional Committee in 1985:

> Land ownership is uniquely significant under Marshallese custom. The ownership of land is vested in the family, including in unborn generations. Landless people are outcasts, second-class citizens. When my people of Rongelap, and others like us, are uprooted from our traditional islands the fabric of our social structure is torn . . .

Our lands are unreplaceable and without price. There *are* no comparable sales since there *are* no sales . . .[1]

On 9 August 1983 the Marshall Islands *Nitijela* unanimously passed a resolution recognising that there was an urgent need 'to eliminate not only the physical but also the psychological effects on the people of Rongelap of their continued residence on a contaminated atoll and their uncertainty as to their safety and well-being'. It concluded that the US be asked to fund the resettlement. In the end the Marshallese government requested $3 million – only 11 per cent of what the Rongelapese had calculated it would cost them to move. Chief Secretary of the Marshall Islands' government, Oscar de Brum, told me they had to be cautious because 'it was at a time when everyone was trying to reduce the US deficit'. No help was forthcoming, however.

Seven months later, on 14 March 1984, Rongelapese lawyer Johnsay Riklon told a US Congressional Committee that as the US had chosen to ignore its responsibility to the Marshallese people, it had accepted an offer of help from the international environmental organisation Greenpeace, who would provide a ship to move them to a different island.[2] Funds estimated at $27 million were still needed for housing, for water resources, public buildings and other infrastructure. The US Administration had offered another study to see if a move was really necessary, but Riklon argued that the Rongelap people could not afford to wait for the money to be appropriated and a survey carried out.

On 11 April 1985, only a month before they were due to move, Senator Jeton Anjain made a last-minute plea, not only for help in moving but also for an independent verifiable radiological dose assessment of all the atolls where fallout occurred, and for a proper clean-up of Rongelap.[3] He secured a promise of two grants: $300,000 to pay for an independent radiological survey of the island, and $3.2 million for the resettlement of its population of 300 to Mejato island if the survey proved the move was justified. Nearly three years later, the Rongelap people are still waiting for the survey to be carried out.

So when the Greenpeace ship *Rainbow Warrior* anchored off the shore of Rongelap in May 1985 to a warm and festive reception, the Rongelap people had received not one cent from the US towards the cost of their resettlement.

Rainbow Warrior

Aloha and welcome to you, now you're here on Rongelap
It is the coolest place and the land of freedom
Surrounded by an ocean and green trees
It is my home, sweet home.

Now you're here on Rongelap you'll find it the best place
Rongelap is in the Marshall Islands, though the waves try to
    wash it away
I'll praise you to the heavens, Rongelap
For there is no place like you
You're my land, my home sweet home.

> Welcome song, written and sung by Rongelap women, translated
> by Roko Laninvelik and Hermy Lang

Europeans and North Americans on board the *Rainbow Warrior* were stunned by the almost unreal beauty of Rongelap: clear turquoise waters, pale sands fringed with palms against a deep blue sky. It was difficult to imagine that an invisible, insidious enemy was relentlessly destroying life on the atoll. As they stood and looked, Rongelap women came to greet them in their small boats, which Marshallese call 'boum-boums' for their noisy engines. The crew were welcomed on shore with *leis* (necklaces) made of fragile white flowers, and with singing and dancing beneath an arch of coconut planks and pandanus leaves. On top of it was a sign: 'Welcome to Rongelap. *Ba Eman Kabjere*. We love the future of our kids.' The crew was offered bananas and fresh coconut milk – delicious, sweet and refreshing and very different from the dried-up version which reaches Europe. At first the crew were hesitant about accepting the local foods, but the radiation sickness experienced by the Rongelapese was a result of a long build-up of radionuclides in their bodies. Consumption of a small amount of local food was probably no more dangerous than walking in Cumbria or South-west Scotland down-wind from Sellafield, or demonstrating on the site of nuclear tests in Rocky Flats, Nevada.

Jeton Anjain, Julian Riklon (now living in Ebeye and working to publicise the problems of both Rongelap and Ebeye) and other Marshallese had joined the *Rainbow Warrior* when it passed through Majuro in order to tell the crew about Marshallese customs and prepare them for the move. Jeton Anjain told journalist David Robie, also on board:

> The people looked to me to find a way to save them, but they didn't really believe a ship would come all the way from Britain. It wasn't until they saw the *Rainbow Warrior* in their lagoon that they really believed me.

The *Warrior* had indeed been involved in many Greenpeace campaigns in Britain: against the building of a nuclear power station at Torness in Scotland; successfully stopping a cull of grey seals in the Orkney Islands, and twice attempting a blockade of the entrance to Barrow Harbour in opposition to spent nuclear fuel being transported through it en route to the reprocessing plant at Windscale. But she had also taken part in actions around Europe, from protests against whaling off Iceland and Spain, to a blockade of chemical waste dumping off Holland. She was later pitted against activities of the super-powers in campaigns against chemical and oil pollution in North America and the feeding of whale meat to minks in the Soviet Union.

Moving the people of Rongelap was to be the last act in the *Rainbow Warrior*'s remarkable history. After leaving the Marshalls for Aotearoa/New Zealand via Vanuatu, she was sunk by a French secret service limpet mine in Auckland Harbour before she could reach the South Pacific atoll of Moruroa and begin disrupting French nuclear tests there. Greenpeace photographer and deck-hand Fernando Pereira was killed by the blast.

Prior to sailing to the Marshall Islands, the *Rainbow Warrior* was given a much-needed $130,000 refit at Green Cove Springs, Jacksonville, Florida, in preparation for one of Greenpeace's biggest campaigns. It had designated 1985 Year of the Pacific, hoping to draw worldwide attention to American testing in the Marshall Islands and French nuclear testing on Moruroa. At first they planned a symbolic gesture in Kwajalein lagoon to protest against Star Wars testing. But Darlene Keju-Johnson and her husband Giff warned Greenpeace that whatever they did must be in close consultation with the Marshallese and be relevant to their *own* methods of struggle. It was then that Jeton Anjain suggested Greenpeace do what the US Administration had failed to: move the Rongelapese to a place of safety.

The *Rainbow Warrior*'s crew had ten days, according to schedule, to move a community of 304 people and about 100 tons of cargo. The islanders had already started the sad task of dismantling their houses. Corrugated iron, plywood and timber lay in great bundles beneath the trees. Their other few possessions were crammed into boxes: cooking utensils, paraffin lamps, clothes, fishing gear. The animals – pigs, hens and dogs – they reluctantly decided would have to be left behind to cut down the chance of spreading the contamination to their new home. One final ritual before leaving was to say goodbye to the coconut trees, sustainers of life. They were counted: 67,000 in all.

For some of the older folks it was their third forced evacuation – in 1946, prior to the first test, to the atoll of Lae, 200 miles south-west of Rongelap, then in 1954, to Kwajalein. For most youngsters, this was the first time they had left Rongelap. It took four trips to ferry everyone, plus the cargo to Mejato, some 120 miles away and on the north-west tip of Kwajalein atoll. Japanese photographer Hiromitsu Toyasaki, a campaigner for radiation survivors the world over, was one of the few journalists willing to make the trip to record the occasion. He later recalled how moved he was by the Rongelap people's silent resolve: as they sailed away on the *Rainbow Warrior*, none of them looked back at their sweet, spoiled home.

If they had done, all that was visible was the bolted church and rows of gravestones.[4]

Mejato

Let us give thanks for the good times
We've had together

chorus
Hello, hello, how are you?
Hello, hello from the Women's Fellowship
The song we sing is to give you peace of mind

We come from our land, where our hearts belong,
The place which reminds us of our past

chorus
On Mejato we try to live as we once did on Rongelap
But we can't forget our home

And the good times
We've had together

> Written and sung by Rongelap women, translated from
> Marshallese by Roko Laninvelik and Hermy Lang

The first job on Mejato was to build a large all-purpose building. It began as a concrete slab, 30 by 40 feet and covered with a corrugated-iron roof – a rudimentary shelter for the first arrivals until they could put up their tarpaulins, brought by Greenpeace, and later build houses. Eventually, the community building was walled and used as a school, a church on Sundays and after school, a general meeting centre, a dispensary (two open shelves for medicines) and a base for the doctors who would continue to visit. It also housed the two-way short-range radio, the only means by which the islanders could keep in touch with other islands. School was often disrupted. One of the two teachers, Lemoyo, told me:

71

We don't have enough space or enough teachers. We divide the kids up according to age into four classes of 12 to 14 a class. On Rongelap we had a building with four classrooms. Each child only gets taught half a day because we can only cope with half the number of children at any one time in that space. As it is, I teach in one half and Aisen in the other and we have to talk very quietly so as not to disrupt the other class. Sometimes the kids just can't hear what we are saying, or there is noise from the other class. We can't divide this room though, because it has to be used as a church and meeting house, too. There's nowhere to put our teaching equipment, it's just piled into the corner in boxes. After class, from 3 p.m., we sit on the floor preparing the next day's lessons. We have very few materials and we're right out of fluid and carbon for making copies. The Department of Education says it can't afford to help. It just isn't fair on the kids – what chance do they have of competing with others to get into the high school on Majuro?

What chance indeed. In 1986 none of the pupils passed the exam for the state high school in Majuro. And as their parents no longer had income from copra, the option of sending them to a fee-paying private school was closed.

When I arrived on Mejato in October 1986, work had just been completed on a dispensary, to be used not only by the visiting doctors but by the local health aide. It had two rooms with beds, so that patients or doctors could stay overnight, and another room with a shower. The radio was brought from the schoolroom. Like the school, the dispensary's lights were run on solar power. At the front was a long verandah, an attractive spot for spontaneous gatherings to listen to radio messages or just chew the cud of life. Shade is rare on Mejato, which has many fewer trees than Rongelap and none of the huge old breadfruit which, with their great fat trunks and generous branches, provide a cool centre for village life in other islands, like nearby Ebadon.

The night after my arrival a party was organised to give thanks for the dispensary which relieved a little of the pressure on the school house. With their usual hospitality, the Rongelap people also made it a welcome ceremony, with *leis* and *wus* (head garlands) of delicate, highly perfumed white and peach flowers. Long tables were arranged outside and loaded with food, brought on the boum-boum with us from Ebeye. I didn't appreciate until later what a relief it was to have some let-up from the virtually unbroken daily diet of tinned tuna, white rice, tinned pears or peaches, and pancakes or doughnuts made with white flour, sugar, water and fat (eggs were too scarce to use in cooking).

Renam Anjain, a livewire young woman with five children, told me later that her people missed not only the food they grew on Rongelap but also the sense of self-sufficiency gained from growing it themselves.

> On Rongelap we had a lot of work to do, tending the trees. On Mejato the trees are old, they've gone wild and don't bear much fruit. We're planting new ones, but it will take 10 or 15 years for them to grow and start bearing fruit. We've tried planting other things, too – pumpkins, tomatoes, beans, cabbage – but they grow a little and then die. We can't understand what's wrong with the soil.
>
> My family had a big plot of land on Rongelap, so I would often go there, clean it, clear the bushes and gather copra. Then we'd have to grate the copra and put it in sacks ready to be collected. We were really busy. We also gathered pandanus, breadfruit and coconuts to eat. Apparently sweet potatoes and bananas also grew well before the fallout, but no more.
>
> On Mejato all we have to do is get up, clean up, make breakfast, do the washing if there are dirty clothes and after that you sit down and you just don't know what to do next.

Roko Laninvelik, a woman who helped me a great deal with translating interviews, showing me around and interpreting her culture, explained the importance of copra farming on Rongelap:

73

When we cultivated copra, the ship came every three months to buy it: they paid 14 cents a pound, maybe less. A family could sell 3 tons – about $1,200 – to buy whatever we needed from the ship – clothes, kerosene etc. They sold things at twice the price you could buy them in Majuro. But at least we were economically independent. The women also sold handicrafts made from pandanus and coconut leaves and the men carved things from a special wood which grows on only a few islands. But here on Mejato the trees are wild and their leaves are no good for weaving – and there is no carving wood.

Side by side with this loss of self-sufficiency the people have had also to come to terms with the health problems associated with their increased dependence on imported foodstuffs – an ironic twist, given that it was precisely for reasons of health that the Rongelapese moved in the first place. Midwife Katrine Jilej explained:

I'm glad to be away from the radiation but I still worry about the children. With so little fresh food, they're just not getting enough vitamins in their diet. They aren't growing well.

Although the traditional Marshallese diet was meagre – coconut, pandanus, breadfruit, fish, maybe bananas and papayas – it was well balanced and nutritional. Rosalie Bertell told me she had asked a Fijian nutritionist about it.

She said coconut is a continuous crop, so that on any one day you can pick it in all stages of development. As the coconut develops its vitamin content changes, so if you eat in any one day coconuts in various stages of development you get a total complement of vitamins. It's a very complete food. They used to use it for intravenous feeding during the war – it's a complete sterile solution for the human body.

Now, at times, there's not even tinned food to eat on Mejato, and it is not uncommon for two meals a day to consist of a small amount of white rice and a milky coffee. Mayor Randy Thomas said:

We often run out of food because the US field ship doesn't bring all our supplies. We should have, for example, a pack of rice – 48 pounds – per person for three months. But often much less arrives. It's the same with all the food. If we complain to the food services on Majuro we're told it will arrive with the next batch, it never does. I don't know what happens to it, whether someone handling it steals it or what. So we have to take money from our Resettlement Fund, made up of donations from groups round the world, and send someone to Ebeye to buy food.

We used to be economically independent, growing food and cultivating copra. This is very bad for us, psychologically. We should be doing something to earn what we get, instead of sitting waiting all the time.

US food aid is essential in keeping the Rongelapese from starvation, but it is a nutritional nightmare. The backs of the Direct Aid cans of peaches and pears in a heavy sugar syrup outline a rudimentary guide to nutrition, telling consumers they must eat something every day from the four categories of food: fruit and vegetables, the guidelines say, can be eaten in any form. This may be true as a temporary measure to ward off starvation, but the Bikinians have now been living for years on tinned, heavily sweetened fruit. The other staples are white rice, white sugar and white flour. A 1985 Department of Energy report on Mejato confirmed that the children were not growing properly, owing to poor nutrition.

The Rongelapese are clearly relieved to have left behind them the worry of daily increasing their already high radiation doses. But Mejato's low fertility and lack of access to fresh foodstuffs is not the only new problem they are facing. Rongelap had its own lagoon, a calm and plentiful fishing ground. Fishing was divided along gender lines, with the men generally going out in the boat. 'Women', said Renam Anjain, 'tied coconut leaves in a long line and made a kind of net we used for fishing together. It's not possible to do that on Mejato: the shore isn't suitable.' (According to Marshallese custom women fish from the shore because it is supposed to be bad luck to have a woman on board a fishing boat. Some Marshallese women say the myth grew up because a capsized boat with a menstruating woman on board could attract sharks. Others say it would have been easy enough to exclude menstruating women and it must have been simply a device of the men, who wanted an excuse to be out on the sea together.) Even fishing by boat from Mejato is not such a pleasant prospect, as Randy Thomas told me:

> The lagoon and ocean around Mejato are much rougher than Rongelap: we've already heavily fished the area around the island and now we have to go further afield. Our boum-boum isn't really sturdy enough for that: we badly need a new boat.

It's not only for fishing that the Rongelap people need a new boat. The journey from Ebeye to Mejato is 62 miles. It takes about 12 hours and is particularly dangerous from November to March when the seas are extremely rough. I did the journey in October: the choice was to sit in the body of the boat and suffer the sickly smell of diesel and the violent shudders, or to perch on the roof. I chose the latter, and at first it was beautiful and absorbing. Four dolphins came and swam alongside us for several minutes; curious about the boat they played around it, arching out of the water in pairs. The sun grew hotter. It was impossible to move around much, though it was just about possible to doze a little.

The Marshalls are near the equator so the sun goes down early and quickly. As it grew darker and colder, and began to rain, the waves grew rougher. We clung on to the shallow wooden ridge around the edge of the roof, soaking and shivering, expecting with every bump to be thrown into the choppy water.

I was glad to admit defeat when the men inside offered to squeeze over and make room for me. Several others stayed on the roof, shining a strong torch beam into the water and keeping a look-out for the shadows of treacherous rocks. The Marshallese have perfected a sophisticated system of navigation, which needs neither stars nor special equipment. They have drawn up detailed maps of the wave patterns around their islands and atolls, and navigators know by heart the wave patterns along their intended route. They can tell by feeling the waves against the boat exactly where they are. It is a precise and reliable system. But the traditional Marshallese flat-bottomed canoes were better suited for their shallow, rocky waters than standard deep-bottomed modern boats like the boum-boum.

I was trying hard not to remember what Lijon Eknilang had told me as we waited several hours on the Ebeye pier for the boum-boum to be loaded:

> I won't take my children on the boum-boum any more. Last time I did it broke down. We had to break off a bit of wood from the boat and paddle for shore. But because the boum-boum is deep-bottomed we couldn't get past the reef. We had to swim for it, with my little daughter on my back. I used to fish underwater among the sharks when I was young, but it's different when you are exhausted and you have a frightened kid with you. We all made it to the nearest island and then had to wait three days to be rescued.

As well as practical problems like food and transport, the Rongelapese are also trying to cope with the deep psychological and emotional upset of being forced to abandon their home. Balkan Anjain's daughter Carol was born with heart problems after her parents were irradiated in the fallout. She was bed-ridden all her life and died on Mejato when she was nine. Balkan Anjain recalled:

> I was one year old when the fallout came. My father died the year after we returned to Rongelap, in 1958. Ever since the fallout he had a pain in his chest. At night I always think of Rongelap, of the graves of my father and my grandparents and how the bushes will be growing over them. There is no one to take care of them.

Boas Jellen, who was 37 when Bravo was detonated, commented:

77

Nowadays I just think of the past and about the next generation, about the small kids. Rongelap is our home, Mejato belongs to someone else. We feel like visitors. In Rongelap, if we felt like doing something we could. We've lost our freedom. God gave it to us as our homeland to take care of. Now we are cut off from our ancestors who are buried there.

What is undermining their community above all else is their sense of being forced into a position of always waiting: waiting for food aid instead of gathering it themselves, waiting for doctors instead of taking the initiative themselves. Now they are waiting for a survey of Rongelap. At community meetings the people have agreed that while they are finding life on Mejato difficult, they do not want to make a move to find a better island until an independent survey can be carried out on Rongelap and on their own health. Helen Boas is a grandmother and an elected councillor who spends a lot of time trying to find out how people feel about the future:

If an independent survey finds that our atoll is too contaminated to clean up then we'll have to decide whether to stay here or find somewhere else. We need the survey to be done quickly, though. Otherwise our life is just waiting, always waiting. We can't build a new one here while there is this uncertainty, while we still have some hope that we can return. We'd like other people to put pressure on the US to release money for the survey and clean-up.

While the US quibbles over money, the people of Rongelap continue their enforced wait. 'The heaven in our future,' said midwife Katrine Jilej, 'is to return.'

5

The Second Generation of Testing: Kwajalein – Refugees and Protesters

For the people of Kwajalein atoll, the first generation of atmospheric testing brought a dramatic and unwelcome change in lifestyle. The US Navy wanted Kwajalein island, the largest in the atoll, as a support and refuelling base for its military scientists and personnel and a temporary home for the hundreds of displaced people from Bikini, Utrik and Rongelap.

Immediately after the Second World War it brought in several hundred Marshallese from other islands to remove the war debris and to construct new military facilities on Kwajalein which, under Japanese rule, had been the launchpad for the attack on Pearl Harbour. At first both the inhabitants of Kwajalein and the other Marshallese brought in to work for the Americans carried on living on Kwajalein. But by 1951, 500 Marshallese were living there, confined to a labour camp of squalid shacks. Nearby lived the North Americans in smart new houses built by the Marshallese. At that point the US decided it wanted Kwajalein for itself and so relocated the 500 inhabitants to Ebeye island, a few miles away. Accommodation was built on Ebeye for only 370 of the refugees, setting a pattern of overcrowding which has never changed.

Handel Dribo is a community leader and one of the most vociferous protesters against the treatment of the Kwajalein people. A grey-haired man with a kind face, he said:

> I grew up on Kwajalein. When the Japanese came after the First World War I was educated by them and employed by them. They treated us different from the Americans – better, I think. When the Americans first came they lived alongside us, but then they evacuated us, first to Kalos and then to Ebeye. We didn't want to leave, but we agreed because we were afraid. They told us that if we didn't leave of our own accord they'd take the land forcibly and keep it for their own.

When the American atmospheric nuclear testing in the Pacific ended in 1958, the US Navy had no further use for Kwajalein. (Since then, the US and the UK have carried out underground nuclear explosions in the Nevada desert. Between 1963 and December 1986, the US has conducted 484 tests, plus another 40 jointly with the UK.) But the next year the US Army announced excitedly that Kwajalein had been given 'a brand new lease of life'.[1] Once again Marshallese land was to be used for military experiments. This was the second generation of nuclear testing, to try out the accuracy and speed of missiles which, in the event of a nuclear war, would carry the nuclear explosives to their target. Kwajalein was to be used as target practice for inter-continental ballistic missiles (ICBMs), fired from Vandenberg Air Base in California, 4,800 miles away.

Over the next four decades virtually all long-range missiles from MX to Minuteman were to be tested there.

Roi and Namur, two islands in the north of Kwajalein atoll, were needed to build monitoring equipment to track the incoming missiles. So in 1960 the US removed the people living on the two islands to Ebeye and Ennubirr, with no consultation, no compensation and no lease agreement. They then filled in the lagoon between Roi and Namur to make one island, big enough for a runway and spacetracking equipment. Ennubirr, like

Ebeye, became an indigenous labour camp, servicing Roi Namur. A year later yet more people were uprooted from their homes and life source when the Navy chose to target rockets at an area of ocean between Kwajalein and Lib island. The families living on Lib were told to pack their few possessions and join the landless on Ebeye.

In 1964 the US Army took over command of Kwajalein from the Navy and decided it wanted more Marshallese land. Rather than shoot its missiles into the open ocean, it preferred the sheltered lagoon, surrounded by the necklace of 93 islands of Kwajalein atoll. Here, said the Army command, the calmer water of the lagoon made it easier to retrieve the shattered pieces of test missiles, which disintegrate as they smack into the surface of the water at 8,000 miles an hour. The new target area was to be the 'mid-corridor', the central two-thirds of the lagoon. The islands that rimmed the lagoon were home to several hundred people: they had their houses on some and used others to gather, to fish and to hunt for seabird eggs.

As the accuracy of the missiles was still uncertain, the Pentagon was nervous lest a duff shot injure inhabitants and attract unwelcome publicity. The 'most practical and economic solution to range safety problems', said a Pentagon report,[2] was to remove the inhabitants – to Ebeye once again. In 1965, 194 people were told to live in cement block housing units in Ebeye and given $25 dollars a month each for the inconvenience.

One of those forced to move was Kinoj Mawilong. She had grown up on Kwajalein but had been relocated to the mid-corridor island of Tarwoj by the Japanese when they built a military base on Kwajalein. When the US took over, she worked in the naval hospital on Kwajalein island 'with my friend Freda and other women – we were the first women to work for the US Navy'. A Marshallese elder and community leader, she remembers the displacements:

I was living on Ebeye the year of the relocation from the mid-corridor islands because my daughter was ill. As far as I remember they didn't try to persuade us with promises of

81

payment – they just told us they needed the islands and we had to leave. We had no choice. I remember that before we left the *alab* asked us to offer prayers. We were brought here thinking it would be temporary but we've lived here in the same small units ever since.

No facilities were provided for the rest of the 1,470 people who had land rights on the mid-corridor islands.[3] Most of them crowded onto Ebeye and survived thanks to the Marshallese tradition of caring and sharing. In June of that year, after five years on Ebeye, the Lib islanders were allowed home, as the island was no longer in the target area.

Ebeye

In 1964, more than a dozen years after they were shunted off their land, the US agreed to sign a lease with the landowners of Kwajalein island. By this time the islanders were desperate for cash. They were having to buy food and pay rent and electricity bills instead of living off the land and the lagoon as they once did. The US offered them $75,000 in cash for 99 years' use of their land: less than $10 an acre a year. With no legal counsel and feeling they had no clout against the US, they accepted.

There were already 4,000 people living on Ebeye. They included people who had been forced off their own land and several hundred other Marshallese who had been recruited to work on Kwajalein Missile Range either in the mid-1940s in the first rush of construction, or in the mid-60s as missile testing increased and new facilities were needed. By 1967, when the US had brought 4,500 people to Ebeye, it was still planning to build housing for only 3,500. Since then, the population of Ebeye has doubled. Kinoj Mawilong told me:

At first it was a few families but since then many more. We're still living on the same small island but there are more of us – so it just gets more and more crowded.

The US authorities blame the Marshallese for the overcrowding on Ebeye, as more and more people come to look for jobs on the base. But people's lives aren't a tap to be turned on and off at will. Marshallese observers reply that the US has fostered a desire for consumer goods; small wonder, then, that islanders gravitate to Ebeye in search of the American way of life. Moreover, the hope of work and the high birth rate are not the only reasons for the population increase in the last 20 years. The shattering of their communities and the quest for medical help has brought many Rongelap, Enewetak and Bikini people to Ebeye.

Lijon Eknilang is one such person. She left Rongelap when she started getting seriously ill with radiation-linked problems, including a thyroid tumour and seven miscarriages. Now she lives with her two adopted children and husband in one tiny room on Ebeye. At one end, bunk beds have been built and a curtain erected so that a little privacy can be snatched. She said:

> I hate living on Ebeye, it's a terrible life here. I'd much rather be living on Mejato with my family. But I've been so ill and now the doctors can't find what's wrong with me – they tell me I have to live here to be near a hospital and so I can get a flight to Honolulu if I need to quickly. I hope to move away one day but right now I don't dare. I'm afraid.

Sail-ins

Ever since they were forced off their islands the people of Kwajalein atoll have tried by every non-violent means available to get their land back. They have petitioned and pleaded with the US Congress, with the United Nations and with their own government. And they have protested in imaginative and peaceful 'sail-ins' to their own islands, disrupting missile testing and forcing the US to the negotiating table. Individually and as a community, they have been punished for protesting; 200 women lost their jobs as maids on the missile range, with no hope of alternative employment. Other protesters were jailed and fined. All the workers on the missile range were subjected to humiliating searches and petty restrictions.

The European and North American peace movements have often assumed that non-violent direct action is a recent creation, inspired by Gandhi but with no wider roots. It is an assumption which ignores the Black civil rights movement in North America, the history of non-violent marches by Black South Africans and the support given to them by the mostly white 'Black Sash' women, the vigils of the mothers of the disappeared in Central and South America, and the protesters of Kwajalein atoll. It forgets that almost all of the liberation movements around the world which finally resorted to guns had struggled for years to make their point in every other way.

The Kwajalein people have said that their ultimate goal is to get their land back. But because they recognise that they are locked into a long struggle with an opponent who holds most of the cards, they also have a short-term aim – to wrestle an agreement from the US which affords them enough money to improve conditions on Ebeye and make life there bearable. In talking to the press, the US Administration has used this aim to demean the islanders, implying that they are greedy and opportunistic.

In August 1967 people displaced from the 'mid-corridor' islands sent a petition to the Congress of Micronesia asking for its aid in 'righting a grave injustice' done by the US government. Only 194 out of 1,470 landowners were eligible for compensation of a mere $25 a month, later increased to $40 a month. 'Electric bills and house rentals exceed $40 a month,' the petition declared, 'and some of us have already been threatened with eviction ... anyone born since the relocation is not considered eligible for compensation . . .' The people had been used to living from farming and fishing, neither of which is possible on overcrowded Ebeye.

The Congress of Micronesia responded by urging the US High Commissioner to negotiate either the return of the land to the owners or a new agreement with more money. When their call was ignored the Congress passed a resolution encouraging the islanders to reoccupy their lands and even promising a Congressional representative to go with them for support. And so, with the blessing of the national government, the first sail-in took place in 1969.

Kinoj Mawilong, a woman elder, church leader and passionate defender of her people's rights, took part in the first sail-in and every protest since. Here she explains why:

Many things prompted me to resettle my home but the main reason was that living conditions on Ebeye really need to be improved. We felt the US had to do something about living conditions on Ebeye, they were unbearable. It wasn't just to obtain the rent money for the land they've taken.

Although my island is nothing but sand and coconut trees, I had a peaceful life there – and more freedom than here on Ebeye.

My home is not like your country. You have big wide open spaces and houses with more rooms. But I had more freedom on my island. We were very self-sufficient. We ate fish and coconuts that we found ourselves. We didn't depend on people. On the small outer islands money isn't very important. During the Japanese period we sold copra – there were only two big companies which bought it – and we also bought imported rice and things from them. But because we had our own native food we were self-sufficient. We didn't have the problems we do now.

When we moved to Ebeye we had to learn a new lifestyle, which was difficult. Living in a small house on Ebeye we felt like prisoners. And although we may get $30 rent a month for our land from the US, it isn't enough to live on Ebeye for a month.

As one of the leaders I had to look to sort out the problems that the people and especially the landowners were facing and to find some ways to help alleviate some of our problems. Having been told by the US government that Kwajalein is very important I had to also tell them that my life and the lives of my people are also very important and they have to not only look after their own interests but also those of the people who own Kwajalein. Therefore I decided, along with other Kwajalein leaders, that we had to work for a better future. It's also appropriate for me because according to Marshallese custom women's voices are also important, not just the men's, and there was a special contribution I could make. I was very active from the beginning and I brought other women into it.

The US Trust Territory authorities were caught off guard, because they did not believe that the people would dare to carry out their threat. The protest reportedly forced two missile tests to be cancelled, and within a week the US promised to consider the islanders' demands. But it wasn't until a year later that the mid-corridor people finally got their agreement – a five-year lease at $420,000 a year, or $285 a year each shared between *all* 1,470 landowners. At least with this new agreement everyone with land rights was getting some compensation. But for the majority for whom it was the sole source of income, it was barely enough to cover even the basic minimum of food and housing.

By the mid-1970s, overcrowding and health problems on Ebeye were becoming ever more acute. The US Army, said the islanders, had not kept its side of the 1964 lease agreement for Kwajalein island, the biggest in the atoll, where the Americans live. The lease promised that the US would 'improve the economic and social conditions of the Marshallese people, particularly at Ebeye . . .' As the US had patently not fulfilled that clause, the islanders decided they would no longer recognise the lease. Ebeye Senator to the Congress of Micronesia, Ataji Balos, told a US Congressional hearing on Ebeye in 1976 as much.

The displaced Kwajalein islanders took no further action over the lease for another three years. But in the meantime the displaced mid-corridor islanders decided in late 1977 to launch another 'sail-in' to protest at restricted access to their own land (where they could still gather food if regular access was guaranteed), at intolerable conditions on Ebeye, and at the lack of compensation. As soon as the Marshallese stepped off their boats onto the shores of their familiar coral islands, Trust Territory officials sent word promising negotiations if they would leave. As talks dragged on over months with no prospect of results, the mid-corridor islanders decided to up the stakes with another occupation in March 1978. This time Peter Rosenblatt, State Department Ambassador to Micronesia on the Compact talks, gave his personal word that there would be improvements on Ebeye and that he would negotiate new terms for leasing the land. The protesters once again said goodbye to the coconut and pandanus fringing their island, returned to the treeless alleys of Ebeye, and waited.

Later that year the Marshallese were told that once they had signed the Compact of Free Association the US would pay $9 million a year for the use of Kwajalein Missile Range. But because for the majority the rent money was the equivalent of a salary cheque – the only regular income they could hope for – they didn't see why they should wait for the drawn-out Compact talks to reach a conclusion before they received a realistic level of compensation. Their assessment proved right: the Compact took another eight years to sign and is still not properly in force.

In July 1979 more than 500 displaced people boarded a fleet of small boats and sailed into the restricted lagoon, heading for eight of their islands. The protest later spread to others, including Kwajalein island itself, where North American civilians were for the first time forced to interrupt their round of social events by the protesters. When the Marshallese had brought their mats and cooking pots to the lawns beside the immaculate tennis courts it was no longer possible to forget the military-created slum only three miles away in which the people who owned Kwajalein now lived out their days. This is how one older Ebeye woman described that sail-in:

I've been involved in all the occupations of Kwajalein. The first time we went we put up tents and stayed on one end of

Kwajalein island. But some of us also went to the beach where the American residents live. They didn't like that. The next time we stayed in the Pacific Club where the officers go, and in the Ocean View Club where the others go to drink and relax. We just walked right in and took our mats with us and set ourselves up in their clubs. We stayed there quite a few months . . . May, June, July, I think.

In the first occupations, the Kwajalein Missile Range authorities didn't do anything to us except follow us everywhere with security guards. They didn't try to get us out of the clubs but they accompanied us from the pier to the clubs and back again whenever we wanted to come and go. Some of the boys tried to go fishing and they put them in jail for it.

One of the islands reoccupied by the protesters was Roi Namur. The people who had once cared for and lived off its soil had been forcibly displaced 19 years previously. A legal brief filed in 1975 against the US on behalf of Roi Namur land-owners seeking compensation said that when they'd been removed in 1960, 'They left behind eight dwellings, a church, and some 30 other structures. No Marshallese person has ever been [permitted] to reside upon or use Roi Namur since.'[4] The landowners had been trying, unsuccessfully, to get some compensation for their lost 600 acres. In 1970 the US Navy hired a firm of Honolulu lawyers, who put the value of the land at $7,666 an acre for a 50-year lease period. The Navy thought it too generous and continued to pay nothing, despite repeated attempts at negotiations by the landowners. It was at this point that the people reclaimed their islands for a few months in 1979. But promises of goodwill combined with inaction had allowed the US to deprive them of any financial compensation. In 1975 the US Court of Claims dismissed their case, saying that the statute of limitations had expired in 1966, a year after the US had promised to begin negotiations. By the early 1980s the US State Department was saying the Roi Namur claims were a 'dead issue' and was refusing to even discuss them.

The occupation of Roi Namur was the first in which the US used violence against protesting Marshallese. Senator Imada Kabua was clubbed by a security guard as he and the first contingent of 25 women, men and children climbed out of their boats and on to their beaches. Senator Kabua later won a court case for assault and battery against the guard.

Back in Washington there was more consternation than usual over the occupations. The Administration of Jimmy Carter was anxious to sign the SALT II treaty with the Soviet Union, but to get Senate to agree it was crucial to promise a definite go-ahead for the development of the MX missile. And that required at least four tests, targeted on Kwajalein. This time the Marshallese had real bargaining power. They might not be able to get their land back – 'no other range would be as good' as Kwajalein, said Captain John Lawrence of Vandenberg Air Force Base[5] – but they could at least secure proper payment. In September 1979 the US signed a one-year Interim Use Agreement worth $9 million a year. Five thousand landowners shared $5 million and the remaining $4 million was entrusted to the Marshall Islands government to carry out development programmes. The Roi Namur islanders were also given compensation.

Rather than deal directly with the landowners, the US has always preferred to negotiate via the Marshall Islands government, RepMar, which has invariably shown itself more in touch with the US than with the mood and wishes of the dispossessed landowners. Any doubts over the government's allegiances were dispelled in 1981 when the government signed a third Interim Use Agreement expressly against the wishes of the landowners, the majority of whom had formed themselves into a mutual help group, the Kwajalein Atoll Corporation. The KAC believed the Kwajalein landowners were entitled to back payments for the 25 years from when the US first took their land to when it signed the Interim Use Agreement in 1979. The $200 million owed them could, they felt, be put to excellent use for the whole community, funding programmes to ensure decent housing, sanitation, recreation and education. The Pentagon would hear none of it and continued to circumvent the landowners, dealing only with RepMar.

In April 1982 the landowners decided it was time for some straight talking. Senator Imada Kabua, president of KAC, announced that the landowners would hold a referendum on 'whether to permit continued development of US nuclear weapons using the land, waters and air space of Kwajalein':

> Our people know from first-hand knowledge, better than most, the perils of nuclear weapons . . . To the extent we assist the development of nuclear weapons delivery systems we are involved in responsibility for their ultimate possible use.
>
> We are not naive. We know the owners of Kwajalein, who number only about 5,000 people living on our remote island in the Pacific, cannot prevent a superpower from developing nuclear weapons. But we can ensure that our islands shall not be used for such a purpose . . .
>
> Many, perhaps most, of my fellow landowners wish to leave Ebeye Island, where we must now live, to return to our home islands. Since the use agreement obligating us to make our islands available expired last year, we are now legally free to do so.[6]

The US response was conveyed by Mr Fred Zeder, then Ambassador to Micronesia, who threatened that any protest disturbing the missile testing would 'be dealt with as any other cases of civil disturbance are dealt with when our national security is at stake'.[7] His comments served to say more brutally what was already obvious: that civil rights which had been fought for so hard in the States did not apply to those entrusted to the care of the US. When it comes to a perceived threat to national security, other principles are secondary. Dr Konrad P. Kotrady, the former Brookhaven doctor who became critical of US policy in Micronesia, had stated flatly in 1970:

> The Army's position was summed up to me one day when a high-level command officer at Kwajalein remarked that the sole purpose of the Army at Kwajalein is to test missile

systems. They have no concern for the Marshallese and that is not of any importance to their being at Kwajalein.[8]

In May 1982 the Marshall Islands finalised an agreement with the Reagan Administration known as the Compact of Free Association (see pp. 179–88) and announced a national referendum to approve it for August the same year. Snubbing the landowners, it included a *50-year* lease for Kwajalein. Almost none of the demands of the KAC was met, not even its plea for an improvement in the Army's treatment of the Marshallese.

At this stage the Compact referendum was to have two options: approval of the Compact, which carried with it huge financial incentives for the region, now economically dependent on the US; or independence. The Pentagon was sure that the Marshallese would opt for the Compact because of the lure of money and because few people realised that the money was, quite literally, in return for Micronesian self-determination.

It misjudged the mood of the Marshallese. Within days of the 30 May 1982 Compact signing, Kwajalein landowners had pledged their opposition to the Compact and their resolve to vote for independence. They were joined by the people of Bikini, Enewetak and Rongelap who still had outstanding claims for compensation from the 1950s nuclear tests. The Compact awarded the radiation survivors compensation but quashed their right to sue in US courts for additional damage (see Chapter Eight).

One of the Kwajalein Senators, Ataji Balos, resigned his cabinet post as Minister of Internal Security in protest, saying: 'If I could not support a Compact which gave the US 15 years at Kwajalein with no hope of help for my people, how can I now support a Compact which gives 50 years?'[9]

Nervous that the Marshallese might, after all, adopt independence, the US Undersecretary of State James Buckley immediately wrote to President Kabua of the Marshall Islands putting off the referendum date, because it did not give enough time to organise a UN observation team or for 'voter education'. Deputy Assistant Secretary of Defense, Noel Koch, quoted in the *Wall Street Journal*, was rather more honest about US motives: 'declaring independence simply isn't an available option to them'.[10]

Thus, in June 1983, a 'new improved' version of the Compact was to be signed, and a ballot set for September which offered only the Compact or the continuation of the trusteeship. Independence was not on offer. Hostage to continuing US goodwill and aid, 57 per cent of Marshall Islanders voted to accept the Compact. Nevertheless, there was a high protest vote: Ebeye and the islands affected by the atmospheric tests gave an emphatic 'no'.

Operation Homecoming

Meanwhile, in May 1982, when independence had still seemed up for grabs, and the Compact would have brought a 50-year lease, Kwajalein landowners made a major bid to reclaim their islands. Operation Homecoming, as it was dubbed, involved at its height more than 1,000 of the estimated 5,000 landowners returning to their islands.

Julian Riklon was treasurer of the Kwajalein Atoll Corporation and has been deeply involved with the protests both from a sense of outrage at the injustices done to his community and because of his opposition to nuclear arms and militarism. This is what he told a US religious-pacifist magazine *Sojourners*:

On June 19 1982, we began what is called Operation Homecoming. About 400 of us went to Kwajalein, and even though we were met by US security guards, we started erecting our tents. The next day more and more people came and when it finally became too crowded we wanted to find another place on Kwajalein for everyone to stay. A group of our leaders and 10 other men went to a beach near the United States' residential area because it had water, houses and bathrooms.

When they got there, they were again met by security

guards and they were loaded into a bus and put in jail. We maintained contact with them over CB radio and about 400 of us marched to the jail. When we got there, we found all the off-duty security guards as well as the colonel and the commanding officer.

Because I happened to be at the front of the group, I was asked to translate the conversation between the landowners and the security guards. The colonel told two security guards to arrest me. They began to drag me to the jail, but some of our women tried to hold onto me. When the women finally had to let go, the two guards grabbed me, choking and beating me down to the floor.

Our lawyers in Washington heard about the situation and they immediately got a court order to release the men who were now in jail. But when we got out, we did not go back to Ebeye. We continued to resist the military people. We were told they would bring in several thousand Marines, but that did not scare us. They cut off the water but some of our men went and started digging wells. Then they turned the water on again, because they were afraid that we might disturb underground wires with our digging.

We stayed on the restricted island for four months and during that time the US conducted two missile tests. We heard that the people in the Pentagon were arguing with each other: some said they should not conduct tests with people in the restricted areas and others said they didn't care about the people. The two missiles landed in the lagoon and fortunately no one was hurt.

We enjoyed the four months on Kwajalein because we were living the kind of life we used to live. The children enjoyed the freedom of going out to fish and climbing the coconut trees. We received lots of support for our reoccupation from people around the Pacific Islands, the United States and Europe.

In October 1982 we came to Washington, DC and negotiated another agreement with the Department of Defense which gave the US the right to use the islands for three years until 1985. The agreement provided that six previously restricted islands be given to us, although Kwajalein was not one of them. The US government also agreed to give us money to improve the living conditions on Ebeye. One of the most important achievements was that the US recognised that it could not simply ignore the landowners and continue operation of the military base.[11]

The US authorities tried to halt the protests in a three-pronged attack of court proceedings, petty revenge and bribery. The Pentagon accused the landowners of 'illegally' reoccupying their land. But five judges, two in the Marshalls and three in Washington, DC, ruled in favour of the Marshallese. The US put pressure on the Marshall Islands government to cajole the people back to Ebeye. It had no effect. As well as the arrests described by Julian Riklon, the US penalised Marshallese working on Kwajalein. Maids and gardeners, deemed 'unessential workers', were sacked: 200 people lost their jobs, effectively cutting off 25 per cent of those bringing home wages from the base. Kinoj Mawilong was one of them:

> During Operation Homecoming in 1982 I was an employee on Kwajalein Missile Range and I was fired for taking part. There was an order for all employees not to take part but I refused to follow it. Instead I went to the camps and stayed there to help the people because I believed we were doing the right thing.
>
> I believe I've lost all the benefits that I would have received being an employee of Kwajalein. But that's alright. For 16 years I worked with Global [the recruiting agency] or the Army. I was a maid. The wage I received at that time was about $4 an hour – good money. I sacrificed that to be with the people and fight for our rights.

The rest of the Marshallese employees had their bags searched every evening as they returned by ferry from Kwajalein. Food, cigarettes and any gifts they had been given by American civilians were seized. Even Marshallese returning from the US or elsewhere via Kwajalein had food confiscated.

At that time there was no bank and no outside telephone exchange on Ebeye and residents had to make the trip to Kwajalein, leaving them vulnerable to the whims of the Army command. So when it became clear that the protesters were not about to leave, the Army shut the bank to Marshallese. Not only did small businesses lose a considerable amount of money in unpaid debts, but food shipments to Ebeye were also halted as payments were not going through. At this point, even the usually submissive Marshall Islands government intervened, and the Army grudgingly allowed Marshallese to use the bank – but only under the scrutiny of an armed guard. Prospective clients had to sit baking in the sun in a school bus as ten people at a time went into the bank. (It wasn't until 1984 that this and other harassments were dropped.) The Army also squeezed the already meagre food supplies on Ebeye by placing an embargo on food shipments arriving via Kwajalein. There is no airport on Ebeye and at that time there was no container yard or warehouse facilities.

The *Marshall Islands Journal* cited Deputy Assistant Secretary of Defense Noel Koch showing a sudden and unexpected concern for the Marshallese dependency upon the US as the reason for the withdrawal of services. He was 'concerned over the potential dependency upon US sources and the resultant negative effect upon independent development of Marshallese capabilities'.[12]

At the same time as using punitive measures the Army tried to cajole islanders into backing down. Kwajalein Senator Ataji Balos wrote indignantly in the *Marshall Islands Journal*:

A missile test was postponed on August 3, when Roi-Namur landowners refused to leave their campsites and move into the shelters. *The Army tried to persuade them with cokes and ice cream. We cannot help but feel amazed by the childish and insulting level by which the DOD [Department of Defense] has chosen to address the Kwajalein people.* (my emphasis)[13]

He wrote too of the Pentagon's astonishing refusal to help get a vaccine to the atoll to curb a typhoid epidemic which Marshallese could only interpret as punitive.

> We feel the US government's ability to get a vaccine for typhoid into the American University in West Beirut is certainly an example of their ability to do so at our atoll. We are amazed that the US doctors, instead of trying to help the Marshallese people of Kwajalein atoll with an immunisation program, have made affidavits *stating that Marshallese have lots of diseases anyhow so keeping sanitary facilities open does not make any difference.* (my emphasis)

Despite the harassment, most of the protesters enjoyed themselves – more so than they usually did on Ebeye. Two of the women were interviewed by the *Marshall Islands Journal* on 9 September:

> 'We came from a dirty place to a clean one' [said Maria Lojkar]. She went on to explain that it is not crowded, muddy, or plagued with stopped-up sewer pipes. 'Why didn't they fix up Ebeye this way?' With the clean water the children . . . stop itching and sores from mosquito bites disappear.' Mrs Lojkar also reported there is no diarrhoea.
>
> 'The old women remember where they grew up, where they played and where the wells were,' Maria Lojkar remarked. Where Mrs Lojkar lives there is a group of four houses that share, in good Marshallese fashion, one cooking fire . . . she explained that there is a lot of sharing back and forth – food, soap etc.
>
> Why are they there? 'We are after the land of my eight children. Where will they stay? Ebeye is crowded' [said Hiromi Kabua] . . . One of the activities of the people in the camps is composing songs. They sing of their ancestral lands and how nothing will displace them – not even a typhoon.

An interview with Kotak Loeak, described as 'a KAC board member who also sits in the powerful House of Iroij, the Marshallese equivalent of the British House of Lords . . . who has been close to the grassroots aspect of the resettling which now includes 13 islands . . .', corroborated their description.

> Our people are happy living as they are now, especially in the islands where there are no military facilities nor armed guards to keep them in restricted areas. After years on crowded Ebeye Island, where we were forced to live by the US, we have discovered the joys of natural living, especially the freedom to move around, fish, plant and build living structures from the surrounding elements. I cannot tell you how good the people feel . . . For the older people the return brings tears of joy . . . For the children it is an all new experience.[14]

During the four months of Operation Homecoming the protest received the support of most of the 5,000 dispossessed landowners and of other Marshall Islanders living on Ebeye. Like every action, those doing the 'visible' work, in this case the occupations, needed support from many others doing lower profile work. Many on Ebeye, who for one reason or another felt they couldn't leave and join the protesters, gave support in other ways. Talking with the people when I was in Ebeye in 1986, I often heard: 'I couldn't go, myself, but I took food out to them and helped in any way I could.' However, a small group of landowners calling themselves Ten-Ten disagreed with the occupations and took the side of the Marshall Islands government and the US. The punitive measures taken by the US Army command were designed to provoke just such a reaction: the suspension of banking facilities hit the small businessmen on Ebeye far more severely than the protesters, whose need for money transactions while they were living on non-westernised islands was more limited.

There was tremendous pressure on workers at Kwajalein not to be involved. And rather than enter into a direct confrontation with the protesters, the Army command put Marshallese workers' jobs on the line in an attempt to undermine community support for the action and isolate the protesters – a not uncommon ploy. The Pentagon tried to make negotiations dependent on the islanders first going back to Ebeye, but they refused to budge until after a settlement. After four months the Pentagon agreed to negotiate, but once again, only with the Marshall Islands government. Kwajalein Atoll Corporation was represented at the talks in Washington, DC, but only as 'an observer'.

When a new three-year agreement was drawn up on 20 October 1982 between the US and Marshall Islands governments (with the approval of the KAC) it embodied many but not all of the protesters' demands. Six islands were returned to the Marshallese, and the mid-corridor islanders were granted access for six weeks three times a year. A fund of $10 million a year compensation from the US was set up for capital improvements on Ebeye, to be administered by Kwajalein people. It has since done much to begin to alleviate some of the worst aspects of life on Ebeye; the desalination plant and improved sewage system being two examples.

And yet people found themselves regretfully leaving their islands – many of them for the third or fourth time – with some of their demands still unmet. One was that the US lease was reduced from 50 years to 30 years under the Compact, pending voter approval, when KAC had been hoping for a much shorter lease. The second disappointment was the refusal to improve the treatment of Marshallese by the Missile Range authorities: it would have cost the Pentagon a fraction of its overall budget to introduce equal pay. Granting Marshallese workers and visitors to Kwajalein greater respect and dignity and ending the searches would not have jeopardised the national security of America. The Army had no such ready excuse – no bomb or weapon had ever been found in the bag of anyone entering Kwajalein. National security was once again used as a catch-all justification, this time for petty harassment.

Women defy the US threat

By 1985 Ebeye's residents were impatient for change to alleviate their lives. In October the landowners asked the US to rehire the

200 maids who were fired in 1982, allow Marshallese students to attend the high school on the Missile Range until one could be built for Ebeye, allow Marshallese passing through Kwajalein in order to catch a plane to eat at the 'Snack Bar', and to provide a lump sum of $6 million to supplement Compact funds to improve Ebeye. It took the Pentagon until February 1986 to reply: 'no' to the money; 'perhaps' to the other requests.

Opting for the only lever they had, in spring 1986 a group of landowners once again resettled their land in a small camp on Kwajalein. Unlike in 1982, when there had been 1,000 to 2,000 people (the estimates were very varied), this time only 100 to 150 people took part: the 1982 resettlement had left many doubtful of their own power against such an aggressor. Moreover, as one participant explained, 'In 1986 the men working on Kwajalein were told they'd lose their jobs if they protested, so we women said, okay, we'll demonstrate anyway.'

When they were threatened with removal the occupiers pointed out that they were perfectly entitled to resettle legally as the previous Interim Use Agreement for the land signed by the US and the Marshall Islands government had run out in September and had not been renewed. It was the US, in fact, which was occupying illegally. The Marshall Islands government hurriedly drew up a new agreement with the US on 15 March, to last until the Compact came into force. When the KAC objected, the Marshall Islands government issued an eminent domain order (which allows it to take private property for 'public use') and sent in its police force to take the land. 'Activities conducted by the United States and the Republic of the Marshall Islands at the Kwajalein Missile Range ... constitute a public use,' [15] said the Marshall Islands Cabinet, which authorised the government to take possession of the land.

KAC leaders were charged with trespassing and assault but won their court cases and the protesters increased to 300. Senator Ataji Balos claimed that a 'shoot to wound' order had been issued by the Army command if any of the occupying landowners strayed into high-security areas. Marshallese police officers were sent from Majuro at the request of base authorities forcibly to remove the protesters, who consisted mostly of older women. Kinoj Mawilong described the bitter scenes that followed:

> The police were asked to physically remove us from the land. We refused and they handcuffed the old women and carried them forcibly away to Ebeye. I was one of those who refused to move but was in the end forced to. I was taken to hospital suffering from exhaustion and high blood pressure.
>
> We refused to move off our land because we knew we were right: there was no legal way they could remove us. The Interim Use Agreement, the lease for the land, had expired so we had the legal right to stay. We did this because it was the only way to tell the US that what they were offering in rent was not enough for us to live on. We never intended to fight with them – we didn't go with weapons.
>
> That they were violent was something new to us: having been brought up with Christian backgrounds it wasn't what we expected. It was beyond our comprehension.

The landowners were particularly angry that their own police force had been used against them. As one elderly demonstrator said:

> The women held onto posts and fought with the young policemen. We yelled that they were betraying their people; we insulted them for doing the US's dirty work and to go back to Majuro.

When the police boat carrying the landowners neared the dock at Ebeye, it was greeted by an angry crowd. Senator Ataji Balos told the *Marshall Islands Journal* of 25 April:

> The boat couldn't get near the pier because there were so many people, so the police left all landowners on South Loi. They just dropped us there. The island has no water, nothing. The landowners walked across the reef to Ebeye.

Their treatment at the hands of the Marshallese police did nothing to reassure the landowners, and they continued their protest at Kwajalein Missile Range's one point of weakness on Ebeye: at the dock, where workers on the base were picked up in the mornings and dropped off at night. When the blockade successfully stopped the ferry picking up workers, Base Commander Colonel William Spin threatened permanently to replace all employees who did not show up to work. He also refused to house them on Kwajalein until the dispute was over, saying there was not enough room – and this despite his threat to bring in outside labour to live on the base. 'The Americans just don't want Marshallese to live on Kwajalein,' charged Senator Balos.[16] About 400 Marshallese workers walked the reef at low tide to get to work. When the evening ferry brought them back, landowners tried to board it to get a ride back to Kwajalein – only to be thrown in the water by security agents.

By this time, US tactics were succeeding in 'dividing and ruling' Ebeye residents. There were rumours – but never any evidence – that landowners were threatening to destroy the houses of workers who reported for duty at Kwajalein before the agreement was settled. As in any dispute when a group feels it is fighting for its future and yet is undermined by members of the same community, feelings run deep and they leave scars. Some workers on the base, anxious to protect their jobs, were angry that the protests might put them in jeopardy.

President Kabua exploited these splits, and on 1 May declared a state of emergency to 'defuse . . . unruly mobs at the Ebeye pier'. He assured Missile Range employees living on Kwajalein, who he called 'innocent victims', that 'the national government will do all in its power to protect your rights'.[17]

The unprecedented state of emergency prohibited interference with the transport of workers to the Missile Range and barred 'unauthorised' people from entering Army-controlled lands, with the threat of a six-month jail sentence or $500 fine. Meanwhile, the US put a freeze on more than $3 million due to the Kwajalein Atoll Development Authority until the protests stopped. Kabua also used the state of emergency to seize $288,000 from KADA's funds and ordered the building of two 200 by 32 foot one-storey untreated lumber barracks on the nearby island of Gugeegue to house the Missile Range's cheap indigenous labour force: 24 units of 48 tiny rooms each. As KADA's lawyer Scott Stege commented dryly to me later:

> Barracks are not exactly our concept of development. What we object to is that the money wasn't spent according to our brief – development. It didn't have the approval of our board and it cost more than it is worth. The government did it through emergency laws instead of using the democratic process it has set up. They didn't abide by their own rules. The President said it was to make a political statement of who was in charge. The reason there was no suit to stop the government taking the money – which I feel would have been successful – is that the government could have then destroyed KADA.

The deadlock was shifted on 6 May when the President promised to 're-examine the payment scheme to the landowners and also seek other development assistance from the US or any other country'.[18]

President Kabua kept to the letter of his promise. The payment scheme to the landowners was indeed re-examined – but was then replaced by one which was specifically designed to disempower the landowners' own organisation, the Kwajalein Atoll Corporation, and at the same time to aggravate any existing divisions amongst them. Kinoj Mawilong described to me what happened:

> Previously it was the KAC which distributed the rent money amongst the landowners but now the government no longer recognises us and so it sends the money straight to the landowners. But it is using a different formula to distribute it. We used to divide the money in two: half would be distributed along a per capita payment scheme, all the landowners getting an equal share. The other half as an increment, divided amongst the *iroij*, *alab* and senior *dri jerbal*. But now RepMar is simply dividing the money into thirds between those three groups. There are only a few *iroij*

and *alab* and thousands of *dri jerbal*. Some of the *alab* are doing as they should and spreading the money round their *dri jerbal* – but not all. So many families who relied on the rent money for their food are now not getting anything.

According to a report in the *Marshall Islands Journal* of 15 August 1986, the *iroij* share amounted to nearly $2 million a year: $960,000 for one primary *iroij* and three others sharing another $1 million.

There are a lot of angry people on Ebeye, according to several sources. They claim that a lot of people 'hate the new distribution formula' because money is being paid to about 80 *iroij*, *alab* and senior *dri jerbal* ... It is common knowledge on Ebeye that a group of prominent landowners were in Las Vegas recently after getting a land payment.

The Army Command and the Marshall Islands government also sought to punish the landowners by charging them 'costs' for the demonstrations, for extra security and police forces, for transportation expenses for officials involved in mediating the dispute, and for 'interfering' with missile tests by their presence. The US deducted $675,000 from rent paid, while RepMar billed KAC for $300,000. The landowners claimed that as there was no lease agreement in force at the time they were entitled to reoccupy their own land.

With their repeated sail-ins and court cases, the displaced people of Kwajalein atoll have refused meekly to accept whatever has been doled out to them by the US military. They have succeeded in wresting control over improvement projects on Ebeye and, with their persistent demands, gained funding for them. Their central demand, however, remains unmet: they are still banished from their home islands, and nuclear missile target practice continues at Kwajalein.

Ebeye's future

The displaced people of Kwajalein have mixed feelings about the feasibility of attaining that demand. The *Marshall Islands Journal* reported on 18 April 1986:

> Landowners from Kwajalein Atoll claim that their highest objective is the complete removal of the American military from their island but they feel that since they are relatively weak and few in numbers this objective is not realisable.

A core group of people have not surrendered their long-term vision of independence, however. Senator Ataji Balos is one of them. In August 1986 he told the magazine *Pacifica*:

> We're a small people but we're not going to give up. If they break up the Kwajalein Atoll Corporation, Kwajalein will be the first place in Micronesia to have a revolution.

Fighting talk, but he and others are worried that as Ebeye residents become even more dependent on the US base, and reluctant to risk losing the possibility of videos, cars and coca-cola, the will to challenge the US occupation will wither away.

I asked two people who have been deeply involved in the protests how they envisaged the future. Marshallese lawyer Johnsay Riklon:

> [People living on Ebeye] have been under the military for so long now they feel helpless. There may be quite a few of them that want to go back but they know it's impossible. They've confronted the US army too many times in their lives now. And almost every time they go out they lose. They get tricked and cheated in the end. The desire is still there but they feel helpless. There's no reason to live on Ebeye.

Can you see any strategy for the future?

Only if the US stops increasing its arms, gives up the idea of Star Wars and of fighting the Russians. We've confronted the

US with all kinds of arguments and we know we're right. We gain a little but in the end we lose what we're really fighting for. Money is so powerful. Each time the US just gives us a little more money to stop asking for our land back and so we go away. It's a sad situation.

Normally, if I own property and you want it, you come and ask me how much and I tell you and I can decide if I want to sell. It's ridiculous that the US can force us to sell and at a much lower rate, just because they are powerful and know we cannot fight them. We may be right under the law, but I've seen the US breaking the law all the time, especially on Kwajalein.

So long as the US says its defending peace in the world, Kwajalein will be needed. I don't see how we're going to break that. We've gone to the UN . . . and now we've just learned to live with this reality. It's so destructive to us. It's breaking our customs and our family life: families are suing each other, brothers and sisters, uncles and aunts, suing each other for the money. So we fight among ourselves.

When we shout louder and try to fight back, then they try to teach us a lesson using our own government. So we're frightened of our own government too. Of course the government is in the pocket of the US. It has taken US money and then the US threatens to stop the money. So the government tells us to give our land to the US at whatever price. We've exhausted all the available remedies to no avail. We've gone to the UN, to the US Congress, and I still haven't seen the light at the end of the tunnel.

We now suffer psychological dependency. Lots of people are secure in their jobs on Kwajalein. They have families to support – they are worried about their employment when the militant types start talking. When we did the demonstration against KMR a few months back some of our fellow Marshallese, the employees on Kwajalein, were angry at us . . . So we don't only have to fight the military establishment but our own government and amongst ourselves. The US just sits outside the picture and watches us – a smart move.

Kinoj Mawilong's reply was at once passionate and sad, moving us both to tears.

If the problems on Ebeye continue then the people will have no choice but to return to their home islands – to go back and face whatever the US does. But if the US is willing to help solve problems on Ebeye, then I think most people will be willing to continue living here.

I thank God that despite the struggle and demonstrations we've suffered no loss of life, like other countries at war. Because we do consider this a war, though we try to wage it without violence.

As far as our customs are concerned the Marshall Islands are owned by women and I believe that I speak for the majority of the Kwajalein landowning women when I say that we have to struggle with both governments – with the Marshall Islands government as well as the US – to bring about a better future for our children and grandchildren. And even if we stay on Ebeye, we will never stop struggling for that.

6

Kwajalein – Base Living

Many islanders have risked their jobs and their safety to protest against both their displacement and the living conditions on Ebeye. Similar conditions of poverty and overcrowding exist in many parts of the globe; but the poverty and indignity of life on Ebeye is made more shocking by comparison with the virtually self-sufficient, structured life previously led on the Marshall Islands – and with the cocooned comfort of life on the Army base built by Marshallese labour, on Marshallese land, only four miles from Ebeye.

Standing on the pier at Ebeye, where children play in the filthy waves, using spent plastic bottles as surfboards, you can see Kwajalein Missile Range. Several times a day an over-loaded Army boat arrives at the pier bringing back workers returning from their shifts and taking others to service the 3,000 US citizens living in spacious surroundings. A slice of Middle America served up on a bed of glittering blue Pacific Ocean.

This chapter looks at the living conditions on Ebeye – and the contrast with life on the base.

A personal history

There was a woman who welcomed me into her house to drink tea with her several times while I was on Ebeye. Each time I saw her she was feeling more and more sick. Every day she turned up at the hospital for an appointment, which was postponed until the next day until on the fourth or fifth day she was seen. She had diarrhoea, nausea, sweating, loss of balance, weight loss. The doctor did not have time to examine her or take tests, and gave her something to block her bowels. A few days later I started developing similar symptoms, which turned out to be dysentry, hepatitis and parasites. Back in Britain, it took me four months to feel better and over eight months to recover, with rest, clean water, a diet low in fat and high in fresh food, drugs and a course of acupuncture. In Ebeye this woman had no access to clean water or fresh food, no possibility of peace and rest in her overcrowded home, and only perfunctory medical care. How much time passed, I wondered, before she felt better? Did she ever feel better?

Cause and effect

Most people on Ebeye spend a lot of the time feeling ill. Some of their illnesses are acute and possibly fatal. Others are chronic, the kind of low-level ill-health which leaves a person feeling constantly drained. 'The most pressing health problems include diabetese, obesity, malnutrition, drinking, VD, unwanted pregnancies, a sky-high birth rate, hepatitis, dysentry, heart disease. I could go on and on,' said Darlene Keju-Johnson.

There are three easily identifiable 'social' reasons for the appalling standard of health: the poverty, overcrowding and unsanitary conditions; the switch to a diet low in nutrition, and the lack of facilities for health education, preventative medicine or treatment. The first two stem from uprooting people and resettling them on Ebeye. But there are two other causes of ill-health which are a direct result of the testing. The first is the poisoning of fish in the lagoon. The second is the effect of non-ionising radiation from the radar installations on Roi Namur and Kwajalein.

To these should be added such psychological factors as unemployment which, according to research in Britain, often makes people prone to physical illness, as well as depression.[1] Chronic depression would be expected, too, among a people who have been robbed of their culture and forced to adapt to an alien world – the kind of painful disorientation experienced, and to a growing extent recorded, by the Maori in Aotearoa/ New Zealand, native Americans, Aborigines in Australia and Indians in Central and Latin America.

Water and waste

For more than a dozen years, reports by United Nations and Trust Territory teams have highlighted some of Ebeye's health dangers. In 1978 a Trust Territory study found:

> As with the shortage of water, the lack of proper sanitary facilities is a major cause of the high rate of sickness on Ebeye. Additionally, foul odors and visible pollution are part of the normal environment in which people must live and work and the children must play.[2]

In late 1978 the Ebeye public works director told the American High Commissioner, based in Saipan, that Ebeye's old and faulty sewerage system was in imminent danger of breakdown. He received no reply. Six months later, when Ebeye residents tried flushing their toilets, human waste filled their sinks.

For years, raw sewage has been emptied untreated into Ebeye's lagoon, where pollution levels have been recorded at 25,000 times higher than the safe level set by the World Health Organisation and 30,000 times higher than the safe level established for Guam.[3] By 1982, when a United States

Trusteeship Council visiting mission reported, nothing had changed for the better:

> The people of Ebeye live in crowded one-room houses with substandard and inadequate community services. The sewerage system never functioned properly as a result of defective construction work. Since the visit of the 1980 Mission, the situation appears to have deteriorated instead of improving . . . The hospital, where only one toilet in 10 is operational, is dilapidated.[4]

Until this decade almost no houses on Ebeye had running water. Even in 1986, when most of the houses I visited had a tap, water would come out of it for only 10 minutes a day. At 8.30 in the morning, just as mothers were trying to get children ready for school, the family would have to gather around the tap with buckets, bowls and bottles and collect as much as possible before the last trickle dried up. The water then stood all day in the heat, the flies and the dust. It had to last for washing the clothes, dishes and bodies of the maybe 12 or 15 people in the house, and to stretch to drinking and cooking and cleaning.

When it was once the home of a few hundred people, Ebeye had enough well water to meet its inhabitants' needs. After thousands of people were resettled there, water had to be barged to Ebeye from Kwajalein three times a week, and the US Army charged the Marshall Islands government for the service. That is no longer the case. One of the gains from the islanders' protests (see Chapter Five) has been the building of a huge desalination plant which went on line in 1987.

Medical facilities

Ever since it became a resettlement camp for dispossessed landowners, Ebeye has suffered an acute shortage of trained medical staff, facilities and medicines. In 1963, polio spread from the US base to Ebeye, where (in contrast to the base) it quickly became an epidemic, leaving 190 people severely paralysed at a time when westerners had been receiving vaccines for eight years.

Not surprisingly, given the state of waste disposal and water supplies, diarrhoea and gastroenteritis have regularly swept through Ebeye. William Vitarelli, the US High Commissioner's representative on Ebeye between 1967 and 1969, described one such epidemic and the tragedy which resulted from the lack of medical facilities:

> I had pleaded with the army colonel from the Kwajalein Missile Range across the lagoon, who was in charge of building water catchment systems, to cover the catchment tanks. I feared they would become contaminated with the filth of Ebeye. He refused. We offered to build new covers ourselves if the army would only provide the materials, again he refused. The [gastroenteritis] epidemic came which was traced to the uncovered and contaminated water tanks. [During the epidemic] the Ebeye hospital ran out of intravenous fluids needed to sustain the lives of the Marshallese children severely dehydrated from profuse vomiting and diarrhoea. I took one Marshallese child who was very ill and put her on a skiff and motored four miles to Kwajalein hospital for treatment . . .
>
> We were stopped at the beach by an American guard who would not let the child enter the island . . . the Marshallese nurse pleaded with the guard that the child was dying and she could not receive appropriate therapy on Ebeye. The guard did not permit the child onto the island.
>
> She died on her way back to Ebeye. Five children died during that epidemic.[5]

In 1975 a severe outbreak of influenza on Ebeye, followed by a minor epidemic of spinal meningitis, left 12 dead and two children with permanent brain damage.

In a special report three years later, the Trust Territory government admitted, rather vaguely, that Ebeye's 27-bed hospital, serving the island's then 9,000 inhabitants, was in 'poor condition' and that 'equipment, supplies and staffing are also major problems'.[6] The hospital on Kwajalein, by contrast, serves 3,000 people and has a '25-bed in-patient capacity with a staff of doctors, nurses, and technicians providing many services in the areas of surgery, pharmacy and X-ray', as the up-beat Kwajalein Missile Range brochure says.[7] A system of virtual apartheid exists, with Marshallese allowed to use the Kwajalein facilities only in extreme cases of emergency – and even then, the 'Marshallese feel that procedures are difficult and arbitrary, [and] that patients are made to feel like second class human beings.'[8] The military command replied that the Marshallese 'abused' this 'privilege'.[9]

A leaked memo, written by Dr George Smith, Kwajalein Missile Range's Chief Medical Officer in the early 1980s, reveals that he was so shocked by the contrast between medical facilities on the two islands he recommended they be streamlined so that Ebeye residents could take advantage of health care on Kwajalein. Nothing came of the suggestion.

When I was on Ebeye in the autumn of 1986 little seemed to have changed: the hospital was still hopelessly overstretched. Sulikau Yoshizawa, the only trained nurse on Ebeye, was in a state of desperation:

> I've had enough. I've been here for years and I can't take any more. I've had it. You have to be somebody really special to survive on Ebeye. I'm worn out – I have to do all the nursing – right now I'm giving kids injections, preventative medicine. I also have to do surgery, help all the doctors, give classes in public health. . . .

A more powerful US visitor to the region, Fred Zeder, US State Department Ambassador to Micronesia, took a rather different view. In 1982 he wrote to Henry J. Nowak, a member of the US Congress:

> [On Ebeye] there are schools, a hospital, commercial enterprises and other amenities . . . It should also be noted that the

US government provides all Micronesians free hospitalisation and education as well as job opportunities that pay well in excess of the local wage level . . . *I can think of nowhere in the United States, or, for that matter, the world, where any government so provides for its citizens or, indeed, for individuals outside its domain.* (my emphasis)

Nutrition

If there's no fresh, local food on Ebeye, what do people eat? According to hospital staff in an article in the *Marshall Islands Journal*, 'a daily diet of doughnuts for breakfast and lunch and ramen (noodles) for dinner is not uncommon'.[10] And if there's such a scarcity of water, what do they drink? The answer to that is washed up on the beach – cans of Coke, 7-Up and fizzy orange: synthetic drinks with artificial sweeteners.

In the same article, hospital staff talk of a two-year-old child admitted to hospital with kidney problems 'as a result of being addicted to drinking cola'. Another article in the same paper of 4 July 1986 referred to the growing problem of children being admitted to hospital with malnutrition caused, not by lack of food, but by a diet of junk food. 'Some of the kids are so weak they don't even have the energy to cry. Others sit miserably with eyes bandaged, hands and feet swollen like balloons and legs covered with scabs.' Deficiency of vitamin A (causing blindness) and protein (causing hands and feet to puff up) are most common.

Lise Sheet is the Director of Food Services in Ebeye. It is her job to oversee the preparation of thousands of school meals a day, including both breakfast and lunch:

All the food has to be shipped in from the outside. It's all canned. We don't have enough freezer space here for fresh fruit and vegetables and then there's the problem with frequent power cuts, we just couldn't risk losing that amount of food. Perhaps when the new power plant comes on [the desalination plant will also provide energy] we can give the

113

kids some fresh food. I really hope so. It's very difficult giving them anything like a balanced diet now.

Unlike Mejato, Ebeye is an urban centre with shops and cafés. Yet it is hard to imagine how even the most well-informed and well-off person in Ebeye could eat a balanced diet. The shops stock almost nothing fresh – a few mouldering oranges from South Africa in one store, a couple of soggy tomatoes in another. Bubble gum, sweetened breakfast cereals, fake maple syrup and chocolate cake mixes pack the shelves. As the middle classes of the west grow more aware of the dangers of artificial additives, preservatives and colouring, and well-informed and well-off households in London, New York and Paris sit down to whole grains grown in India, local vegetables and salads, and fruits from the Caribbean and the Pacific, the manufacturers of junk food are seeking new markets.

The only salad I saw in Ebeye was grated cabbage with Thousand Island dressing in the harbour café. Two days later I was leaving from Kwajalein US Air Base and dropped in to the snack bar, the only place where Marshallese and other 'visitors' can eat – the least prestigious café on Kwajalein, in other words. There, in the refrigerated counter, were salads of crunchy lettuce, tomatoes, cucumber, at half the price of the café on Ebeye. The menu offered main dishes served with vegetables and the only bananas I saw during my whole time in the Marshall Islands. In Ebeye, people pay 100 per cent more than Americans on Kwajalein do for their subsidised food, and for items of incomparably poorer quality. They also pay 20 per cent more than people do on Majuro.

Even fresh fish, normally a staple for the Marshallese, is now rarely tasted by Ebeye residents. On days when no test flight is booked, they could, in theory, go fishing in their lagoon. But the incoming missiles, which crash into the lagoon at 8,000 miles an hour, have broken the coral reef below the waves. This has stimulated the growth of an odd-looking brown seaweed, which thrives only on broken, dying coral. When the fish eat this seaweed, they become poisonous to humans.

Known as ciguatera, this fish poisoning is thought to kill 1,000 to 2,000 people a year on Ebeye and in French Polynesia where the French government continues to test nuclear weapons, and in Kanaky/New Caledonia where there is a great deal of French military activity around the ports.[11]

Eating fish from the lagoon is made yet more hazardous by the fact that although the weapons tested do not carry nuclear warheads, they are tipped with 'spent' uranium-238. When they break up beneath the surface of the lagoon, their cargo of uranium is dumped into the Pacific waters. According to the US military, the uranium is used to weight the missiles and to simulate a nuclear warhead so that it will show up in the same way on their radar screens. Strategic Air Command Lt. Col. Richard Kline, in Kwajalein, has denied that uranium-tipped missiles have been targeted to land in the lagoon. However, Army Public Affairs Officer Ed Vaughn in Huntsville, Alabama, has admitted:

> We do have a clean bottom policy at Kwajalein. We send a submersible and divers out to recover the debris from the re-entry vehicles that break up . . . We don't claim that we get it all out, by any means, but we attempt to get as much of it as we can locate.[12]

In the *Pacific Daily News* of 16 July 1979, Col. Robert A. Parsons maintained that there were no 'significant uranium concentrations in the lagoon and the health and safety of the local populace will not be affected'. Ebeye residents have protested about it repeatedly. But so far, requests for a proper survey of the lagoon and the health of the people who eat its fish have met only with silence and inaction.

Young Ebeye

Half of Ebeye's population are teenagers. For these young people, Ebeye is their only reality. Parents who still nurture hopes of reclaiming their land from the US worry that their children would not know how to live on a traditional outer island. They have never learned how to build an outrigger canoe or climb a coconut tree to pick the fruit or make a house from pandanus leaves and wood.

Darlene Keju-Johnson has spent time in Ebeye but now lives in the capital, Majuro, where she runs a youth group in the evenings. She talked about what young people on Majuro and Ebeye have to look forward to.

> These kids are really missing out and it's not their fault that they haven't had a taste of their own culture because it's been bombarded by the US. That's one of the reasons I decided to come back from the States. I was in Hawai'i for 17 years. I learned about the US culture and their language and I wanted to return. I had enough of what they had. I wanted what I had before I left – an island way of life, which is everything you own you share, you work together as a team, you have your songs and dances, your Marshallese language, your beautiful lagoon and your fish . . . everything that is your own identity. I missed that and I wanted to come back to it. Unfortunately when I came back I was wrong – everything I'd left had gone from Majuro and Ebeye.
>
> If there's a place I want to bring up my kids it's on the outer islands. Not on Majuro or Ebeye. I think they deserve to know about their own culture. Kids should be able to choose between their own culture and the one thrust upon them – in this case by the US. Kids on Ebeye and Majuro haven't got that choice and I think it's very unfair. Everyone should know about their own identity and culture and choose which society to grow up in.
>
> That's why we're trying to get the youth in Majuro together, using the family planning clinic as a centre, so we can teach the culture – we want to teach both health and our own traditions.

Unfortunately, the young people of Ebeye have no similar project. There there is hardly even space for the young ones to play, for all land is built up apart from one area where fire swept through the jammed-together scrapwood houses. For the older ones, there is no work, no college and nowhere to hang out but the bars.

Irene Paul is the director of a 'head start' programme for four- and five-year-olds and takes a keen interest in teenagers, too. She's trying to encourage others to press for better facilities for Ebeye's children and young adults:

> Activity on the island is very limited – they are really bored. I've talked to some of the kids who are supposed to be troublemakers – 11- and 12-year-olds. And deep down inside they are really beautiful boys but they've got nothing to do – what else but get into trouble? We've not even got a youth centre – we need a place for youth activities and to provide counselling for both boys and girls. Drugs, coming in from Kwajalein, are a problem, and alcohol even worse.
>
> People have been here to study the problem but I think it's high time to start doing something about it instead of just studying it. Everyone seems to identify the problems but we already know what it is. What we need is something done. It's the main concern of the community now.
>
> They need activities – all sorts of things, besides jobs, because not everyone's going to get work. A place where they can come in and have table games, with a gym for exercises . . . and a must is a counsellor working with them who could gain their trust.

Lack of places in the elementary school means the children attend in split shifts. At any one time, half of them will be playing in the garbage-strewn streets. But according to an article by Johannes Elaisha,[13] the forming of an all-woman Parent Teachers Association in 1987 has given huge support to the demoralised education system where there is a 50:1 student–teacher ratio. Still, there is no high school – except for one three miles away which teaches more or less the same curriculum that teenagers on Majuro would follow. It is on the American military base and Marshallese children are not allowed in its classrooms. Instead, if they go on to secondary education (and, according to Mayor Alvin Jacklick, fewer than half those who complete elementary education do), they must travel 300 miles to Majuro or thousands of miles to Guam or the US. That entails expensive air fares and money to keep their daughters and sons at boarding school or with relatives.

I asked Irene Paul if there was a lot of violence among young people. 'No – suicide is more of a problem,' she said. Almost all of the suicides are young men: another young lad killed himself while I was there. As well as the burial, there were gatherings in the house of friends of his parents. Most of the community went to offer their support and sympathy.

Ebeye is shocked and stunned by the frequent suicides, and in 1987 the community began organising 'suicide prevention meetings'. Young suicides also preoccupy Ebeye's Mayor, Alvin Jacklick. I was talking to him in his office one day when a high-pitched whine broke out. 'What's that?' he said, getting up and looking out of the window. 'Police sirens make me panic – another suicide most likely.' The noise turned out to be a drill from the neighbouring building site where the desalination plant was nearing completion. Jacklick explained that he was jumpy because he feels it's up to him to do something concrete about the suicides:

We have a lot of high school graduates on the island who are not able to find work on Kwajalein or anywhere, so we are asking the US Army to bring in a recruiting officer to see if they could at least take half of those young people and put them on an AROTC [Army Reserve Officer Training Corps] programme and give them skills, so that they can come back and work for the people of the Marshall Islands or stay and work in the US.

Last month we had three suicides. Being the chief executive of Kwajalein Atoll Development Corporation and the mayor of Ebeye and the one responsible for the wellbeing of these people, I'd rather they went to the US and learned some new things, learned how to be themselves, rather than stay here and commit suicide in my face. Once again someone comes to wake me at 2 a.m. to tell me there's been another suicide.

Given the overcrowding and stress in Ebeye, there is a low rate of street violence compared to western cities. I asked Jacklick if he was not worried that if Marshallese men joined the US Army they would be killed fighting for it or would return to Ebeye with the skills to be *effectively* violent.

> I would rather our young people went to fight a justified war on behalf of the US than fought amongst themselves here over a can of beer or bottle of rum. It doesn't make any sense to me that my two cousins beat each other up because one guy doesn't give the other a sip of the drink he's holding in his hand. I feel so bad about that. It's not justifiable.

I suggested that those sorts of petty fights happen in the army, too.

> That's not my concern, because I don't want to join the army. But if these guys are willing to go – and they'll know what they are letting themselves in for because it will be explained to them – then I don't have anything to do with it because they will sign the paper. But here I am responsible for them, and for problems I didn't create.

Jacklick is a self-avowedly ambitious man, who was once one of the most vociferous opponents of the US presence in the Marshalls. Ironically, he now finds himself in a position of responsibility in which he must negotiate with the authorities that run the base. It is a measure of how few options are open to Ebeye that Jacklick is now proposing that the US should give military training to Ebeye's young men.

With the attention of the community drawn most acutely to the crisis amongst the island's young men, the difficulties faced by young women have assumed a lower profile. But as Irene Paul pointed out, the increasing incidence of early, unwanted and repeated pregnancies is a major concern:

119

The birth rate has really gone up – 100 per cent in the last year, I reckon. Last year an average of one and a half babies were born a day – now it's two or three. And it's still going up. Many of the mothers are 12 and 13 years old. We don't even have a health educator here. The kids might have heard about family planning but they don't know where to go to get anything.

I asked Midnight Nathan a woman of 22 with a daughter of seven and a son of 18 months, whether in her experience young women were told about contraception by teachers or health workers.

No, that's the big problem – so they don't use family planning. There's a lot of babies with no fathers. Seems like they go out with married guys and get pregnant. *I think it's because they don't like their lives, that's why they do it.* (my emphasis)

At one time the Marshallese had their own methods of limiting the number of babies a woman had. These traditional methods have been largely forgotten or abandoned, said Neimon Philipo, a Marshallese elder and now one of the judges on the Traditional Land Rights Tribunal:

When a woman was eight months' pregnant she stopped sleeping with her husband. She would go to a special house and be looked after by the women in the family on both the woman and the man's side, and by other older women. After the birth of the baby the women would bathe the mother in hot salt water and coconut milk and prepare a medicine out of *kinnat* leaves which the female turtles eat after they've laid their eggs. The tea made out of these leaves is good for keeping the mother strong while she's breastfeeding.

The husband was not allowed to sleep with the woman for a year – until the child can swim, we say. In fact, any time a woman is taking local Marshallese medicine, she's not allowed to sleep with her husband.

That was the old method of family planning. Women still had quite a few babies, but not 10, 11, 12 like they do now. Sometimes they get pregnant now as soon as they've given birth. At least then they had gaps in between.

In the Marshall Islands the promotion of dried baby milk has, of course, led to a decrease in breastfeeding, once regarded as a protection against pregnancy, as well as a vital source of nutrition for the baby.

Darlene Keju-Johnson has been talking to midwives on the outer islands about old-style family planning: 'As well as breastfeeding and staying away from the husband for the first year, they tell me we also used menstrual calendars. The men must have been very good and understanding about it because these things need co-operation.' She and others are concerned not only that contraception should be widely available, but that it should be safe and that women be properly informed about their bodies.

Significant numbers of heterosexual western women are returning to barrier methods of contraception (condoms, caps and spermicide), having learned of the dangers of taking the pill over a long time, the risk of infection from a coil and the benefits of condoms in preventing the spread of sexually transmitted diseases including AIDs. Pharmaceutical companies are meanwhile looking for new markets in the First World where women, particularly those living outside urban centres, rarely have access to information on the risks associated with different contraceptives such as the birth control injection Depo Provera which has only been granted restrictive licence in a number of western countries.

In spring 1987, six months after I'd spoken with women on Ebeye, a women's clinic was opened there to advise on family planning, sex education and sexually transmitted diseases.

Overcrowding

Forced relocations, a high birth rate and the attraction of urban centres for people in search of jobs means that Ebeye – and to a growing extent Majuro – are horribly overcrowded. The majority of Ebeye's scrap plywood and tin dwellings are no larger than 500 square feet, housing an average of 13 or 14 people. It is seldom possible for everyone to sleep at one time.

It is hard to get away from Ebeye: all the nearby islands are in US hands and are out of bounds. Traditionally, the Marshallese would walk the reef at low tide to visit friends on a neighbouring island or sail to another island to picnic, to gather food or to be alone and escape from anything bothering them back home.

On outer islands children will spend the day out playing, adults will be farming copra and fishing or will gather with their friends to chat or play the ukeleli or a game of cards under the shade of a tree. That's just not possible on Ebeye. There's barely a tree in sight and the few that are left are hardly surrounded by pleasant clean beach or forest floor to sit on. The only escape from Ebeye is by aeroplane – too expensive for the majority of people – or to wait for a field ship to pass and hope it will take you to another atoll. So claustrophobia and pent-up frustration compound the problems.

Relieving overcrowding on Ebeye is one of the priorities of the Kwajalein Atoll Development Authority, as its chief executive, Alvin Jacklick, explained:

> We have to work within our present framework, given the fact that we've been modernised and westernised for the last forty years. One thing we *can* do is to reduce the population here on Ebeye and relocate the people on northern islands by building a causeway between here and the island of Gugeegue, given back to us as a result of the 1982 demonstration.
>
> Unfortunately, it will be more expensive for people to live there if they work on Kwajalein because they'll have to hire a private boat to get to work. Or if they come to Ebeye they'll have to use taxis or buy a car. But I'm convinced we'll be able

to relocate half the population of Ebeye to Gugeegue and the other northern islands – and I'll be very relieved when we do.

The problem is that other Marshallese may then be tempted by the idea of a job on Kwajalein and want to come here. The government doesn't understand how desperately overcrowded we are and gives entry permits to people coming here to work. So we are bringing in a regulation to stop this. It is to protect the people of Ebeye who've been here a long time and also to protect those who would end up living in a slum here, whereas they are living in much more comfortable conditions on the outer islands. It's inhuman of the Marshall Islands government to let more and more people come here looking for work: senseless and immoral.

Until the causeway is complete, life on Ebeye, says lawyer Johnsay Riklon, is 'brutal. It's an assault.'

Living cheek by jowl with other people is new to the Marshallese, and highly stressful. And the situation was exacerbated further in January 1988 by a typhoon which left more than 2,000 people homeless. Winds averaged 50 knots and huge waves pounded Ebeye, less than five feet above sea level at its highest point. Its wood and corrugated iron houses are particuarly fragile and Mayor Jacklick estimated over $5 million in damage, with a third of Ebeye's homes destroyed and another third badly damaged.[14]

According to a report commissioned by the Marshall Islands Social Services Department and conducted between December 1984 and January 1985 by an American, Dennis T.P. Keene,

The amount of crowding varies from one society to another, but this tolerance results from the gradual evolution of institutions in adaptive response to steady increases in population. It is highly unlikely that Marshallese populations were ever near to being as densely concentrated as they are now on Ebeye and Majuro. It would be unreasonable to expect natural social evolution to generate institutions to cope with the new stresses of overpopulation in the few decades in which the population growth has occurred.

Dr Merliss noticed the high incidence of hypertension in the Marshallese people, estimated at between 24 and 40 per cent, compared to 5 per cent in the average white American male. He blamed, in part, the cultural upheaval that has been induced directly or indirectly by the testing. 'Hypertension is a stress disease' and 'often related to crowding or breaking of social patterns by individuals or by groups', he says.[15]

Under the stress of living ten or twelve people to a room, with nowhere to go for physical exercise or relaxation, something has to crack. The report pointed to anecdotal evidence of a rise in child abuse. I asked Darlene Keju-Johnson if this was something new – or if it was only now being talked about:

> I wouldn't say it was completely new, but it's getting worse. As well as the current overcrowding, we've had four different cultures telling us different directions on how to bring up your family. The Germans, for instance, were very strict. No rights to other members of family, only the husband. If the children don't do as you say, you whack them. But what happens when you keep whacking the kid's head or you actually burn them with matches? Yet you hear this from friends – there's almost no research or statistics to say this actually happened in 1979, but you know it's happening. You see it in your community. You smell it, you feel it.

Biram Stege, the only woman school principal in the Marshall Islands, is concerned at the number of girls and young women who run away from home:

> Some of our girls really want to get on and do something with themselves, be something . . . but a lot of them, as many, don't even finish school. They run away from home, they float back and forth, go with someone, then with someone else . . . They think, what's the use of going to school?

The Keene report found that according to police records on Majuro in 1975, six young women were brought to police attention that year: none of these was a runaway. In 1983, 28 women were reported, 16 of whom were runaways. In 1984, 12 out of 16 were runaways. 'Older informants believe that the problem of runaways is a new phenomenon in Marshallese society. All agree that it is a growing one,' it reports.

Two years ago a project was set up on Majuro for runaway girls, organised by Evelyn Lanki. She has also held workshops on Ebeye, where even more girls run away.

> From talking to the girls I think they're often trying to escape family problems. One reason they drop out of school is that the older girls are expected to stay at home and look after younger kids. They get behind at school. Maybe the parents are fighting between themselves because they are depressed with their living conditions. Or maybe they favour other kids and this girl feels left out. Sometimes she's been abused – hit, or worse still, sexual abuse.

Many also believe that they are running *to* something: independence, money, a more 'American' way of life:

> On Ebeye they are often girls who've come from the outer islands hoping to earn money, maybe at the base. They stay with relatives who perhaps expect them to do the housework. So they go with men – sailors, Americans, local guys. They get them drunk then steal their money. They want money for drinking and going to the disco . . . everyone is trying to be American now.
>
> They're very confused in some ways, caught between being American and being Marshallese. But often they think theirs is a good life because they have some independence. And they're good to one another, they're loyal and look after each other. Some would prefer to get into a regular relationship and move away from the kind of life, though.

The young women are said to live in gangs, looking after each other, sleeping rough – in containers at the docks – or on board visiting foreign ships. Most drink, which is disapproved of in women by many Marshallese. Because they're labelled as outcasts simply because they've left home and rebelled against social norms, they find it difficult to compete for the few jobs available. With no family support either, prostitution is one of the few choices open to them.

Prostitution and venereal disease

All over the world where there are military bases there is prostitution. The military expects women to service its requirements: cooks, cleaners and seamstresses look after practical needs; wives, girlfriends and 'pin-up girls' keep up the fighters' morale; jobs vacated by men in times of war are filled by women who, at the end of the war, are told to return to home and make way for the returning men. And most soldiers also expect to have their 'sexual needs' met by local women. That may involve rape, particularly when the military is at war with the local community; it invariably involves local women in prostitution.

Kwajalein Missile Range is quite different from most bases in that it is first and foremost for research and development and for radar tracking and so is staffed mainly by civilians. It does not, for the present at least, house a large number of soldiers. Moreover, a considerable number of American women live on the base, as wives or in their own capacity as skilled technicians, and socialising is a major preoccupation. Social interaction with Marshallese people is definitely discouraged. Marshallese base workers are not allowed into leisure facilities, restaurants and bars, and they have to be off the base when the last shift ends. There is one exception to this rule, however. I was told by several Marshallese women that an officially sanctioned list of women is allowed on to the base 'after hours'. At one time it was, they said, easy to get a night pass, but after the land protests by Ebeye residents regulations were tightened up. American men are of course free to come to Ebeye themselves, and are much in evidence, hanging around bars and discos.

The correlation between a military presence and prostitution is not, however, a static one, determined only by the number of men living on a base who want the services of prostitutes. In the case of Kwajalein it is also about how the military occupation has changed the local economy, replacing subsistence fishing and farming with a cash economy, and making consumer goods – TVs, videos, cars, alcohol and cigarettes – available in the shops. Yet there are jobs for less than 10 per cent of the

Marshallese population, and very few of these are open to women. In a rapidly changing society, consumer lifestyle and American-style independence are the models for women – and also out of reach to the great majority of them. At the same time, the base and the commercial opportunities on Ebeye act as a magnet for ships whose crew may also be in search of prostitutes.

Darlene Keju-Johnson recalled:

> Men off the boats are always on the look-out for prostitutes. Women didn't used to need to go into prostitution because families would help each other out. No one was hungry, you didn't need cash because it wasn't that sort of economy. It's really changed in the last 15 to 20 years. It's just gone pheew – to a cash economy.

Dr Keene likewise concluded that the rapid increase in the number of young women turning to prostitution could be seen as a direct or indirect result of American military presence and rapid westernisation:

> The substitution of wage work and a cash economy for subsistence fishing/gardening and reciprocity undermines values such as sharing and hospitality. Constant change weakens respect for the elderly, for the long accumulation of experience no longer guarantees the most relevant knowledge for the problems at hand. The young shift from being economic assets to being economic liabilities. Group tasks are individualised. Individual independence emerges as an alternative to group interdependence and solidarity.

However, as Evelyn Lanki pointed out, certain Marshallese traditions still survive:

> At least here in the Marshalls the girls are accepted back into their families if they want to go back, even if they've been missing for months. We don't have attitudes about children of an unmarried mother being 'bastards' – they're just accepted. Meanwhile, our women's organisations are fighting to get more child support from men.

Venereal disease is rife on Ebeye. It was at its peak in 1984, then dropped off in 1985 after a concerted effort was made to encourage people to come forward for tests. Even so, in December 1985, 55 new cases of syphilis and 28 cases of gonorrhea were reported; in a mass screening in September 1986, 8 per cent of people tested had syphilis.[16]

When I asked Midnight Nathan about issues for young women on Ebeye, she named syphilis as one of them. 'Girls don't really know about VD – they think syphilis is just a little illness so they don't know to be careful.' Evelyn Lanki agreed. 'They don't realise how serious VD can be, and think it's worth having it as long as they can get money to buy what they want.' When she ran a workshop for young women on Ebeye, many were found to have VD:

Two of the girls were in a particularly bad way. One had probably had it for three years without knowing. She didn't know till she was pregnant. The baby was born blind then died. Another girl of 14 had had it for two years without treatment. The bacteria was eating away her vagina. She must have been suffering horribly but not daring to tell anyone.

It's difficult to halt in the early stages because people don't want to say who they've slept with. And if they're prostitutes maybe they don't know. We have a problem with the American military men. We'll have a terrible situation once AIDS gets here.

While Evelyn Lanki implied that North American men from the base carried and spread VD on Ebeye, others I talked to disagreed. They said people working on the base had medical check-ups both before they came out to work on Kwajalein and while they were there; it was more likely to be spread by sailors from the boats that call in to service the base or bring imported food and western goods to Ebeye.

I asked Darlene Keju-Johnson what she thought was most important for solving Ebeye's health crisis. 'Education and self-help,' was her reply:

128

We have a lot of the health problems of industrialised nations but they have higher standards of living than us and their health care is at least 30 years ahead. We're fighting just to survive.

And what have we learned from the industrialised nations? Well, women have learned to feed their babies powdered milk, which isn't as nutritious as breast milk and so leaves babies prone to infection; it's virtually impossible to sterilise bottles here; and mothers end up watering it down because they can't afford to buy enough. So now we have to begin at the beginning again, encouraging women to go back to breastfeeding.

People here have almost no access to information. If the ad says it's good for them or if it's in style and fashionable in the States they'll buy it. The challenge here is to make people aware of what's really happening, of what's really healthy for them . . .

Kwajalein Missile Range

In the minds of certain military planners, Kwajalein atoll clearly exists for the convenience of the US military – right down to what time it is there. The Marshall Islands are on the other side of the international dateline, but Kwajalein runs on an American schedule: if it's Friday in Majuro, it's Thursday in Kwajalein, Ebeye and Washington, DC. The Pentagon insisted the atoll change in case they fired missiles on the wrong day.

The Marshallese themselves were clearly also seen as a bonus – cheap labour to build and service the base. The US authorities, however, were never keen on seeing too much of them, and since the sail-ins, when Marshallese people once again made themselves at home on their land – and in the country club at the base – they've made it plain that the islanders are not welcome. Even the 600 or so workers are made to feel that they are temporary visitors. Every day they are subjected to strict security, receiving a pass which indicates where they are allowed to go on the island, or, as is more often the case, where they are not allowed to go. It is not only 'militarily sensitive' areas which are off-limits, but also almost all the shops, amenities and recreation facilities. Marshallese workers must be off the range by the end of the last evening shift. To keep the numbers of Marshallese down, the US even insists that its employees of lower rank who marry Marshallese people must go and live on Ebeye.

Anyone arriving on Kwajalein to catch a plane is subjected to even greater restrictions, as Evelyn Konou, the only woman senator in the Marshall Islands government, explained:

When my sister Rosalie and I and another woman were coming back from Ebeye, we had to get the boat at 6 p.m. – it was the last one. But the flight didn't leave till 12.30, so we went to sit in the snack bar: our passes said that's the only place we could go. But soon the snack bar closed. So there was nowhere to go but one of the restaurants. We went and sat down and tried to order a drink but the waiter asked for our passes and said we couldn't sit there. I don't see what they think we were going to do to them, three Marshallese women sitting in their restaurant. It's not like there's anything to spy on there. How can they say Communists are bad when they won't even let Marshallese people sit in their restaurants? We're just expected to wait for the plane for five hours in the terminal with nothing to drink. We can't even go to the Yokwe Yuk [Marshallese for 'welcome'] Club when we're thirsty.

When you go to Kwajalein you enter the terminal and they say STOP!, so everyone has to stop. SIT DOWN! and we all sit down. You feel like everyone does what we're told, when to stop, when to sit, when to go. So that's democratic government.

As well as the normal military notices, forbidding photographs and so on, Kwajalein's security terminal has a huge board with a list of regulations. These include restrictions on the amount of water and cigarettes that a Marshallese person working on the base is allowed to take out. Many workers felt the rules, instigated after the Operation Homecoming protest, were an excuse to search – and thereby intimidate and humiliate – the Marshallese.

Few journalists are allowed on to Kwajalein Missile Range, unless they are simply passing through on their way to catch a plane. When I rang the US Embassy in London to ask permission, the official said Kwajalein was not on his list of military bases and he'd have to telex the Pentagon. I then learned that you need a special permit from Huntsville, Alabama, headquarters of Army Command. In the end, I let the matter drop, as by then I'd talked to another journalist who advised me that if you do pursue such a request you draw a great deal of attention to yourself and may find even your way to Ebeye is blocked. (Ebeye requires a special pass, unlike the rest of the Marshall Islands, which ask only a US visitors' visa.)

It was hot and thundery the day I arrived on Kwajalein. I'd flown from Majuro with Jeton Anjain, senator of the Rongelap people, and his brother Abel, a preacher. It was already raining in Majuro, torrential sheets of rain that turned the road to a series of unnavigable potholes. Jeton's daughter Abacca drove us to the airport. Twice we had to turn around and seek alternative routes, though there is only one main road which stretches the length of the narrow strip of an island. Abacca took the small back roads which lead to houses by the shore and only sometimes take you back to the main road. She got us to the terminal just in time. We arrived with an extraordinary amount of luggage, and had to pay extra on the local airline, Air Mike, as Air Micronesia is fondly called. The cases and packing boxes were full of provisions for the Rongelap people now living on Mejato where we were eventually headed. Partly because of the luggage, which we could only just carry between us, we didn't hang around on Kwajalein that day. There would be a ferry leaving soon and we'd have no excuse for still being on the Missile Range: I worried that I might be searched and my tapes and films confiscated. Jeton and Abel also had to be careful;

Abel's daughter was married to a North American and living on Kwajalein, and the family needed passes to come and visit her.

On the way back, however, I had an hour and a half to kill between the ferry arriving and the plane leaving. There's a shuttle bus between the ferry terminal, the airport and the snack bar, the only other place we were allowed to go. I first checked in at the airport, then decided to walk to the snack bar to have a look around on the way. The streets on the Missile Range are really avenues – wide and smooth, lined with coconut palms planted in regimented rows. They seemed sterile and artificial in comparison with the lush groves of working coconuts, planted and harvested for food on outer islands: Kwajalein was like that once, before the raging battles of the Second World War destroyed all its trees.

Private cars are banned on Kwajalein and the inhabitants ride round on bicycles of every size and style, including ones with elongated Easy Rider handlebars. It's one of the many bitter twists that Kwajalein is populated with cheap, safe, clean bicycles which are healthy to use and which last longer than cars and therefore present less of a waste disposal problem. Meanwhile US cars are a status symbol on tiny Ebeye, which you can drive around in ten minutes.

It was Sunday on Kwajalein – play day for the Americans on the base. I walked past a baseball pitch where two women's teams – coached by men – were playing, urged on by cries of 'Go team, go!' and 'Yeah, Carole, yeah!' from supporters sitting behind the diamond, protected by wire netting. Across the road men played American football on one field; on another a few individuals practised their throwing. Further on there were tennis courts and then a leisure complex with darkrooms. A copy of *Kwajalein Hourglass*, a daily broadsheet published on the base, advertised a men's bowling league, a softball team needing more players, aerobic classes in the gym, golf, windsurfs and yachts for sale . . . Evidently adults have a lot to amuse themselves with on Kwajalein while on Ebeye children play in the street, in the polluted surf or, when it's raining, in the one room of their house.

Every now and again, an article appears in a US newspaper written by a journalist who has clearly been shown round Kwajalein but has either not ventured to Ebeye or has chosen to ignore it. As most of the US workers on Kwajalein are civilians doing technical jobs for companies with defence contracts, they are there in a voluntary capacity rather than being assigned by the military to the Missile Range. So a colourful blurb focusing on the advantages of life on Kwajalein never does recruitment any harm. Here's an excerpt from a report which appeared in the *Hartford Courant* (published in Hartford, Connecticut, with a daily circulation of around 222,000) on 17 October 1985:

Kwajalein is in many respects a determinedly ordinary place. The Defense Department has gone to great lengths to create an exquisitely mundane environment in one of the world's most exotic settings.

'This is just a small town like any other,' said Lt. Col. Tom Macey, deputy commander of Kwajalein. 'It's just a nice bunch of people doing their jobs in a nice place – that happens to be a defense site on a bunch of remote tropical islands.'

Kwajalein has its own American Legion Post, Boy Scout troop, elementary and high schools, radio station, newspaper, movie theatres (two of them), baseball diamonds (also two), library, department stores (called Macy's and Gimbel's), Bible study class and Alcoholics Anonymous chapter. There is a Surfway supermarket with a fair stock of commodities ranging from fresh California vegetables to peanut butter.

The day I arrived, a military cargo flight brought in a bounty of new items such as anchovies, pizza sticks, and mineral water, and the store did a land-office business. The Post Office branch was unusually busy that day too. The twice-weekly flight carried letters from the mainland.

Only 34 of Kwajalein's 2,585 residents are in the Army. There are 46 civilian employees of the Army. The rest either work for defense contractors or are the dependants of those who do. As civilians they aren't required to wear uniforms. In the intense heat, most people wear shorts and sandals, adding to the relaxed atmosphere.

At dusk, as the blinding tropical sunlight diminishes and the heat lets up, joggers pour out in force onto Ocean Avenue and the tennis and basketball courts fill up.

Swimmers splash in the water off the public beach and bikini-clad young women ski behind motorboats on the calm surface of Kwajalein Lagoon.

'It's a heck of a pleasant place to live,' said Dave Miller, a 26-year-old meteorologist who arrived six months ago with his wife and 5-year-old daughter from a small town in Oklahoma. 'The streets are safe, it's clean, and there are plenty of social and sports activities.'

For Ebeye residents, working on the Missile Range only serves to highlight the poverty of their own situation. Nietok Anjain, who at one time worked on Kwajalein at Macy's Store, told me the Marshallese employees weren't even allowed to buy anything from the shop.

Most Marshallese on base are employed as cooks, gardeners, warehouse workers, maintenance personnel and, formerly, as maids. Occasionally they may be secretaries or mechanics. Whatever their job, they are subjected to systematic wage and job discrimination. A US Congressional Subcommittee was told:

> Close to 90 per cent of the workers said that they felt they are being discriminated against in terms of jobs and pay because they are Micronesians . . . Approximately 75 per cent of the workers were able to provide the names of specific non-Micronesians who do the exact same job but who receive significantly higher pay for their work.[17]

They are rarely promoted, particularly into positions where they would be supervising others. Peter Coleman, former acting High Commissioner, gave his own reasons for this in 1977. He is particularly revealing about the attitude of the American 'visitors' in the Marshalls:

> While some of the Micronesian workers at Ebeye may have the technical ability to warrant promotion, *they do not have the ability to be in charge, to supervise people, particularly Americans.* (my emphasis) [18]

Kwajalein may have all the comforts money can buy, but many civilians working there are uneasy about the military regime, as a report in the *Guardian* on 15 July 1984 by Harold Jackson, one of the few journalists who has reported on both Kwajalein and Ebeye, highlights:

> American foods, clothes and other goods are flown the 4,500 miles from California at vast expense. According to the base adjutant, Captain Tracy Puritz, it needs 580 flights a month to sustain Kwajalein's standard of living. There is also the attraction of high pay and tax concessions; but Kwajalein is still not the happy little gathering that all this affluence and leisure might imply.
>
> The first adjustment required – not only from the scientists but from their wives and children – is that they become subject to a constant and heavy stress on military security of all kinds. The base's phone book has large printed warnings that calls are 'subject to monitoring' . . . There is also the overwhelming presence of the private police force run by another of the contracting companies, the Washington Security Force, with roughly one policeman for every five workers on the base.

Both Jackson and journalist David Robie, who was denied official clearance for Kwajalein, were slipped copies of a poem composed by a disillusioned base dweller which read:

> We can't voice our opinion,
> Our phone lines are tapped,
> With one patrolman for five
> We've a feeling we're trapped.

Base living it's called
But one wonders for who;
It's more like an encampment
With 'who' watching 'you'.

But discontentment with their own lot does not necessarily spill over into empathy with the Marshallese. While waiting for an interview with the commanding officer, Colonel William Spin, which proved fruitless, David Robie started chatting to a security guard, Don Smith, who offered his perhaps not untypical view of the deal doled out to the Marshall Islanders by the guardians of the Trust Territory.

They don't know how well off they are. If the US left Kwajalein, they would only lease it out to someone else – and that would be the commies.

It's far better that the US remains here. We give them freedom . . . we don't interfere or invade their lives.

Look at the ferry . . . it has a canteen and the Marshallese workers can have a cup of coffee or something when they come over. And when the boat goes back it sells cut-price beer, so they're pretty happy really.[19]

7

'Dealing with the Outside; Keeping What is Ours': Women's Experiences of Colonialism

In this chapter, ten women who live in the most westernised islands of Majuro and Ebeye talk of both the dramatic changes and the subtle contradictions brought about by the presence of the US in their islands. The chapter is presented in interview format.

Until now, I have focused primarily on the impact of nuclear weapons testing on the lives of the Marshall Islanders. However, four centuries of colonisation and particularly the last 40 years have had other far-reaching consequences. When the Spanish came to Micronesia seeking spices and the Germans came seeking copra and other goods they also brought with them their customs, their language, their religion, their way of looking at the world. Like other colonialists before them, the North Americans have brought more than their bombs.

Chailang Palacios, a Chamorro woman from Saipan, told a British audience how she felt the US had colonised her people's minds:

You have heard it, and I have heard it too from the older generation: 'Oh, we are so grateful that the Americans won the war. They saved us from the Communists, from Russia.' Yet right after the war the Americans came, like the early missionaries, in the name of God saying. 'We are here to Christianise you, to help you love one another, be in peace.' We still have the Bible while the missionaries and their white governments have all the land.[1]

Women have played a particularly important role in resisting the destruction of Micronesian culture, as Belauan lawyer Roman Bedor told film-maker Gina Kalla:

When the western peoples arrived, they took away the men's rights in society. They thought that if they took power away from the men, they would be able to control the society. But as our society is matrilineal, women play an important part. The women continued to organise, they kept on meeting, they kept the culture alive, as well as the language. So we are one of the Pacific islands which has maintained its language and its culture despite 400 years of colonisation.

But even while fighting for the survival of their culture, there can be traps and barbs for women if they are expected to take up the role of preservers of tradition with no thought to the contradictions inherent in their doing so. A RepMar paper on women's status shows how women are both powerful and trapped within a particular role:

Since the Marshallese culture is matrilineal, Marshallese women traditionally have great influence and power. As 'nurturers' women are recognised as the givers and sustainers of life, especially in relationship to children. In traditional stories, it was the women who established new clans (*jowi*) and new lineages (*bwij*), women unable to have children could usually adopt and any woman was considered a mother to her sisters' and brothers' children.

Traditionally Marshallese women have always been 'peacemakers' with the oldest woman of her lineage within the immediate family dealing with family problems. Even today the oldest women in the family may have the final say in family decision-making. Marshallese women, also, are known as 'benefactors', for when a woman marries, the family does not lose a daughter. Even when women marry outside the Marshall Islands, they are concerned for their families and relatives and will help them in any way they can.

Traditionally, too, Marshallese women play the role of 'encouragers'. In long ago battles, the women would beat the drums. Today, in sports, girls encourage the success of the event by singing, dancing, and beating on any available object. And to this day, men have come to rely on women's organisations and clubs for the planning and implementation of their political platforms and rallies.[2]

Traditions may ensure a community's survival and enrich its culture. They may also suffocate the development of some members of the community – most often women. Vanessa Griffen, a Fijian activist, has written:

Culture, or custom, is the commonest argument used against any call for a new image of women in the Pacific. Even aware women are confused about this question because in the postcolonial period, cultural identity is an important part of national rehabilitation and pride. We as women need to deal with this question and present a clear statement of custom and tradition in relation to the liberation of women. Vanuatu, in a country paper presented at the South Pacific Commission conference, summarised the argument succinctly: 'Cultural activities have a potentially freeing effect on women. However, the confusion between these rich historical traditions of culture and the social convenience (to men) of custom practices has led to the retention of attitudes which ensure that women find it difficult to escape from their traditional roles.'[3]

When considering the devastating impact of western-style development on the Marshallese, it is easy to become nostalgic, as if harking back to a utopia which perhaps never existed. It is clear that in countless ways the subsistence island lifestyle was much preferred by most Marshallese people. But even if tomorrow we were to succeed in pressing our governments to call a halt to the arms race, if Kwajalein Missile Range were to put up a 'closed' notice, if the Pacific were no longer a fulcrum of Cold War hostility, there could be no turning back the clock to a previous lifestyle. As each of the women interviewed in this chapter says, women in the Marshalls today are struggling with a delicate and demanding project: to retain and keep vital all that is good in their own culture, to extract what good they can from western culture, that is attempting to suffocate their own and to synthesise the two. Rather than being pulled apart by conflicting demands, they are attempting to draw on a whole host of resources in their fight for self-determination for themselves and for their region.

Lijon Eknilang was a child when the fallout showered over her. She has since suffered seven miscarriages and a thyroid tumour, and is constantly plagued by ill-health which the doctors can never seem to diagnose. She feels she has to live on Ebeye, though she dislikes the way of life there, because she is frequently in need of medical attention. 'I'm very frightened of what's happing to me,' she says. Nevertheless, she is very active in fighting for justice for all the Marshallese. She was hoping to run as mayor if her health improved enough for her to live on Mejato. She also has a wicked sense of humour and a wide appreciation of life: 'I think you should have fun in life, I've always believed in enjoying myself.' At one time she was a professional singer.

I urged her, 'Write your life story, tell the world what's happening here.'

'If I wrote down my story it would be this thick,' she laughed, demonstrating with her finger and thumb. 'There'd be good stories, bad stories and sad stories. And there'd be lots of funny stories.'

The colonising of the Marshall Islands has set in motion

emigration to the US as people start to rely on a cash economy and are obliged to look further afield for work, and as Marshallese marry Americans living on the base and go with them when they return home to the US. The Compact of Free Association allows Marshallese entry into the US to work and study and allows Americans free entry into the Marshall Islands; at the same time, only a quota of Marshallese are allowed to work on the US base on their doorstep, and only in the most menial positions. And like immigrants to European countries from their former colonies, despite legislation enshrining their right of entry, when the invaded knock on the door of the invader's house, they find hostility and racism. This is one of Lijon's stories.

'When I was growing up, I was always different. I climbed the trees, went diving . . . I fell in love with the underwater, it's so beautiful. I used to play with the small sharks, bang a rock with my fishing spear, and the shark would come. He'd circle around me and we'd play. One day a strong wave came and hurled me on to the reef and I hurt my back. Then the shark came right after me, when he smelled blood. But I swam back slowly.

'At that time I could stay down a long time, no trouble, walking around on the bottom. When I tried again recently I could only stay down a minute or two, then I'd come right back up. I'm not used to it any more.

'I wasn't allowed to go to school because I played with the boys, did all the boys' things. They wouldn't let boys and girls play together. But I organised for us all to go to the beach one day, to take food and have a good time. They wanted to know who did it, who was responsible. That's when they stopped me going to school. But I wanted to read and write so I taught myself.

'When I was young I thought people who spoke English were smarter, were different, knew more, so I wanted to learn. I worked with people from the Peace Corps and for the first three months, listened. Every time I heard a new phrase, I would try to remember it. Then I would ask someone I knew who spoke

English, what does "How are you doing mean? And how do you respond?" After three months I could start speaking back.

'I married an American guy who had been in the military but got out. He lived in Kwajalein and worked for a company on base. We went to live in LA. I thought – all those girls at home are teachers or secretaries. There's too many of them. I want to study electronics. So when I went to school, I had to ask the teacher if I could take a tape recorder into the lessons. At night I would listen three, maybe four times to each sentence, till I understood it. Sometimes I understood only one word and had to work it out from there. When the exam time came we had to watch and listen to the teacher set up an electronics kit and then set up our own. I couldn't understand what he was saying, so I just watched very carefully and copied it. There wasn't one thing wrong with my kit, so they offered me a job in the school.

'In my next job my supervisor didn't like me because of the colour of my skin. There were only three other black or brown women in the building, but they were right down in the basement, so he didn't have to see them – I was on the second floor. The other workers told me after a couple of days to work more slowly because I was finishing the jobs too quickly and then we'd all be given more work. That's how I knew he couldn't have taken a dislike to me because I was no good.

'He told me I had to leave because there were other, poorer people than me who needed the job. He said I was rich because I dressed nicely. I wasn't. I really needed overtime and he would never give it to me. When I resigned the company president told me he was sad, because I'd worked well and never had time off. I told him it was the supervisor who was forcing me out.

'The day I left the supervisor said he was sorry I was leaving. I told him to look around the room. Everyone was staring. I said, "You don't see any, do you?" "See what?" "Women with black skin?" I told him not to say he was sorry I was leaving because he wasn't and I didn't want to see him, didn't want to hear his voice any more. I said, "This is your key and these are your tools, take them." And I walked out.

'I came back to the Marshall Islands. I was supposed to go back to LA but I can't live in the US. I have to live here.'

Neimon Philipo works for the Traditional Rights Court. She is an 'elder' of the Marshall Islands and a very wise woman, both kind and shrewd. She has a vast knowledge of her culture and strong opinions on the need for women to organise together. We met for the first of several talks in the Likrok 'restaurant and entertainment centre' in 'downtown' Majuro, as the small town centre is called, with some intended wit.

Can you tell me about your work with the court?

It was set up in 1984 and deals with disputes over our land and customs. It's particularly important now that people are losing their land to the Americans and because American and Marshallese ways are clashing: suddenly we're having to deal with money. Our land is our security. As long as we have coconuts, breadfruit and pandanus we have what we need to live. And it's important in a spiritual, an emotional way. So when one member of a family is tempted to sell the land for money, the others are often angry and come to us. I think money is to blame for a lot of our current problems. It's harder to share money than it was to share food. Young people now forget the land belongs to everyone.

There are nine people on the Court: three from *iroij*, three from *alab* and three from *dri jerbal*. Only two women applied and I was the only one to get on: we were elected by our leaders.

It's a very challenging job. I thought I knew all our customs and language but I find I don't. I learned from my grandfather when I was young: he was an *alab*. And things are changing. Some women now use their power as landowners, whereas before they left it to the men to take care of things.

To tell you the truth, I don't know if the Traditional Rights Court is working, really, because we're not truly independent. We're under the umbrella of the *Nitijela*, the parliament. In one case recently it stepped in and changed our judgment. Originally we were nine full-time judges but then the *Nitijela* made only three permanent – the rest of us are paid only for particular cases. It's hard for only three to be impartial because they end up handling cases of friends. The *Nitijela* just decided who would be the three, with no discussion – it was a political decision. It's now October and I've only been called in for one case this year: they needed me because it was so complex.

At the Traditional Rights Court we invite old Marshallese from the outer islands to tell us about the language. I try and learn from the old people: in Marshallese, one word might cover a whole sentence in English. But I hate it when some people call themselves 'experts' in our ways and customs. It means they can't be wrong.

In the old days – long before the Americans, before the missionaries first came – we had a god by a different name. But it is curious how many of our old religious stories and customs coincide with the Bible. Our Marshallese chant is like the Bible and still used by many ministers. We had a story of 12 brothers, like the 12 sons of Israel and one like Jonah and the whale. Another one warns of a time of sickness, famine, war, when brother will fight brother . . . like in the book of Matthew.

How do you think life has changed for women, with the arrival of the US?

We've lost much of our culture. Traditionally, in the Marshall Islands when a young woman has her first period we give her a bath, rub her down with oil, put flowers on her head. She goes to stay with the old women so they can help her understand. In Yap, every time women have their period they go to a menstruation house. It's like a celebration. I think these rituals and wisdom are important and it's sad we're losing them.

We have many sayings about women: *Kora Lep Jaltap* meaning women are like a basket where you put what is precious. *Kora Em An Kel* means every woman is different. *Kora Em Ajese* means women may be weaker than men in body but in mind, and in other ways, they are strong. Women stay up all night looking after a sick child and then work the next day. *Kora Lijman Juri* means women are the peacemakers, especially the older women, who intervene and make decisions. *Kora Menunak* means you are descended through your mother – it is her blood which is important. *Ailin Kein An Kora* means the Marshall Islands belong to women.

Women here are starting to organise themselves. Before, most women weren't active, but we no longer sit in the background with good ideas and don't say them. I'm glad. So there are good things we've learned from the Americans.

But they've also brought military men with money to spend on prostitutes. And when I was young I only remember two suicides and they were very particular cases. Now young people are generally very depressed. It's terrible to be living in the shadow of these suicides. Sometimes the young people think their parents don't care enough about them because they don't give them money – but they can't give what they don't have. Yet at the same time, the Americans have encouraged young people to be open-minded and free to do what they want. They can stand up and say what they believe now, so for that I admire the Americans: young people and women didn't used to be able to express their ideas.

What about life for young women growing up now?

Most of my contact with girls has been through the Girl Scouts. I was President from 1979 to '83. When we first set it up, we were given the US rules but we said, 'We can't follow these, they're against our customs', so we just changed them to fit with our ways. We try to encourage girls to stay on in education. That's one thing that's changed for the better. My mother and father stopped me from going to high school. They said, 'Girls only need to know how to read and write.'

When I asked the Secretary of Education what girls wanted to be, she said some want to be nurses, doctors and engineers. More want to be lawyers, secretaries and aviators. Girls in my troop want to be computer programmers. So it's good they don't just want to be in traditional female occupations.

I used to be a teacher. I had no qualifications except for love. If you know how to show love to children, that's when they learn.

145

An old Japanese lady, a scholar and a graduate of Harvard, taught me to teach. Within two weeks I took the slow learners and found they were just like other children – only people had told them they were stupid. They weren't. One is now an outstanding pupil. His mother thanked me and I said, 'Thank the child for being willing to learn.'

When I was in school I could tell you the population of every state in the US and its geography and history – but nothing about the Marshall Islands. I'm pleased that's changing.

I got into an argument with the Seventh Day Adventists because they punish children for speaking Marshallese in schools. I told them they should teach in the mother tongue, at least while the children are young so they can read and write in their own language.

Mary Lanwi organises handicraft shops run by women's clubs on a co-operative basis, to give women some degree of financial independence. She is an older woman, a grandmother, and very energetic. When I talked to her she had been working in the shop in Majuro during the day, then attended a funeral and turned out again at night to open the shop at the airport to catch visitors who might buy last-minute souvenirs of the Marshalls. We talked in the airport café at midnight.

Where did you grow up?

I was born in 1921 and grew up on Jaluit. My parents were working with the Protestant missionaries. My grandfather was part-German and part-Austrian. He was killed by the Japanese during the war. Both he and my father were very strict. They didn't allow us to go to school, but taught us at home from text books. My mother taught us too. I went to school for the first time when I was 12 and finished schooling in Kusaie.

Tell me about the work you've done with women.

I was first a teacher, then I worked in the social services as a women's interests officer. We began a women's programme in 1960. At that time there weren't many women in politics and women wanted to learn to do better the things they were already doing – to cook, sew, take care of their families. In the last few years I think women have really opened their eyes.

When I was still employed with the government I went to Saipan to work as a health planning co-ordinator for the Federated States of Micronesia. But later the Marshalls separated from Micronesia: I was amongst those who didn't agree with it because we were stronger when we were together, especially when dealing with the US. We've been shown to be right by what's happened, haven't we?

What about your work now?

The handicraft centre gives women some economic independence. They make all sorts of things – vases from shells, weaving fans from pandanus leaves, shell jewellery. At one time girls of ten arriving from the outer islands could make them, but the skills are being lost now.

It's important that women should earn their own money so they can decide what to spend it on. Many end up paying for the medical fees or school fees for their children. Many people are unhappy that we now have a money economy instead of a subsistence one, but now it's here women have to learn to cope, to take responsibility for their own future.

What do you think are the effects of westernisation on the Marshalls?

There's a lot of confusion, people just don't know anymore what's right . . . there's more education, more jobs open to women, they used to only be teachers or nurses. But for some independence comes too early. I see girls of 13 drink till they can't walk, quitting school . . .

My son and daughter-in-law work at the hospital in Ebeye. People there badly need local food, not imported stuff which doesn't give them any nutrition.

What do you think about the Compact?

I don't think we're ready yet for independence . . . there's been no encouragement towards it from the US. But I just feel we don't know enough about the Compact. It hasn't been explained clearly ... we don't know what we're agreeing to. I feel sorry for the Kwajalein landowners though, I think they've been treated very badly.

Rosalie Konou

When I was on Majuro, many people said, 'You must talk to Rosalie Konou', the only woman lawyer in the Marshall Islands. She works for Legal Services, a government-funded organisation, and works a lot with women, representing them in child-care/custody cases. She was so busy she was impossible to reach. Then when I was on Ebeye, her brother-in-law, Senator Imada Kabua, asked me if I had anywhere to stay when I went back to Majuro. 'Phone Rosalie – you'll get on well and she'll put you up.' She and four children were living in a small two-bedroomed house; nevertheless she made me welcome.

What has been the impact on women's lives of US influence on your islands?

In some ways it's made women more dependent on men because of the cash economy, with men working and women staying at home looking after the children. It means she needs his income ... Before, and now on the outer islands, she could gather her own food, so if the man left she and the children wouldn't starve. And on the outer islands you don't live alone, you live with your relatives so they will look after you if you break up with the husband. Relatives of the man would also come and bring food and look after the kids.

But nowadays everyone has to work and look after their own children. There's also a saying 'father of others' – you might not know who your father is, or he might have lots of children you don't know about. But you know your mother, she's the centre. Like my children's father: he was here because of me, now he's somewhere else taking care of someone else. In the old days there was nothing women could do to get help from him but relatives would come and bring food, share custody. Of course, there are *some* really good fathers, men who want to look after their children: that's a strength in a man.

148

Tell me about your work representing women?

The most difficult is getting child support. Divorce is easy enough – according to Marshallese custom you just don't live together any more . . . but then the problem is that men just go and forget their childcare responsibilities.

Are you generally successful in getting child support? Does it normally end up in court or once the man knows the woman has a lawyer, does he start paying?

Sometimes they make an agreement with her; sometimes they get mad and become violent, beat them up, break things; sometimes their new wife doesn't want them to pay. The judges are pretty good – sometimes they tell the man off in court. If they think they're going to hide money they try and squeeze everything out of them. The courts say the priority is the children, not the car or the house or the bank loan. Though of course, the father has to have something to live on. I've represented a lot of women and I haven't lost a case. I identify very strongly with the women I'm dealing with.

Are more women now training to be lawyers?

No. They need government support and the government is cutting its staff – and they employ very few women. It's terribly difficult for kids growing up now, with the American dreams of careers but no jobs. I also grew up as part of the post-war generation: even in high school I always wanted to do law, and was always interested in government and politics, but it was a struggle to get training.

Do you think women identify strongly as Marshallese, are proud to be Marshallese, or do you think the American way of life is held up as better?

They feel patriotic, but if they examine their feelings . . . I don't know. Sometimes I think it would be easier for me to practise as a lawyer in the States, but then it would be even more difficult to raise four children on my own there and it's so competitive. But women are better treated by the law. I don't know – we're in a confusing position.

Hermy Lang is 21, married with two daughters aged two and three. I met her on Mejato, where she was visiting relatives. She'd just left work at a pizza take-out on Majuro and was having a holiday before going back to look for work. We got talking the first night I was there when we found ourselves sitting on the same mat at the celebration to give thanks for the new clinic building (described in Chapter Four). While I was on Mejato we went swimming together and one hot and rainy afternoon we sat indoors while she taught her mother and aunt and other women traditional Marshallese dances she'd learned in school. First, they made a tape recording of themselves singing and playing ukeleles so that they'd have music to dance by. Late that afternoon Hermy was going to teach other Rongelapese the dance for a celebration they were planning when a group visited them from another island later in the month.

Hermy described vividly the dilemmas and contradictions of being brought up to respect traditional Marshallese values, but living in a semi-American environment.

Where are you from?

I was born in Majuro but my mother's from Rongelap, so in a way I'm from there. When I was 15 I went there on a visit, but only for a few months.

What did you think of life on Rongelap compared to yours on Majuro?

They didn't have modern things on Rongelap. I prefer life on Majuro. I like going to the disco and the movies. On Rongelap I was a bit bored, though I liked it for a holiday. I just wouldn't choose to live there.

Do you have paid work on Majuro?

Yes, at Gibsons, the hypermarket, in their pizza place. I resigned my job when I came here and I'm not sure that I'd want to go back. It was really hard – hot and long hours. I started at 6 a.m. and quite often I had to do overtime to cover up for someone else who didn't show up. Then I'd work till 10 p.m. So although I was supposed to work eight hours, I often ended up working 16. I was paid one dollar an hour. Most employers on Majuro pay that – or maybe $1.50.

Who looked after your children? Your husband?

No, my mum, because my husband works at Robert Reimer's [another big store]. She usually does the cooking, too. Or I do, or my husband. He helps look after the children sometimes, or washes the clothes. I give my mum some of my wage.

When do you get time to go to the disco?

Only at weekends.

Who do you live with?

My husband and kids in my mother's house. My sister lives there, too. That's our custom, to all live together.

Did you finish school?

Yes and I really wanted to go to college after I graduated from high school, but I didn't have enough money. I wanted to be a medical secretary. I'd have had to go to Hawai'i or to the mainland [USA] to study for it. Only two girls in my class went on to study more. Their parents had the money. One is studying nursing; I don't know about the other. Most of the others are married now, with children. I can only think of one who isn't. She's working at the new hospital as a secretary.

Is it difficult for a young woman not to get married?

Yes.

Do you think it's better to get married than to stay single?

Maybe. If we're pregnant, so they have to support the child. Though some men say they won't get married *or* support the child.

151

Did they teach you family planning in school?

No, but I think it's a good idea. I think they do now. I only want two children – no more. It's too much work otherwise. My husband agrees. He's still studying at the Community College of Micronesia – the University of Guam has courses there. He's working part-time and also studying to be a teacher. I also want to work part-time, study part-time when I go back.

Is life better for young women now than when your mum was young, do you think?

No, I think their life was better. Nowadays girls go to parties and get drunk. Almost all the young girls in Majuro now have American boyfriends – or British ones, working at the power plant. But those men are already married. They'll go home and leave their Marshallese girlfriends. Girls now think they have to be American, they don't care about Marshallese customs. Ladies aren't supposed to go to bars, only men. Today women don't care, they're like men, they do what men do.

Is that good or bad?

Sometimes good, sometimes bad.

But you say you like going to the disco?

Yes, I enjoy it. My mum doesn't like me going, but I still go. I don't drink – only cola. The other girls drink screwdrivers – rum and coke. I don't smoke either.

Are there things that men are allowed to do that you'd like to do?

Well, I wouldn't want to go fishing. But they like to study – I like to study. They like to have their own job – I do too.

Do you think women are able to do any job, or only certain ones?

We can do anything. We can do what men do.

Is Majuro a good place for your daughter to grow up, do you think?

I think here on Mejato is better – it's peaceful, not dangerous. I'd like to come back sometime.

What do you think of the way the US has treated the Marshall Islands?

I don't like the nuclear testing and the Missile Range. They're cheating Marshallese people – they don't care about us. They don't want Marshallese people to live with them on Kwajalein. They only give us the worst work and don't pay us as much.

Abacca Anjain is a secretary for Majuro local council. She grew up on Rongelap and Majuro and lived with a family in Hawai'i for several years while she studied. When I spoke to her she was living with her husband and small baby but was hoping to go to the US to study for a degree: she would like to be active in politics in the Marshalls.

We talked in the back of a pick-up truck on the way back from taking her younger brothers and sisters swimming at the far end of Majuro, away from the built-up urban centre.

What do you think has been the effect on women's lives of having the US take over after the war?

The change, the big change and a shock to the Marshallese, has been catching up with western ways of living. It's really hard – from what I hear from my parents and my grandparents, there are sicknesses now that they never had before. I think that's because we don't know how to eat American foods, how to handle it, what's good for you and what isn't. That's why there's a lot of diabetes.

What you see by the road [she gestures to stalls we've stopped at], people selling coconut and pandanus – there's a programme going on to encourage people not to sell their local food so that they have money to buy canned food. It's been in the news-papers and on radio, not to sell local food but to feed it to their children instead of imported stuff so they won't get malnutrition.

Also, our culture is changing quite a lot. In our culture, if your family, your parents, know you're going out with someone, that means you're married to him. The guy is accepted into the family. Not like America where you have to have a ceremony. But nowadays, you might be living with the guy but you feel he can't really be your husband because you didn't marry him. That's because a lot of people now are Christians. They read the Bible. We are used to doing one thing in our culture but the Bible tells us to do something different, so there is a lot of confusion.

Are women made to feel ashamed if they have a child without a man there, whether or not there's been a ceremony?

It's not really a big deal if a woman gets pregnant and everyone knows she hasn't got a husband. People just like to talk: 'Whose baby is that? Who's she going out with?' Things like that. But they don't really care. They don't say, 'We shouldn't hang around her because she's not married.'

Do the men take part in childcare?

Today? Mostly they think they should go out and get a job. If women stay at home, they're the housewife. But in some families of course both parents feel they need to work because everything is based on money now.

And then does the man help look after the children when he comes home?

Some do, some don't; some men care, some don't. They might cook, or bed them. The men don't think it's their job. If the woman doesn't do the housework, people talk: 'What kind of woman is that? She's supposed to do it.' Her husband is doing it for her. So it's like if a woman wants to do something that might give her a bad reputation, she has to do it in secret. But if a guy wants to do something that the public thinks is bad, he'll just do it in public anyway. People will just say, 'He's a man.' But for a woman it would be a big deal.

In Britain, there is a widespread problem with violence in the home, with men beating the women they live with. Does that happen here?

Maybe in four out of ten homes – it's starting to be a big thing.

Why do you think that is?

The way of life is changing – they watch TV. There used to be more respect for women. Men are more powerful nowadays. I guess it's because women don't know they have rights.

Women in the west have begun to make rape and child sexual abuse a public issue . . .

There are cases like that. There is a guy in jail right now for raping a three-year-old girl. If you do something publicly like that, all the island knows about it. Last year there was only one case we heard about, but who knows what goes on in the home? Maybe their husbands rape them. Maybe they don't even know what rape means – maybe they think they just have to be committed to them. But there's yes and there's no. Here whatever happens in the family is supposed to be in the family – for the protection of their family's reputation. But seeing a little kid – it's totally rape. You can't say he's a male, she's a female. If you look at the body of a child – raping her, that's murder.

Around military bases in Europe the presence of military men is a spark for drugs and prostitution. Do you think that's the case on Ebeye?

Before the occupation, they used to give out 30 passes every evening – first come, first served – to go to Kwaj. One time I asked one of the girls, 'What you going there for?' 'There's lots of handsome guys,' she said. 'And we have fun – drink, play games.' Then they come back at midnight. Now there's fewer passes and they are much stricter. Some men from the base come to the disco on Ebeye too, looking for Marshallese women.

Now that your way of life is changing and people need to have a job to support themselves instead of living off the land, do you think parents think education is as important for girls as boys?

155

No, families don't put so much into the girls' education. They think it's a waste – she'll only get pregnant. It's something to laugh about if a girl finishes school. 'Are you going to college?' they ask. And she says 'yes'. And they laugh. Like, 'You won't finish, you'll just get pregnant.' It always makes me mad when men talk like that. Like – what do you think women are? It's the men who give us the problem. Women can do a lot of things, not just get pregnant. I wish there were a way to change it all around, see who's the smart ones then.

In Majuro and Ebeye some women have jobs, live on their own. But in our culture the women don't generally leave the family. And if my father dies, my husband takes care of the whole family, my brothers and sisters, my mother too.

You want to get into politics. Do you think you'll be able to encourage other women to be active?

Yes, other women might say, 'She's strong, she can do it, I can do it.' But at the moment women say, 'I'm just following what my husband says, or what my leader says.' There *are* women's organisations but they're not very active . . . only for something like when the President of the US comes – they make the food. I think things will change. If I go into politics I expect I'll be in the Opposition, so I won't have an easy time. People don't like you always asking questions, objecting to things.

Evelyn Konou, sister of Rosalie, is the only woman in the *Nitijela*. She has served for eight years, representing the island of Jaluit, and has always been in the Opposition, although the former Opposition coalition, 'Voice of the Marshalls', has for some time been fairly fragmented. When I visited her at home she was gardening. Her house is surrounded by tropical plants and flowers, bearing witness to what could be grown in the Marshall Islands if the infrastructure were laid for economic independence.

What is your opinion of the Compact?

In Jaluit we voted 'no'. We thought that because the people

affected by Section 117 didn't like it, it shouldn't be passed, even though in Jaluit we weren't directly affected. [Section 117 stipulated a set sum in compensation for those displaced and injured by atmospheric testing, and disallowed any further court cases.]

What do you think about the fact that America still controls the military and foreign affairs?

In general when it comes to international security we feel good with the US. People are afraid of the Russians, of the Communists. I really feel loyal to the US. We don't want to be called Communists. I expect they're nice people, like you and me – I'm sure when you're hungry they feed you, when you're in their home they look after you. But we've never met any Russians, so we only know what the US has told us. When I was young, I heard about Communists, that they were bad, and that's all I know. But when we compare democratic and Communist governments, maybe neither is better than the other.

We've been sold the American way of life, but it hasn't brought any real development. On the outer islands, there are no schools or health programmes. You expect people to read and write, but no. There aren't enough people writing our own books – like geography books, for schools. The US just cares about its own military schedule. Everyone knows about the US – they don't spend billions of dollars in Latin America for nothing. But just wait till Russia starts putting money in here.

We're supposed to be better off under the Compact than as part of a Trust Territory because we have a constitution. Yet we still have to ask the US to agree to what we want; our constitution is weak in comparison to US law, and the Compact is part of US law. The US can still amend the Compact if it wants to. Even after the referendum the US made a lot of amendments to the Compact. People didn't really understand it when they voted on it. People don't generally read about what's happening here – they listen to their leaders. That's why we need a better education system.

Do you think the impact of Americanisation on women's lives has been good or bad?

Both. A lot of women smoke and drink a lot, like they see the Americans do. But in education and growing, then it's good, because women didn't read before. They'd just stay home and look after the kids. But we're in the twentieth century, so we have to learn to read and write and know more.

What other ways do you think life has been changed by the west?

We still share everything. If you have food, you share it. But we're having to change to a money economy instead of living off the land. Not everyone's in work, so those that do work feed those that don't. Here I see people starting to live like Americans, centred around money – you have to know how to budget your pay cheque and when it is under $50 for two weeks, it's hard. People come to stay here with their extended family, and then there's more strain on the money.

In Jaluit and the other outer islands, do women use family planning?

The new Catholic mission is teaching the rhythm method, but you need to know a lot about your body, and work with your partner. He has to understand and co-operate. People listen to the health education on the radio, which includes family planning, but there's no one there to really explain it. Girls here have kids too early – at 15 and 16. If they're at high school their mum looks after their kids while they're at school. Parents feel sorry it happened, but they'll still take care of their grand-children. If it's your son who has got someone pregnant, you'll go over to the family and say, 'I want to help take care of the kid', or 'I want to take it in.'

If a child is related to you, you'll take care of them, adopt them. We don't need papers to adopt, you just take care of someone. Sometimes there are arguments, if someone later wants their child back, but as it's family, they don't go to court, just argue it out. You adopt and look after the kid because it's your sister's or your cousin's. Like when I was a teenager I looked after my older sister's son from when he was three months. But it's not common to adopt a kid non-related to you – like you're investing in something which isn't going to benefit you in the future. If a woman can't have children, someone in the clan, in the family, will give you one. Then you know the child will look after you later. Sometimes you might adopt from your husband's sister, but then people worry that if he dies or you divorce, the child won't look after you.

There's no paperwork. The system is there, it's just not written. But now courts prefer paperwork.

Do women come to you with particular women's issues?

Some do. But I'd like them to more. Women are still paid less than a man for doing the same job. And if a woman and a man apply for the same job, even if the woman is more qualified, the man gets it.

I saw a newspaper article on a women's group getting together a petition opposing across-the-board taxation, saying it would penalise the poor. Is it unusual for women to join together to oppose the government?

Yes. Those women are secretaries, mostly. They work for the government. So they are more confident, they have strong leaders amongst them. They are organised but I don't think they're a chartered union.

Has it been difficult being the only woman senator?

I've always felt comfortable – I believe that everyone should be represented. I didn't feel uneasy about it, even at the beginning. I was involved in campaigning before, in the debate over whether we should belong to a Federated States of Micronesia, for example. More women would like to be in the *Nitijela* but we're not organised, there's no point to start at. Some women are really bright and capable but they're married and their husbands don't support them in their work. Even if they have kids, they can solve the problem of childcare more easily than the problem of their husbands. If the woman gets more

159

education than her husband, he feels she should stay down and not go higher. The male leaders in general think it should be men making the decisions. But there are a lot of women in the Marshalls who'd be better.

Are there women in other political posts?

There are only two or three female mayors. One of them is Amatleine Kabua, the Mayor of Majuro and the daughter of the President. She ran against me to be one of the two senators of Jaluit last year. I thought it was a really bad approach. As a woman she should have run in a different place. Her family has land rights everywhere, so she could have run anywhere in the Ralik chain. It's really bad – instead of getting more women in the *Nitijela* she runs against the one woman senator. When her father told me she was running I said she should have run from somewhere else. But anyway, she lost.

What do you think it is which makes people here vote for one candidate rather than another?

I don't think we get elected because of our family, or even for the promises we make. It's more because people have confidence in us as individuals – especially me, as a woman. Maybe now they have more confidence in women, I feel confident I can do the work, I can talk, I know where to go to get things done. I go back to Jaluit several times a year to talk to people. They want to know you're capable and honest. It's also your political party. It helped me that I'm in Voice of the Marshalls, in the Opposition. It's not because my family's famous: it isn't. It's difficult to make election promises. You can't say I'm going to do this or that because the money situation isn't stable. So even the ministers can't make true promises.

One good thing about the people from Jaluit is that they'll talk to you, tell you what they think, criticise you. In the Marshalls people generally don't like to criticise. They're polite. So being in Opposition makes you look like a bad guy – you talk and stand up and complain and criticise the government and you get thought of as a troublemaker. But I like it when the

Jaluit people criticise me – they should. Leadership should be given true and valid criticism. I, on the other hand, often criticise the government in the *Nitijela* and I get a negative response, especially from the other party. I try to explain why I do it, but they don't understand. Maybe they will in 10 or 20 years – so I leave them be and carry on. It's hard.

In the following testimonies two women, the first from Majuro, the second from Ebeye, talk about the impact of the clash of western and Marshallese cultures on their relationships with their husbands and children. Both interviews were abruptly stopped when the women – who wish to remain anonymous – asked me to switch off my recorder so we could talk privately. Although the interviews are short I include them because they highlight how, with the imposition of a cash economy, women in the Marshall Islands are facing some of the same conflicts and challenges as urban women in other parts of the world and how, at the same time, their situation is very particular to a colonised society.

'My husband hated me going off to study. I wanted him to come to America with me but he wouldn't. So after I was there a year, I called for my children to come and live with me, I really missed them. I found an apartment for us and a car. I couldn't have made it otherwise, I needed them. Strange, he doesn't seem to miss them now we're separated.

'He was insecure because I studied and now I earn more than him. He wanted a woman who'd just stay at home. Well, that wasn't me. I wanted someone who'd be a friend and be supportive of my work. He must have been the only person who wasn't proud of my work. All my family was.

'He hated me to drink at all – he said it wasn't "sexy" or feminine. But he'd go out and come home at 5 a.m. drunk. If I went out drinking with my friends, he'd shout at me when I got home, lock me out or kick me. Of course, it made me want to drink even more, so when he went out drinking I'd stay at home and watch TV and drink. It was no good, it was destroying us both.

'He made it seem like the whole world was a fight between men and women. "When you're at work you may be a professional, but when you're at home you're nobody", was his attitude.'

'I worked on Kwajalein for several years in different jobs; then I got married to a Hawai'ian guy living on the base and I quit working. When we got divorced he took the kids – I knew I couldn't afford to have them here, my wages at the base wouldn't have supported them. I haven't seen them since. When they left my son was nine and my daughter seven. He's 20 now. I looked after my kids for nine years, but I haven't seen them for eleven years.

'Once my mother-in-law wrote and said why didn't I go and live in Hawai'i. But I'd been there with my husband to stay for maybe six months or so and I got very homesick, I couldn't live there. She said if I wasn't going to live there to be near the kids I shouldn't write to them. So I stopped for a while but I missed them and started again. I'm hoping to go next year if I can save enough money, but what will they think of me? They haven't seen me for so long. Will they be angry with me for not being able to keep them?

'When they left I was kind of lost for a while . . . I was pretty awful. I would drink a lot, just drink and drink and drink, for one whole year. From December to December. We have a big celebration at Christmas . . . I started drinking on Christmas Day and just kept drinking and all of a sudden it was Christmas Day again. What happened to all those months, I thought . . . gee, I better stop.'

Biram Stege is the only woman school principal on the island of Majuro. She works at a private Catholic school, where the majority of children pay for tuition, though a small number get their fees paid from a 'needy students fund', for which the school does small-scale fundraising. She is responsible for the elementary school, where children go from between the ages of five or six and 13 to 15. There are 388 students.

Do you teach the children in Marshallese?

In the lower grades we do, primarily in kindergarten and first grade, but as they grow up it's bilingual. In the upper grades it's mainly English, but with particular courses in Marshallese.

Can most of the children read and write in Marshallese?

Yes.

Why is it felt necessary to emphasise English after second grade?

The earlier you learn, the easier it is to catch on and be able to cope at that level. Most of the books we have are in English – there are very few materials in the Marshallese language. Even in our Marshallese language and arts classes it's very difficult to get useful material. The Department of Education is tackling it, but slowly. We need Marshallese writers in order to have materials.

Do the children still feel good about Marshallese if they are being taught in English? Doesn't it make them feel bad about their own language?

They are still very hesitant about speaking English – they find it embarrassing because their friends might say, 'Ah, they're trying to be like an American.' Most children would prefer to speak in Marshallese. What we are trying to do is to help the children learn English but at the same time respect their own culture and language. That's difficult because if you require them to learn English it could be an unspoken message that your own language isn't good enough. But at the same time we realise the only time the student is exposed to an English environment is at school. At home it's all Marshallese. Kids can really suffer if they go on to high school lacking basic skills in the English language – reading and writing. If you try to get a job here and take a test, you're really at a disadvantage if you don't speak it. You have to prepare a child for what they're expected to do or produce.

Does the US federal assistance that you get come in the form of consignments of books in English or in money so that you can decide?

No, money. We can spend it on anything except the religious programme.

Is it difficult to teach local history and geography if there are so few books?

Very difficult. I find that very hard. Father Hezel, a Jesuit historian, wrote something on Marshallese history and background and when he was here last I asked him if there was something we could use in our curriculum in local and Pacific history. I'm hoping to find something on Pacific history, at least.

So at the moment it's up to the teacher to do it orally?

Yes, pretty much, the teachers have to create their own materials.

What were you taught in geography and history when you were young?

I knew about how many rivers and lakes there were in the US but nothing about here. I knew nothing of my own region. The curriculum was such that no time was spent on local culture and history. But we now have a programme where older Marshallese people come to the school here to meet with classes and tell Marshallese legends and stories. Sometimes they teach the children weaving or skills. It's done orally. So the students now know more than I did when I went to school.

Do the parents put as much importance on the education of girls as boys?

Yes, pretty much, especially today when they see women can get into fields that men are in. In this culture, women are a lot stronger than men.

In what ways?

Anything you want done, you go to the women because they are the force behind everything. In this community, anything the parish wants to accomplish, it's the women who organise themselves and do something about it. Women are the great movers. Not that men aren't – they're in there, in the background, but to really move it, you need women. Maybe it's because of the land inheritance. And generally women are more serious.

The girls who go on to high school, what do they want to do after?

That's a big question we're asking ourselves – what are we educating our kids for? Up till now it's been for college, but then we realised that less than half the class goes on to college. But we haven't really sat down to do some serious thinking and planning. More people, fewer jobs, more competition to get jobs.

In Britain and the US we are just beginning to talk about child abuse and to realise how widespread it is.

Child abuse isn't talked about much, not because it's not there but because we're just not talking about it . . . both physical and verbal child abuse. Being a parent is hard. Maybe we need to be taught how to be *kind* parents. We need to give parents confidence and they need to pass that on to their children. That's something about we Marshallese – lack of self-confidence. We're embarrassed, ashamed, shy. Why won't kids speak out in class? Why are they so anxious? You wonder where that comes from. A majority of the kids are like that, and I think it comes from their home, from our culture. I don't know what it was like before we were colonised but now that's how it is.

And it's also from western influence which says that anything Marshallese isn't good, anything imported from outside is good, no matter what it is – like food. Marshallese don't know the difference between what's good and what's bad in imported stuff. If it's on TV, if it's white people's, it must be good. We automatically think of ourselves as down here, as little people, and they're big people.

We pass it on to our kids, you can see that. The challenge in education is to teach the kids to be proficient and handle the English language and culture so we can deal with the outside world but at the same time to keep what is ours, to know well our own culture.

That's a really hard challenge but I think it can be done. You can be really good in something else but at the same time be really solid and strong in yourself.

PART TWO

The Pacific Picture

8

Solomon's Solution:
US Policy in Micronesia

Part One of this book looked specifically at the effects of colonialism and nuclear testing on the people of the Marshall Islands. Yet in the last 40 years the general world trend has been away from the most blatant colonialism. During that time, many First World countries have gained their independence, although the west continues to maintain its supremacy through economic means. Against that trend, the US managed to secure Micronesia as a testing ground – first via the Trusteeship and now via the Compact of Free Association. How has that been achieved?

Kennedy's headache and the Solomon Report

In 1971 key sections of a confidential document were leaked to the *Young Micronesian*, the newsletter of the Micronesian students at Hawai'i University, which shed fascinating light on US policy in the region. The document had been commissioned by President Kennedy in 1962. Two years previously, a UN

Visiting Mission had deplored the extreme lack of economic development in the US Trust Territory. The Micronesian economy was indeed stagnating: the US had not replaced the Japanese infrastructure which it had taken down with chauvinist abandon; scrap metal, the leftovers of Second World War battles was Micronesia's second most important export. US funding for the whole territory did not exceed $6.1 million a year.[1]

Then in 1961 an outbreak of polio on Ebeye and other Marshall Islands hit the international press. Kennedy foresaw a potential problem if the US did not clean up its image in Micronesia during an era of strong anti-colonialist sentiment. He was also determined that the US should not give up its convenient testing ground.

On 18 April 1962, Kennedy signed a National Security Action Memorandum which 'set forth as US Policy the movement of Micronesia into a permanent relationship with the US within our political framework'.[2] This has been the theme tune of US policy ever since.

In order to implement the plan, Kennedy turned to a friend, Harvard economist Anthony Solomon, asking him to write a survey of Micronesia and to recommend how best to proceed. Solomon's commission visited the islands during the summer of 1963, and the Solomon Report, as it was known, was issued in October of the same year. Extremely sensitive, it was immediately classified and has remained so ever since, only a sanitised version being made public. However, after the first leak, a fuller copy has since been circulated. Two decades later, it is still an embarrassment to the US government, stating frankly the problems created by the US presence and how the US could manipulate the situation to its advantage in the Pacific. Solomon surmised that 'time was running out for the US in the sense that we may soon be the only nation left administering a trust territory'. He made concrete suggestions designed to avoid any such embarrassment while retaining an asset 'said to be essential to the US for security reasons'.[3]

What was needed, the report stated, was for the people to

make 'an informed and free choice' about their future political relationship with the US, while 'insuring a favorable vote in the plebiscite'. A plan for the next five years was drawn up, with two particular objectives: 'winning the plebiscite and making Micronesia a United States territory under circumstances which will satisfy the somewhat conflicting interests of the Micronesians, the UN and the US' . . . and 'achieving rapidly *minimum but satisfactory* social standards' (emphasis added). In so doing, Solomon recognised that the US would 'be moving counter to the anti-colonial movement that has been sweeping the world and will be breaching its own policy since World War I of not acquiring new territorial possessions'. Thus, if the UN Security Council vetoed any new arrangements, 'the US might have to decide to proceed with a series of actions that would make the trusteeship agreement a dead issue, at least from the Micronesian viewpoint'. That is, the US would have to persuade Micronesia that a more concrete 'relationship with the US' – annexation – would be preferable to trusteeship under the ultimate guidance of the UN.

One obvious factor which did not endear the US to the Micronesians was, as Solomon pointed out, 'the economic stagnation and deterioration of public facilities that has characterised the US administration of the trust territory in contrast to that of the Japanese'. While it was clearly Japanese businesses and individuals who had been the main beneficiaries of the vibrant economy between the two world wars, 'per capita Micronesian cash incomes were almost three times as high before the war as they are now and . . . the Micronesians freely used the Japanese-subsidised extensive public facilities'. Solomon dismissed the possibility of there being any great passion for independence, but he warned of 'an inchoate insecurity' about US policy in the area. What was needed, he recommended, was a quick injection of cash and then a plebiscite in late 1967 before the results of the 'aid' faded. After that, the area could be reopened to Japanese investment to make up for the reductions in US subsidies. In the meantime, a nationwide legislature would have to be established to take on some of the responsibilities after the relationship with the US was changed.

The means by which Solomon recommended the plebiscite be won make illuminating reading. Not only was aid to be used to buy votes – and once success was ensured it would be abruptly terminated – but 'Washington should facilitate the general development of . . . loyalties to the US'. That was to be done by bringing leaders to the US, 'introduction in the school system of US oriented curriculum changes and patriotic rituals', and increasing college scholarship to the US for Micronesians. Interestingly, he urged the launching of a Peace Corps programme 'because it is of critical importance to . . . the plebiscite attitudes'. The Peace Corps had been formed on 1 March 1961, ostensibly to help people of interested countries meet their needs for trained personnel, to foster a better understanding of Americans, and to foster a better understanding of other people by Americans. However, successive Administrations have used the Peace Corps quite cynically to try to 'export' American culture, to soften the ground for the US to dig deeper into a country's political system and to spy on the population for likely dissidents. Solomon envisaged just such a role for them in Micronesia:

They should be responsible for the development of favourable political attitudes towards the US through a systematic program of information through various communications media . . . and act as reporters and evaluators of all activities and attitudes that might have an important bearing on the outcome of the plebiscite . . .

According to former State Department official Donald F. McHenry, Solomon's idea was taken up in a big way:

The Micronesian Peace Corps program was massive – for the Peace Corps and for Micronesia. At one point there was almost one Peace Corps volunteer for every one hundred Micronesians.[4]

It was the highest ratio of volunteers to host recipients in the history of the Peace Corps. Nearly every inhabited island in the territory was assigned Peace Corps volunteers.[5] However, the real influence of the Peace Corps volunteers was more complex and varied. Some individuals, of course, fulfilled Solomon's design. Others, who had volunteered for the Peace Corps because they believed in its stated intentions and wanted to be of help to the Micronesians, found that their presence helped only to spread American lifestyles and promote the belief that Americans were better educated and therefore in some ways superior. William Vitarelli, a one time Peace Corps co-ordinator, says that even the well-meaning 'came to the islands with American habits, American values and sophisticated skills that functioned well in a technological society, but in most cases did not prepare the Micronesians for self-sufficiency'.[6]

Yet there were some who became openly critical of the role of the US in Micronesia and who began to use their skills – as lawyers, educators and so on -- to assist the Micronesians in asserting their rights and organise against US abuses. On their return home, many of these volunteers continued their work, publishing *Friends of Micronesia* and lobbying in Congress.

While many of Solomon's recommendations – such as the Peace Corps influx – were put into practice, his hope for an early plebiscite did not materialise.

Nevertheless, the US continued to press for an arrangement which, in Solomon's words, would give 'a reasonable appearance of self-government ... but on the other hand retain adequate control'. Although Solomon expected independence to be presented as an option on the plebiscite, he thought it would be possible only if there were 'continuing US subsidies' in return for 'permanent ceding by Micronesia of exclusive defence and military use rights to the US'.

His list of wrongs committed by the US was also more frank than anything the Trust Territory administration has publicly admitted before or since. Solomon kept coming back to the question of the economy, but also broadened his scope to include the US 'custodial' attitude, which meant that 'initiative has been stifled' and a 'psychological pattern of dependency' encouraged. But when it came to abuse of trust, he singled out the Marshall Islands for special mention: 'no other district has had so much cause for suspicion, doubt and resentment towards the US.' First came the atmospheric tests, and then

> to make room for a military base, the people of Kwajalein atoll have been moved to a barren, dirty slum on another islet in the atoll, Ebeye . . . They can work on their home island but they cannot live there.

Solomon's basis for criticism was not so much that the US was acting badly towards Micronesia but that sooner or later the rest of the world would tumble the fact. He was particularly keen that the US should be seen by the world to be

> providing Micronesia with a reasonable degree of self-government. Without that we would be defenceless against charges that we were grabbing Micronesia to thrust it into a colonial status without consideration of the interests and rights of its people.

His recommended version of 'self-government', however, included a US High Commissioner with the power to veto any Bill, annul any law, remove any official or assume the executive or legislative power 'for security reasons'.

Solomon in practice

When President Kennedy read Anthony Solomon's remarks on the Marshall Islands' economy, he would have been in no doubt as to what must be done to secure the future of Micronesia. Although the report was never officially published the sudden changes which took place in its wake indicate that it was very quickly translated into policy.

Economic aid shot up: in 1963 it doubled to $15 million. Yet as a Hawai'ian-based observer Robert Kiste noted, the aid programme was totally inappropriate.[7] The islands were available

for welfare programmes which included large-scale food subsidies in a subsistence economy, job training schemes designed
for urban Americans, and aid to the elderly in a society where, in
the words of Chailang Palacios, 'We have no nursing homes for
the aged. They are our books. They are our encyclopaedia.'[8] All
the while, there was no investment in establishing a local
economy which would lead to self-sufficiency.

From 1969 to 1975 the US concentrated on obtaining a
favourable result in a future plebiscite. First, however, it tried to
entice Micronesia into the most 'extreme' option outlined in the
Solomon Report – Commonwealth status akin to that of
Puerto Rico. All the Micronesian island groups rejected it bar
the Marianas – the most intensely colonised since the first
Spanish intruders – which agreed to it in a referendum in 1975.
The US was particularly keen to secure the strategically sited
Marianas as it was beginning to retreat from Indochina in the
early and mid-70s and wanted other secure bases in the region.

The separation of the Marianas from the other islands started
a rot which quickly spread and led to the fragmentation of
Micronesia. As Glenn Alcalay observed:

> The Marshalls, which had the highest yield of copra in
> Micronesia, also had the largest tax and wage revenue from
> the Kwajelein missile base and therefore gave them a larger
> financial base than the other districts. Reluctant to share the
> wealth, the Marshalls opted for separate negotiations with
> the US. Belau followed suit and the remaining island groups
> merged into the fourth entity, the Federated States of
> Micronesia.[9]

After the Marshalls split away they became known as the
Republic of the Marshall Islands, or RepMar. At the time, there
was some opposition from progressives in the different island
groups who saw danger in fragmentation. Most, however, went
along with government arguments that they should keep what
dollars they received from the US for themselves. Jeton Anjain,
Senator for the Rongelap people, told me:

175

I now realise that allowing Micronesia to split up has made us much weaker when it comes to negotiating with the US. We should have listened to people like Rosalie Konou [see pp. 148–50] and stuck together.

Economic dependency grew ever more acute from 1975 onwards, as the US plumped for the second option outlined by the Solomon Report and worked to ensure it would get a vote in favour of its proposed Compact of Free Association. Aid continued to mount up until the Compact was finalised: $30 million in 1969, $60 million in 1962, $114 million in 1984. But it was never designed to meet the needs of the people.

The welfare programmes brought Micronesians flocking into the administrative centres in the hope of getting jobs or benefits. Over one half of all Micronesians now live in urban centres, many of them in shanty towns.[10]

Trade became wildly imbalanced and remains so today.[11] Tobacco, beer and tinned fish accounted for 61 per cent of imports into the Marshall Islands in 1981.[12] The value of exports as a percentage of imports in the Marshalls stood at 4 per cent in 1981; copra – subject to intolerable fluctuations in price – is the only export of any significance. Food imports alone for the 70,000 people of the Federated States of Micronesia were worth $3.591 million in 1980.

During the years of Japanese occupation, the Micronesian-based fishing industry had thrived. Under the US, however, it dwindled into virtual insignificance at the same time as the US and other nations themselves plundered the Pacific for its valuable harvest. According to Kwajalein Senator Ataji Balos, the Marshall Islands government received $2 million annually in return for leasing its 750,000 square miles of fertile fishing grounds to Japanese, Taiwanese, Filipino and US commercial fishing firms. The Commerce Committee of the Marshallese *Nitijela* believed nearly $100,000 million worth of fish was caught every year from their waters, he said.[13]

Fishing has recently become a source of controversy in the region, as the Pacific nations realise the value of the resources in their ocean garden. The US has persistently refused to sign the Law of the Sea Treaty and to recognise the normally accepted 200-mile limit (which excludes foreign powers from fishing a country's waters) off the coast of Micronesian atolls, respecting only a 12-mile zone. Sixty-six per cent of the world's tuna harvest is from the Pacific, with 600,000 metric tons of the world total of 1,750,000 metric tons caught in the Western Central Pacific. According to a US Commerce Department official:

> It can be expected that US fishermen will continue to fish heavily in Micronesian waters. Deep ocean fisheries of the governments of the Marshall Islands and the Federated States of Micronesia remain relatively unsurveyed and under-exploited, and will be more likely to benefit by supporting foreign tuna fleets.[14]

When Kiribati, to the south, opened talks with the Soviet Union in 1986, it sent US officials into a spiral of Cold War talk, warning that the Russians were using fishing as a front for spying on Kwajalein Missile Range, several hundred miles away. The US issued Kiribati with threats of economic sanctions. The charge of spying may be true, but the result of the US reaction was to firm up the Pacific island nations' determination that the US knuckle down to some serious negotiating over fishing leases. The *Marshall Islands Journal* made it a subject of a feisty editorial on 15 August 1986:

> The United States is the only nation that refuses to pay up or respect island jurisdiction over marine resources. Fishing is *the* issue in the Pacific and the sooner Washington figures that out the better it will be for all concerned. Until then, Pacific islanders have to contend with continued American arrogance: US officials are refusing to pay $20 million annually for access to the entire Pacific. Paradoxically, even the American negotiators acknowledge that the talks are for more than just a simple fishing treaty, but they are unwilling to pay the price and wonder why the Russians are getting such a receptive hearing everywhere in the Pacific.

Eight months later, on 24 April 1987, the same paper reported that 16 Pacific nations including the Marshall Islands had together succeeded in obtaining a better deal, with the US recognising their 200-mile exclusion zones and paying 10 per cent of the catch value to the Pacific nations. The payment, however, is in the form of aid, not cash, once again tightening the bond of dependency.

The Marshall Islands have also struck a fishing deal with Japan: in 1986 it brought in $950,000 in fishing fees and $160,000 in goods and services. But a deal with the Soviet Union, also angling for fishing rights, looks highly unlikely. The Marshallese government chief secretary Oscar de Brum told me they would need US permission to do a fishing deal with the Soviet Union.

> The Compact of Free Association leaves us free to develop contacts with other friendly nations – *friendly to the US that is*. But before we do that we'd need to consult with the US because they have strategic defence rights in our area. If the US approves of it, on an economic basis, I'm sure we could go ahead with other nations, too, because we do have the fish. (my emphasis)

Given the US panic over any hint of Soviet presence in the Pacific and its stranglehold over policy-making in Micronesia, there seems little likelihood of de Brum's government operating a free-market policy and negotiating a better deal with the Soviet Union.

The countries of Micronesia have not been able to take advantage of their own abundant fishing grounds because they have not had the infrastructure necessary for a fishing industry – large boats capable of deep-sea work, even during the stormy winter months, and refrigeration and freezing facilities.

In 1985 a UN visiting mission recognised that although the islands appeared reasonably prosperous and '[al]though the infrastructure on Majuro was adequate, the economy appeared to be an artificial, service-orientated one, lacking in capital investment'. Local fishing industry would have been capital wisely invested. Only in the last couple of years has that slowly begun to happen.

The Mission later went on to remark that it:

> could not help but observe that a generalised lack of initiative seems to have impeded the development of a more productive economy in the Marshall Islands. The Mission feels that a stronger desire among the people to take responsibility for their own development would go a long way towards overcoming the obstacles imposed by nature.

And yet the delegates – from other nuclear and colonial powers, Britain and France, shown round by US tour guides – did not question the root causes of the Marshallese psychological dependency. What they had accurately observed, however, was that Micronesians had become used to a way of life they could not afford, abandoning their own traditional small industries and collapsing into dependency and a 'dollars-today' mentality. The US had thus manoeuvred itself into a position where it had merely to threaten to withdraw funds and compromised island leaders would toe the line. This was, in other words, the very context in which Solomon had envisaged a 'favourable' outcome for a plebiscite on the Compact.

The Compact of Free Association

> Of all the colonial powers that have ruled Micronesia, the US is the most perfidious. The other regimes made no bones about it: their interest in Micronesia was self-interest and their policies were openly formulated to serve those interests ... The US has steadfastly maintained that its primary concern is the Micronesians' welfare, while doing everything in its power to destroy the validity of the Micronesian people. As for me, I would prefer an honest tyrant to this treachery any day.[15] Micronesian critic of the Compact

179

On 21 October 1983, President Reagan appeared on American television to make an appeal to the people of Micronesia:

Under the trusteeship we have come to know and respect you as members of our American family, and now, as happens to all families, members grow up and leave home. I want you to know that we wish you all the best as you assume full responsibility for your domestic affairs and foreign relations, as you chart your own course for economic development, and as you take up your new status in the world as a sovereign nation. But you will always be family to us.

The previous month, Micronesians had had to decide in three plebiscites whether to accept the Compact of Free Association, with its slight variations for their three nations, the Federated States of Micronesia (Yap, Pohnpei and Kosrae), Belau, and the Marshall Islands. The result went in favour of the Compact, but there was considerable opposition. Out of the 60 per cent of Marshall Islanders who voted, 58 per cent were in favour; meaning that a little over 32 per cent actually voted yes. Many ballot slips with a 'yes' vote included a written opposition to one section which curtailed the rights of those injured by radiation to pursue their compensation claims in US courts (see page 238). And all the atolls most directly affected by US military activity – Kwajalein, Bikini (whose inhabitants now live on Kili) and Rongelap – voted overwhelmingly against: 70 per cent on Kwajalein, 90 per cent on Bikini/Kili and 85 per cent on Rongelap. In all, 10 out of 24 atolls voted against. In the Federated States, Pohnpei voted against but Yap and Kosrae went in favour. The most fraught situation arose in Belau which, in 1979, had approved the world's first anti-nuclear constitution. There, 62 per cent of the people approved the Compact, but 75 per cent approval is needed to overturn the nuclear-free constitution (see Chapter Nine).

President Reagan's speech may have brought tears to a few eyes. But while the Compact promises independence, its subtext reveals otherwise: it is in fact a virtual US annexation of the islands for military purposes, a denial of self-determination and a shrugging off of responsibility for past actions. The US has 'full authority and responsibility for security and defense matters', which includes the option of establishing military bases and facilities on the islands which may be nuclear-capable. Nuclear-armed ships, planes and submarines have the right to pass through and stop over.

Moreover the governments of the Marshall Islands and the Federated States of Micronesia are required to 'consult' the US over their foreign affairs. And the US can veto any item of domestic or foreign policy or any business or trade agreement which it deems threatening to its security – a catch-all clause which, it has been established, could include a fishing deal with the Soviet Union, for example. In the final analysis, legal and government experts agree, US security interests overshadow every other consideration.[16] Self-determination is a mere gloss.

This exchange, during a hearing on the Compact between Senator Johnson, chair of the US Senate Committee on Energy and Natural Resources, and Mr Fred Zeder, US Ambassador to Micronesia and a central Compact negotiator, is particularly revealing.

> Senator Johnston: Is it understood that we have full plenary power to say that any activity is military even though we may be wrong?
> Mr Zeder: Yes, sir.
> Senator Johnston: Any activity whatsoever, we could determine to be military and prevent it?
> Mr Zeder: Yes, sir.
> Senator Johnston: I just want to be absolutely clear.[17]

In recognition of the 'scarcity and special importance of land' in Micronesia, the US promised to request the 'minimum necessary' for extra military bases. However, the governments of Micronesia, states the Compact, 'shall for their part sympathetically consider' US land requirements. Ambassador Zeder told the Senate Committee that this ensured the US whatever land it wanted, although prior to the plebiscite the Marshallese were told that there was no need to worry about the US military taking more land.

Micronesia is also expected to comply with any other defence or security treaty which the US enters into and which it decides should also apply to the islands. And while the US can deny the military of any other nation access to Micronesia, it can invite its own allies into the islands. In return, the US promises to defend them. But as the State Legislature of Pohnpei pointed out, the presence of the US is more of a liability than a reassurance: the Central Pacific becomes a nuclear target only when a major power establishes nuclear bases there. Pohnpei voted against the Compact because the people 'are desirous of a truly nuclear free Pacific, free from any form of nuclear weaponry'.[18]

Large sums of money are tied to the Compact, but state aid (as opposed to compensation for individual groups of injured or displaced people) will actually *drop*, in line with Solomon's recommendations.

The Marshall Islands will take a significant cut from $47.93 million in 1985 to $36.45 million a year for the initial 15-year period of the Compact. Funding to the Federated States of Micronesia and the Belau will drop less drastically: for the former from $78.36 million (1985) to $76.41 million; for the latter, from $21.09 million (1985) to $19.77 million. Given the rate of inflation in the US, from which the islands import goods, however, the real decrease will be more severe. At the same time, the population is expected to have doubled by the time the Compact expires.[19]

The aid, moreover, has strings attached which lead straight back to the Pentagon. The Compact has been sold to Micronesians as a 15-year bridging arrangement until the islands are ready for complete independence. But Ambassador Zeder expressed his confidence that 'US grants and services which cannot be matched from other sources' would ensure that Micronesia will not break free until the US chooses to cut the knot of dependency.[20] Where aid is concerned, there is never a free – or even cheap – lunch.

But just in case the islands should turn their backs in the

future on the lure of western comforts and choose what would be an economically stringent path of independence, the US has an automatic 15-year extension option on the use of Kwajalein. The web is tighter still: an indefinite Mutual Security Agreement automatically comes into force on termination of the Compact, which allows the US military virtually unrestricted access to Kwajalein.

Not only does the Compact push the people displaced from Kwajalein atoll into the arms of the US military for the next 30 years – and indefinitely, if the Mutual Security Agreement comes into operation – it does so at a level of compensation well below what should have been the realistic asking price. Kwajalein senator Imada Kabua (cousin of President Kabua but often in political opposition to him) said, 'Our government should have either booted out the US military or used Kwajalein as a lever.'

The US has invested a billion dollars in Kwajalein Missile Range: it would be costly to replace and would involve the difficult task of making another small nation give over its land. Nowhere else, says the Pentagon, is quite so convenient. In that context, the compensation-cum-rent paid to Kwajalein land-owners seems even less realistic: $12 million a year from the less than $40 million a year paid by the US to the Marshall Islands government.

Even the seemingly fair clauses of the Compact carry a sting in their tail. And so it is with Section 177 under which, 40 years after the first nuclear tests, the radiation survivors of Rongelap, Enewetak and Bikini are compensated. The US has paid $150 million to the Marshall Islands government in compensation. This has been invested and Bikinians can expect to share a total of $75 million, Enewetakese $48.5 million, Rongelapese $37.5 million and Utrikese $22.5 million. At first site, that seems a fair deal, particularly when one considers the 200,000 North Americans living downwind of the Nevada test site, the US military personnel also irradiated by the tests, or the survivors of the mutating chemical toxin, Agent Orange, used in the war against Vietnam, who are still struggling for compensation.

Section 177, however, carries not one, but three stings. Firstly, the compensation money is grossly insufficient to support three communities who, for generations, will have no way of being self-sufficient. Even if the people of Bikini and Rongelap were able to return to their islands, they could not grow food for themselves or for sale for many years, until new trees grow in new soil.

Secondly, Section 177 cuts off any further rights of radiation survivors to sue in US courts. Should late effects of radiation become manifest in future generations, or should more people have been damaged than is now known, they will have no recourse to compensation from the US. The latter is well within the bounds of possibility, given the 1978 Department of Energy report which revealed that 14 atolls were in fact contaminated during the 66 nuclear tests: medical follow-up has been done on only two – Rongelap and Utrik. So while Section 177 provides $150 million in compensation it effectively wipes out lawsuits claiming damages of $7 billion still pending in US courts.

Thirdly, 177 carries with it an 'espousal' clause. This means that should US courts overrule the previous clause, the government of the Marshall Islands will indemnify the US for up to $150 million. In other words, a tiny nation has been forced to agree to take on the responsibility for the crimes committed against itself by a superpower when it was not even a sovereign nation.

Compensation

No amount of money, of course, can compensate for the loss of health, culture and independence suffered by the Marshallese. Compensation is needed, however, not as an act of revenge but as the only way of surviving and re-establishing some kind of self-respecting lifestyle. But money can dramatically change people's relationships with each other. The sudden injection of large amounts of money into a society whose economy has only recently been based on cash has rocked Marshallese traditions of sharing and caring.

The *iroij*, or chiefs, of Rongelap are the family of Amata Kabua, President of the Marshall Islands. As soon as the radiation compensation in Section 177 was announced, the *iroij* staked their claim: 33 per cent of Rongelap's $2.5 million a year for 15 years. Randy Thomas, Mayor of the Rongelap people at the time, explained:

> There are only 50 *iroij* out of 1,000 or so Rongelap people now scattered around the Marshalls – yet they are asking for a third of the money. They justify this by saying that according to our traditions, *iroij* are entitled to one third of our harvest. But traditionally they wouldn't actually claim all of that for themselves – they would redistribute it to people who needed it.
>
> My people have met and talked about this and we will offer the *iroij* 10 per cent: even that is a lot, given their numbers. And none of them has lived on Rongelap recently, or moved with us to Mejato. They don't need the money like we do, to build houses and a school on Mejato and to support ourselves now we cannot grow food.
>
> We've budgeted for the $625,000 we'll be getting every quarter: education will get 5 per cent, people injured by fallout 20 per cent, people's general needs 15 per cent, and the *alab* 10 per cent. We'll put 10 per cent into insurance and will invest the rest – 30 per cent – into our trust fund for the future.
>
> There are only five or so *alab*, but they get 10 per cent because if the *dri jerbal* come to them with needs, the *alab* must look after them. The *iroij*, on the other hand, will keep all their money for themselves.

Meanwhile, the people displaced from Kwajalein are deeply unhappy about the handling of their compensation and rent provided by the Compact. Kinoj Mawilong, grandmother, owner of land on Kwajalein and one of the leaders of the sail-ins:

The money is being paid to RepMar instead of directly to us. We are afraid that, because of the huge debts our government has, it will start spending the money on other things instead of sending it to us. Already, they are refusing to recognise the Kwajelein Atoll Corporation, which we landowners formed to fight together for our rights. Money is being paid only to the *iroij*, the *alab* and a few senior *dri jerbal* – one third each. So instead of being shared between 5,600 families, as we used to do, it is staying in a few hands.

During the plebiscite campaign those who opposed the Compact suggested, in a seemingly contradictory move, that the Marshalls should opt for some kind of commonwealth status. Although this would not free them of the demands of the US military, it would, they reasoned, at least cut through the pretence of independence and would block the US attempt to shrug off responsibility for radiation damage. To think that the Reagan administration would treat members of a commonwealth any better was perhaps a touch naive. That they felt there was no point even in going for the independence option is a measure of just how trapped by economic dependence many Marshallese people now feel. Jeton Anjain, one of the most frequently dissenting voices in the Marshall Islands *Nitijela*, summed it up: 'We were led to depend on US assistance and now we're afraid to stand up for our rights in case the Americans stand on our heads and push us back down.'

Even President Kabua had to admit that Section 177 was hardly ideal. Under questioning in the *Nitijela* he said that at the time of signing the Compact, 'he did not know what he was signing as he was sick and without his advisers'. A great pity, then, that he did not admit as much to his electorate and either advise them to vote against or insist on reopening negotiations.

In April 1987 Tony de Brum, Marshallese Minister of Health and former Minister of Foreign Affairs, lifted the lid on the negotiations between the Marshalls and the US.[21] He confirmed that the US had used its economic power over the Marshalls to force it into accepting the worst aspects of the

Compact. Early in the negotiations the US 'held out the carrot of early termination of the trusteeship and the establishment of economic independence' by 1981.

> The government of the Marshall Islands, in reliance on these promises, began to establish the infrastructure necessary to maintain an independent nation following termination. Relying upon these promises, money was borrowed for many projects including power plants, air transportation and other things necessary to an independent government which had not been provided by the US as Trustee. The US Ambassador to the Status negotiations encouraged and participated in the promotion of these projects utilising loan funds. Once the government of the Marshall Islands was burdened with this debt, the carrot was removed, the trusteeship was not terminated and the government of the US refused to assist with relief of the burden of debt assumed in reliance upon the American promises. The US government informed us that we had been unwise to rely on a policy commitment from a former US administration.[22]

At that point, said de Brum, the US used the debts to pressure the Marshallese government into accepting the Compact in full, including the espousal clause. And as, under the trusteeship, '100 per cent of the funding of the Marshall Islands depended upon the US', President Kabua had his hands tied. The Marshalls held out 'as long as it could against this pressure' but eventually 'an ultimatum was issued' by the US: accept the Compact or remain as wards of the US.

However, worse was to come. 'The US unilaterally changed the provisions of the Compact through its internal legislative process by withdrawing from the Compact ... provisions which had induced some of us to support it.' These included tax concessions, free importation and recognition of the right of the Marshall Islands to control its own territorial waters. The final insult, says de Brum, was that the Marshall Islands accepted the 'illegal and unconstitutional' clauses such as espousal in order to

187

achieve sovereignty. 'Even that has proved illusory.' In all its attempts to open negotiations with other countries, only one – the former government of Fiji – recognised it as independent from the US.

9

Cold War in the Pacific

The previous chapter showed that although the Marshall Islands are akin to a US colony, the primary source of US interest in them does not lie in exploiting the natural resources of the region. Its goal is different from that pursued by earlier rulers, which followed the classic colonial pattern whereby under-developed countries produced commodities – minerals or cash crops – for export to the 'colonial metropolis': that is, they were a source of profit.[1]

The US has made a financial loss, rather than a profit, in the Marshalls, despite a good deal of clawback in the form of aid which has been used to buy back US goods and services, and lucrative spin-offs for US industries, from fishing Marshallese waters to the anticipated mining of mineral deposits on the sea bed. Indeed, the US has allowed and later positively encouraged economic dependency. That in itself is not so unusual. A number of First World countries are dependent on aid while also providing industrialised countries with markets for technology and manufactured goods, with cheap labour, and with cash crops and minerals. But the goal of the US in the Marshall

Islands has been more than economic: it has been, single-mindedly, to use the islands for military purposes. To do that it has had to ensure that the Marshall Islands government is malleable: a small economically dependent country finds it hard to fight back.

What has happened in the Marshalls has been called 'strategic economic dependency':[2] it is part of a pattern which also involves other countries.

As this book has so far focused on the Marshalls and looked at the rest of Micronesia only in general terms, it is worth describing the situation of other Pacific examples of strategic economic dependency.

The Philippines

The relationship between the Philippines and the US is one such example. Under Spanish rule until 1898, when the islands were taken over by the US, the Philippines only gained their independence in 1946. But by that time the country had been devastated by the Second World War and agreed to allow 23 US bases in return for aid. The US later backed the corrupt and cruel regime of Ferdinand Marcos for two decades because he was largely loyal to the US and his presence guaranteed the bases, the most important of which are Subic Naval Base and Clark Air Base, regularly visited by nuclear-capable bombers. The Philippines also play host to military exercises 'Cape Thunder' and 'Hawkeye'; Command, Control and Communication Centres for submarines are located at San Miguel, and a satellite operations centre links the Philippines with Hawai'i, South Korea and Diego Garcia.

Although President Corazon Aquino has promised a referendum on whether the lease on US bases should be renewed when it runs out in 1991, she is under enormous pressure to accept the bases in return for US aid: she inherited an economy in tatters and $26 billion in foreign debt. The New People's Army is meanwhile fighting a guerrilla war in the countryside;

amongst its central demands is the removal of the bases and the scrapping of plans to build a $2.1 billion nuclear power plant at Bataan. The US is therefore jittery about the security of its bases in the Philippines and wants the option of using Belau, in Micronesia, as a part of a 'fall-back arc'.

Belau

As part of the original entity of Micronesia and therefore under the Trusteeship, Belau was also subjected to Solomon's recommendations. In 1979, however, Belau's 16,000 or so inhabitants voted to adopt the world's first nuclear-free constitution. They have since come under constant and unrelenting pressure from the US to overturn that constitution and adopt the Compact of Free Association, which would allow the US free military access. The US Administration was deeply worried that in refusing all things nuclear Belau would set an example which could become an inspiration to others. 'It sets a very bad precedent,' US Senator William Cohen told US Public National Radio. 'I think you'll see consequences flowing to . . . possibly Australia and Japan and other regions.'

After 10 plebiscites in eight years, including one which changed voting rules, Belau finally agreed to accept the Compact in August 1987. Spearheading the pro-Compact campaign was Belau's President, Lazarus Salii, who came to power after the mysterious assassination of the former President, Haruo Remelik, on 30 June 1985. The issue has divided the population of Belau against one another and Salii now faces a domestic revolt unprecedented in the history of Belau, with its strong traditions of respect for leaders. Seven lawsuits have been taken out against him and members of his administration alleging corruption, bribery and misappropriation of funds.

Despite the US pouring money into the campaign to approve the Compact − $400,000 in the December 1986 referendum alone − there was strong opposition. Teacher Lorenza Pedro told me why:

Huge numbers of us were killed when the Japanese and the Americans fought out World War Two on our islands. We don't want nuclear bases because we don't want to be caught up yet again in someone else's war.

But by the latter half of 1987, the opposition was facing severe intimidation: homes had been firebombed and the father of two staunch anti-Compact campaigners was shot in a death-squad-style assassination. Fifty traditional women leaders filed a suit challenging the referendum which changed voting laws, but pulled out after the attacks: the judge noted that the suit was suspended owing to intimidation.

Under the Compact, Belau loses one-third of its land for the next 50 years. The US is planning a Trident submarine base, an airfield for nuclear-capable aircraft, an amphibious base and a jungle warfare training centre. In return, Belau will receive around $20 million a year in US aid. President Salii insists that Belau has no alternative but to accept: the country is virtually bankrupt. Belau's leaders have been persuaded to overinvest in a power station which is way beyond its foreseeable needs and which has landed it in a nightmarish circle of debts. Behind the deal was a British firm, International Power Systems Company (IPSECO), which sold oil-fired power plants to Belau and the Marshalls in the early 1980s. It was a deal which was bound to run aground. Belau signed a $32.5 million deal with yearly repayments of $8 million: the country's total annual budget is only $12 to $15 million. Belau bought a 16 megawatt power plant: its projected needs were less than 9 megawatts. Its population is less than 15,000, many of whom live from subsistence farming and fishing.

And yet a deal was worked out where two British banks, National Westminster and the County Bank of London, shared the loan, which was underwritten by the British government-backed Export Credit Guarantee Department. This was in turn guaranteed by a consortium of five banks headed by Morgan Grenfell and insured by Lloyds of London. The US State Department gave its blessing despite warnings by the US

Interior Department's Inspector General in 1983 – before construction began – that the project was ill-conceived, poorly executed and would result in financial disaster for Belau.

IPSECO head, Gordon Mochrie, claimed the plant would be totally self-supporting. Yet Morgan Grenfell director Richard Halcrow told *Euromoney Trade Finance Report* in 1986, 'there was never any illusion that the power station would be self-financing. This was always perceived as an infrastructure development . . .'[3]

Ibedul Gibbons, high chief and traditional head of Belau (as opposed to the elected president), told the UN that he and the plant's opponents thought it was:

> a misguided, self-serving and totally inappropriate but cleverly conceived scheme by which the present administration came to accept an outrageously expensive public project which is financially doomed to failure.[4]

The plant has not produced a single watt of electricity and has broken Belau's frail economy. On 21 March 1986, IPSECO declared bankruptcy. Later the same year it became clear that Belau could not meet even the interest payments on its massive loan: Morgan Grenfell filed a $35 million suit against the tiny island nation.[5]

The strategic importance of the Pacific to the US

The strategic importance of the Pacific to the United States is attested by the fact that five of our eight mutual security treaties are with nations of the region. The world's six largest armed forces are in the area of responsibility of the United States Pacific command: those of the Soviet Union, China, Vietnam, India, North Korea and the United States. Five of these six have been at war within the past 11 years and the sixth is North Korea who, some have said, is at war all the time.[6]

Richard Armitage, US Assistant Secretary of Defense, and Reagan's 'Pacific Architect' in the Pentagon

The strategic importance to the US of the Pacific has its roots in the Second World War and in the Cold War which followed. The Japanese bombing of Pearl Harbour in December 1941 brought America into the war and it was towards the Pacific that America's fire power was first turned. Until 1943 more Americans fought in the Pacific than in the Atlantic and 53 per cent of Americans thought that Japan was the number one enemy, according to polls that year.[7]

But even before the war in the Pacific had ended, the US and Britain were laying plans against their new arch enemy: Communism and its embodiment, the Soviet Union. After the war, the US was determined to hold on to the Pacific islands it had captured and to establish 'forward bases' stretching across the Pacific from Hawai'i through Kwajalein, to Guam and on to the Philippines. The military thinking behind this was in part to ensure loyal outposts on the doorsteps of the Soviet Union and, later, China. To the west the US is separated from the USSR and China only by the Pacific Ocean and the islands of Micronesia. The forward bases were also intended to draw fire from the US mainland, in event of war, protecting it like 'pawns in front of the king on a chessboard.'[8]

Integral to the US anti-communist crusade was the possibility of using the 'powerful atomic blow'.[9] In fact, as former Defense Department official Daniel Ellsberg has documented, the use of the 'atomic blow' was repeatedly threatened:

> Every president from Truman to Reagan, with the possible exception of Ford, has felt compelled to consider or direct serious preparations for imminent US initiation of tactical or strategic nuclear warfare, in the midst of an ongoing, intense non-nuclear conflict or crisis.[10]

Of the 11 examples Ellsberg gives up to 1981, nine were over interventions in the First World. Of those, six conflicts were in the Asia–Pacific region.[11]

Military or expansionist powers have always used other smaller or weaker countries either to consolidate their 'forward defence' or as launch pads for their armies, ships and, more recently, aircraft. As the world is divided into 'spheres of influence' and the web of bases, ports and radar equipment grows, so the thirst for 'strategic dependants' becomes greater.

If the US is to fight a nuclear war, it has to ensure not only that its submarines and bombers and missiles can destroy the Soviet Union, but that it can knock out any possible retaliation from Soviet bombers and subs. To that end it has encircled the Soviet Union with chains of radar systems to prevent bombers flying outside Soviet territory. These are situated in Japan, Korea, Taiwan, Canada, Alaska and the Philippines. Then there are flying radar stations, called AWACs, Boeing 707s with dish antennae. The Pacific Ocean is also wired up to listen for Soviet submarines, with arrays of hydrophones – called SOSUS – sited off Hawai'i, Japan, Okinawa and Guam. Detected submarines would be destroyed by P-3 Orion aircraft, which carry nuclear depth charges and are based in Hawai'i, Japan, Okinawa, Guam, the Philippines, Australia and Aotearoa/New Zealand. From Australia, Guam and Hawai'i the US controls a network of spy satellites and has huge electronic eavesdropping antennae in the Philippines, Okinawa, Guam, Japan and Hawai'i. Their job is to evaluate targets for future wars. To find out what orbit Soviet satellites are in, the US has electroptical tracking facilities on the Hawai'ian island of Maui and in Korea and the powerful space radars of the Pacific Barrier on Kwajalein, Guam and San Miguel in the Philippines.

All of these islands and Pacific Rim countries, then, are caught in the web of nuclear war preparations – and all will be priority targets in any nuclear confrontation between the superpowers. In the meantime, they have all, to a greater or lesser extent, come under pressure from the US both to provide facilities and to quell any domestic opposition to the US military role.

The Pacific jewel

US Administrations have also fixed their sight on the economic prize which lies beyond the islands of Micronesia, in the Pacific Rim countries of South East Asia and in the countries of the South Pacific.

> In the mountains, river valleys, jungle plains and thousands and thousands of islands which make up the totality of 'the Pacific' there are no cocoa trees and no diamonds, but virtually every other kind of resource is there in abundance ... there is more than half the coal, natural gas, and uranium ore. In raw materials the region accounts for 94 per cent of all the natural silk produced, 87 per cent of the natural rubber, 67 per cent of the cotton and 63 per cent of the wool.[12]

In the late 1960s a number of US corporations, including the Bank of America, were laying plans to carve out a slice of lucrative markets and suppliers of raw materials and cheap labour in the area. By 1979 A.V.Hughes, Permanent Secretary to the Finance Minister of the Solomon Islands, could predict:

> We are probably witnessing the start of the second scramble for the Pacific, just a hundred years after the first such carve-up. This time, populous and powerful Asian nations will join those of America and Europe, together with multinational corporations based around the world (themselves as powerful as medium sized nations), targeted on natural resources exploitation.[13]

When Ronald Reagan, a Californian, was elected to the White House he brought in his tail wind a new generation of policymakers who scorned the East Coast liberals with their faces turned to Europe. The region of the world which made *their* hearts beat fastest was the Pacific Basin, which includes the world's fastest-growing economies of East Asia. The drive for the Pacific was accelerated under Reagan: by 1983 US trade with Pacific nations outstripped its trade with Europe by one third,[14] and 40 per cent of US trade now passes through the Pacific. It was a 'dramatic and probably irreversible switch,' said Peter Wilsher in the *Sunday Times Magazine*.[15] Gough Whitlam, Prime Minister of Australia from 1972 to 1975, predicted:

It is likely that by the year 2000 the gross domestic product of Japan and China, including Taiwan, together with Korea, will be greater than the GDP's of North America and the EEC. This represents one of the most momentous shifts of economic strength in world history . . . If the last three centuries were predominantly the Age of the North Atlantic, the 21st Century will be the Age of the Pacific.[16]

When he was appointed to the Joint Chiefs of Staff in 1985, Admiral William J. Crowe, Commander-in-Chief of the US Pacific Command, which stretches from the Arctic to the Antarctic and from the west coast of America to the east coast of Africa, wrote an article demonstrating how the imperatives of economy and anti-Soviet warfighting strategy are intimately linked in the minds of the policymakers.[17] He cited South Korea as one example of a Pacific Rim country where US trade and strategic links are intertwined: it is not a 'strategic dependant' like the Marshalls and Belau but rather part of the 'neo-colonial' pattern.

As well as stationing radar and satellite spying equipment, there are 40,000 US troops on South Korean soil. The repressive regime of Chun Doo-hwan is, in return, backed by the US. The two are tightly linked by trade, with the US taking 40 per cent of South Korean exports in the first half of 1986. But the relationship is not all milk and honey; the US is increasingly edgy about its $6 billion trade deficit with South Korea, and the latter is distinctly unhappy with encroaching US protectionism. However, with growing student unrest and a strong challenge from the parties – illegal until the first election, in 1987 – Chun Doo-hwan is in no position to turn his back on his superpower ally, particularly as relations with North Korea remain very chilly. Nearly four decades after the war, families are still divided by the border. In 1988, elections and the staging of the Olympic Games in South Korea have spotlighted world attention on its domestic and foreign policies.

As US trade with the area continues to outstrip that with any other region of the world so an increased military presence is thought to be needed to protect trade routes. That is, the Soviets are now perceived as a threat not only to the US mainland but to its trade routes and the countries which keep the US wealthy.

Hence the attraction of a naval base at Belau, for example, is economic as well as military, even though Belau itself is not profitable. According to a study by the Library of Congress Foreign Affairs and National Defense Division, a naval base would:

> enhance the US ability to defend sea and air routes east of the Philippines. These routes from the Indian ocean to Northeast Asia . . . are already used by the large cargo carriers for whom the shallower routes via Malacca are impassable. Soviet forces based in Vietnam would be at a disadvantage in trying to interdict these routes.[18]

And hence Indonesia is of consuming interest to the US as it controls access to all three deep-water straits through which nuclear submarines and warships, oil tankers and other trade ships travelling between the Pacific and Indian Ocean pass. Indonesia is officially non-aligned but increasingly westernised and dependent on the US which, along with Britain, supplies President Suharto's military regime.

The military-trade equation works in other ways to increase tension in the region. Because the area is deemed strategically important, any hint of the Soviet Union establishing trade links is immediately assumed to be threatening, both to trade and military supremacy. Hence, for example, American panic over Kiribati's fishing deal with the USSR. The Administration was worried not only about losing lucrative fishing but about the Soviets gaining a commercial – and then military – toehold in its 'American lake'.

The Soviet presence

How much influence *do* the Soviets have in the Pacific? A 1984 US State Department Study dismisses fears of a Soviet build-up out of hand. 'The fact is,' says the report, 'that in no other major area of the world is the USSR so completely without friends, access, or influence.' The authors assume that 'under the right conditions' the Soviets would involve themselves in regional affairs, but their current access is limited to a minor aid network which has largely been rebuffed.[19] The report acknowledges that nuclear activities and hard-line attitudes towards fishing regulations have not endeared the US to Pacific islanders. (But it points the real finger of blame at *French* colonialism: 'By any rational and objective assessment it is clear that France has created the greatest opportunities for Eastern bloc penetration.')

In July 1986 the Soviet leader, Mikhail Gorbachev, gave a key speech in the city of Vladivostock, on the Soviet Union's Pacific coast, in which he indicated that he intended to reverse the decline of Soviet relations with Asia after two decades of neglect. He made it plain that he considers his predecessors' policies in the region to have been a disastrous catalogue of ignorance and miscalculation and that he intends at least to improve the climate of opinion and trade. He has already begun to do this by making overtures to the Chinese. Gorbachev made several concrete proposals for a demilitarisation of the region. Most observers believe he is sincere, though they variously attribute his motivation to a wish to get Soviet industry on its feet – and, in so doing, slash military expenditure – or a wish to ease superpower tension, or both.

Admiral Crowe, in charge of the US Pacific Command, argues that 'the Soviets are turning to the one alternative they can develop and exploit unilaterally – their military power', and he warns of an 'increased and determined Soviet threat'.[20] A rather different picture is evoked by Pacific watchers Lyuba Zarsky, Peter Hayes and Walden Bello.[21] Their analysis shows that the Soviet Union has far fewer forward-based conventional or nuclear-capable ships and aircraft or personnel in the Pacific than the US. Most of its facilities are on or near its own territory. At present its only known foreign bases in the region are in North Vietnam: an air base at Da Nang and a naval base at Cam Rahn Bay. Instead, the Soviet Union relies on a home-based nuclear arsenal. This, they argue, is also very threatening and destabilising.

In attempting to analyse the number of US and Soviet weapons and forces in the Pacific, a confusing picture emerges. If we take the Pacific and East Asia together, the Soviets appear dominant. If we look at the alliances of the Pacific Rim, the US and Nato appear dominant. William Arkin, writing in the *Bulletin of Atomic Scientists*, says that because the Soviets are deploying land-based nuclear launchers while the US is putting sea-launched Cruise missiles in the ocean, 'assessment of a "balance" in the region is therefore difficult to imagine and somewhat passé'.[22] For most people, the finer points of number crunching seem an incomprehensible exercise. What is impor-tant is that both sides are bristling with arms which could in seconds devastate their home, their village, their city, their island. The people of the Pacific are left in no doubt that this is so. Long before people in western Europe were blockading missile bases and marching through the streets to protest at the deployment of Cruise missiles on their soil, US submarines were prowling the Pacific armed with sea-launched Cruise missiles and with Trident warheads, and Soviet missiles were aimed at US Command Control and Communications Centre on Kwajalein.

10

'Dump it in Tokyo, Test it in Paris, Store it in Washington . . .'

If it is safe,
Dump it in Tokyo,
Test it in Paris,
Store it in Washington
But keep my Pacific nuclear free!

As this Pacific Conference of Churches poster suggests, the nuclear powers use the Pacific for many parts of the nuclear cycle (the stages necessary for manufacturing nuclear weapons), cuckoos laying monstrous eggs in the nests of others. Uranium mining and milling; processing and reprocessing in nuclear power stations; research and design at weapons labs; testing of nuclear explosives and delivery vehicles (i.e. missiles); dumping of waste radioactive materials, and storing the weapons until they are used: these are the components of the nuclear cycle, and all of them take place – though not exclusively – in the Pacific. This section examines those components of the cycle which contribute to nuclear colonialism in the region: powerful nations have consistently chosen to test, dump and store nuclear weapons and waste on someone else's land because the cycle is dirty and dangerous.

The US is not the only nation to have carried out nuclear explosions in the Pacific. France is responsible for an estimated 93 underground and 41 above ground tests since 1963 in the South Pacific atoll of Moruroa. Britain carried out a dozen atmospheric tests in Australia and half a dozen on Christmas Island between 1952–8.

A tribute to her loyalty to France

When Algeria's uprising against France finally won it independence in 1962, France was forced to stop nuclear testing in what is now the Algerian Sahara and look for a new site. When French Polynesia – scattered islands with a small population away from the eye of the world's press – was chosen, it was 'a tribute to her loyalty to France', said President de Gaulle.[1] After the humiliation of the Second World War and the loss of two colonial wars in Vietnam and Algeria, the French people were, for the most part, only too happy to believe in de Gaulle's vision of 'grandeur' and 'independence', predicated upon a French *force de frappe*.

In 1963 French legionnaires began arriving in Tahiti and, in the face of unanimous opposition from the Polynesian Territorial Assembly, occupied two atolls, Fangatuafa and Moruroa (known in France as Mururoa and meaning, in Mangarevan, 'a place of great secrecy'). They began constructing testing facilities and assured the Polynesians that 'not a single particle of radioactive fallout will ever reach an inhabited island'.[2] In May 1966 the Centre d'Experimentation du Pacifique (CEP) announced the first test at Moruroa, promising they would never explode a bomb unless 'winds are blowing towards the southern portion of the ocean where there are no islands'.[3]

Unimpressed, the recognised leader of the indigenous Tahitians and representative in the National Assembly, John Teariki, met President Charles de Gaulle when he arrived on 6 September 1966 to witness the first test. He told the President:

> [Now] a widespread uneasiness exists in Polynesia and is worsening from day to day. It is due to the Fifth Republic's policy since you took over the helm, a policy consisting right from the beginning of a long series of attacks against our liberties, threats and acts of force aimed at reinforcing the colonial system and the military occupation of our islands . . . as has become evident, your policy has had only one aim, that of being able to freely dispose of our country as a testing ground for your nuclear weapons. Since then our destiny, our health, our social, economic and political institutions have been geared to your military needs . . .
>
> You made this decision without consulting us Polynesians, although our health and that of our children will suffer from the tests. This is a serious breach against the French constitution and the charter of the United Nations. Your propaganda department disregards the most elementary truths by alleging that these atomic and thermonuclear blasts are completely harmless to our health . . . The reports of the UN Scientific Committee on the Effects of Atomic Radiation for 1958, 1962 and 1964 have firmly established that each radioactive dose, however small, is harmful to those exposed to it, as well as for their descendants – that it is consequently recommended to avoid increasing natural radioactivity – that there exists no efficient method of protection against the harmful effects from widespread radioactive fallout from the explosion of atomic and nuclear bombs. Which is why all these reports reaffirm the necessity of stopping all the nuclear tests . . .[4]

Teariki went on to make a fierce and emotional plea to de Gaulle to take his bombs back to France. 'If you do so, you will never be accused of having caused cancer and leukaemia here in our islands. If you do so our descendants will not blame you for the birth of monstrously deformed children . . .' De Gaulle's response was to pocket Teariki's speech, shake his hand in silence and leave the room.

Four days later, Teariki's worst fears were realised. De Gaulle had come to Moruroa to preside over the first test, of a 120-kiloton bomb. Prevailing winds, however, were blowing towards neighbouring inhabited islands. One test was cancelled, but the following day De Gaulle ordered it to go ahead. The French have never released any radiological data on the resulting fallout. The New Zealand Radiological Laboratory continually monitored the radiation released from French tests and announced that radiation levels there rose substantially during the atmospheric testing programme.[5]

Twenty years – and 133 tests – later, huge underwater cracks have developed in Moruroa's coral reef and these are thought to be leaking radioactive waste into the ocean. With each underground test, the atoll is sinking another three-quarters of an inch into the sea.[6] In 1981 freak waves swept stored plutonium from former tests and drums containing radioactive waste into the open sea. A clean-up operation of the atoll has been ordered but it is a near-impossible task.

Successive French governments have blocked any independent comprehensive study of the effects of testing on the structure of the atoll, the ocean environment and health effects. The only outside report on the radiation hazards was carried out in 1983 by Mr Hugh Atkinson, who led a five-person delegation from Australia and Aotearoa/New Zealand. They were allowed to spend only four days on Moruroa and were prevented from taking the samples they needed; nevertheless, they reported that there was no hazard.

Publication of health statistics in the French colony was abruptly suspended in 1966 when the testing began and has not been resumed. The French say they are a military secret, but Polynesians are putting pressure on Paris to release statistics showing incidences of cancer among islanders. The only evidence that exists, therefore, is anecdotal. Dorothée Piermont, a Member of the European Parliament for the German Greens, talked to Tahitians in 1985.[7] Manarii Teuira, a 36-year-old Polynesian man who worked in Moruroa from 1966 to 1972 told Piermont how three of his closest workmates gave in to temptation and ignored the ban on eating fish from the lagoon there. They suffered diarrhoea and skin complaints and one man, his father-in-law, had internal problems which led to five stomach operations. All three eventually died in a Paris hospital, of cancer. A woman whose husband worked on Moruroa for 15 years from 1969 told Piermont that she'd suffered six miscarriages. When the seventh child was born, its skin peeled away from its flesh shortly after birth. Another woman whose husband worked on Moruroa told how her fourth child had been born without an anus.

In July 1981 the French magazine *Actuel* reported that Polynesians suffering from cancer were being flown out in secret by military planes to French military hospitals. The number of evacuations seemed to be on the increase: 50 in 1976; 70 in 1980; 72 during the first six months of 1981. A mother whose son had been flown to Paris, where he died, told Piermont that her son and the other evacuees were told that their treatment was conditional on their signing a declaration not to tell anyone of the nature and cause of their illness.

The French testing programme has been criticised by Australia, Aotearoa/New Zealand and other Pacific nations in virtually every international forum. In the face of sustained protest, France announced in October 1984 – while a socialist president, François Mitterrand, was at the helm – that it would continue testing at Moruroa for at least 15 years to 'perfect our nuclear strike force'.[8] The Maohi, the indigenous people of French Polynesia, however, have not been passive bystanders. Long prison sentences have been and are being served by outspoken critics of France's activities. As Oscar Temaru, leader of the Front de Liberation Polynesian, an independence party which opposes the holding of atomic tests, has said: 'The colonial age began in Polynesia when it was coming to an end everywhere else.'[9] It belongs to the new era of nuclear colonialism.

Tahitians have protested against the multitude of ills which have flowed from the French military presence. Like Micronesia, Tahiti has been transformed into a dependent colony, whose economy would most likely collapse if the French abruptly withdrew. An intense effort has been made to instil French values and mores: whereas only 600 French lived in Polynesia in the early 1960s, the French population has now increased to about 22,000, with 1,000 new arrivals every year, alongside the 114,000 Maohi. Although about half the French settlers work directly or indirectly for the test centre, Maohi were enticed from remote Tahitian islands to work as unskilled or semi-skilled casual labourers, with no job security and no unemployment benefit. In 1980 it was estimated that for every Maohi in an urban centre on a decent income, ten live in slums.[10]

For the most part, the French government was right to calculate that its actions on Moruroa would escape the glare of global publicity. Some international support for the Maohi has been forthcoming, however. Greenpeace took direct action against the test programme in the early 1970s, and was joined by a boat sent by the government of Aotearoa/New Zealand. In 1982, Greenpeace again sent two ships on protest voyages through the region. Then in 1985 the Greenpeace ship *Rainbow Warrior* was blown up in Auckland Harbour on the orders of the French government, to prevent Greenpeace from disrupting tests.

Field of Thunder: British testing

In the second half of the Second World War, the US was racing to beat Germany to the secrets of the bomb – secrets Germany was not, as was later revealed, close to unlocking. But at the same time the US was desperate to prevent the Soviet Union from obtaining the same information. Britain was at first party to the experiment, contributing its own clues to the puzzle, but so anxious was the US to sew up the post-war atomic energy market that it eventually excluded Britain, too.

In the early 1950s, therefore, under a Labour government led by Clement Attlee, Britain became a third runner in the nuclear arms race. When Britain exploded its first bomb in 1952 the now-defunct *Daily Graphic* ran an open letter thanking Britain's atom-bomb expert Dr William Penney. 'The fact that you and your team have made it possible for Britain to make and store atom bombs has made the country a world-power once again.'[11]

Attlee's request to use the US test site on Eniwetak had not been greeted with enthusiasm and so in September he approached Australian Prime Minister Robert Menzies for permission to use the Monte Bello Islands, just off the north-west coast of Australia. Menzies was enthusiastic, and Australia was to play host to a dozen atmospheric nuclear tests between 1952 and 1957, despite the early danger signals. After the very first test at the Monte Bello Islands, Operation Hurricane, clouds of radioactivity drifted towards the mainland.

In December 1985 an Australian Royal Commission, headed by Judge James McClelland, reported its findings on the British tests. It had been set up as a result, in part, of 30 years of lobbying by Aboriginal people injured and displaced by the tests and by veterans breaking their vow of silence. McClelland's abrasive, outspoken criticism of the nonco-operation of Mrs Thatcher's government and the British civil service stung the British government into releasing a welter of documents – many of them classified – which threw a little light on some shameful moments of British and Australian history. From 1953, nine tests took place on the Australian mainland, north-west of Adelaide, two at Emu Field and seven at Maralinga, a name derived from Aboriginal and meaning 'Field of Thunder'. An estimated 1,000 to 1,500 Aboriginal people lived in the area around Emu Field and Maralinga before the British moved in, and Aborigines were also most at risk from the fallout from the three tests on the Monte Bello Islands. Yet at no time were they consulted about the tests. Mostly they weren't even warned. According to evidence which has emerged during the Royal Commission, if they were found to be living within one of the poorly guarded areas, they were either perfunctorily rounded up and hosed down, or they were ignored.

The British and Australian authorities claim they know of only one incident when Aborigines were found on a firing range, though three others have been documented by the *Observer*.[12] The Royal Commission was told by an Australian ex-serviceman how he saw what he believed to be the bodies of four Aborigines in a crater and was later told by his superiors to keep quiet about it. The one government-acknowledged incident happened on 14 May 1957 when a family of four, Edie and Charlie Milpuddie and their children Henry and Rosie, known to the Aborigines as 'spinifex people', or nomadic bush people, spent the night in the bottom of a bomb crater. The bomb, codenamed Marcoo and exploded in October 1956, was relatively small – 1.5 kilotons – but as it was a ground-burst, caused severe contamination. Edie Milpuddie was pregnant at the time and later miscarried. The Royal Commission was told how the authorities, terrified of a public scandal, warned troops to keep silent about the family on pain of death or 30 years in jail. Rudi Marquer, a captain in the Australian Army, described how the Aborigines were forced to shower; no one explained to them why it was necessary. 'There was quite a lot of cahooing and screaming going on because the female [sic] didn't want to have anyone else wash her under a shower and her husband apparently also objected.'

Little wonder, then, that soldiers who met up with Aborigines in test areas did not, on the whole, report their presence. It must have seemed too much of an ordeal to put themselves and others through. British Royal Engineer Gordon Wilson told the Royal Commission in 1985 that he'd found Aboriginal people in the 'yellow area' – the hottest spot – at Maralinga several times. Asked why he hadn't reported it, he replied: 'Let's face it, it was their country.'

After Totem I, a 10-kiloton bomb exploded on 15 October 1953 at Emu Field, Aborigines saw a black cloud which drifted over Wallatinna and Welbourne Hill, their encampments to the north-east. Yammi Lester was 10 years old at the time and living at Wallatinna:

I looked up south and saw this black smoke rolling through the mulga. It just came at us through the trees like a big black mist, the old people started shouting 'It's a mamu' [an evil spirit] . . . they dug holes in the sand dune and said, 'Get in here, you kids.' We got in and it rolled over and around us and went away.

Everyone was vomiting and had diarrhoea and people were laid out everywhere. Next day, people had very sore eyes, red with tears and I could not open my eyes. I lost my sight in my right eye and could only see a bit with my left eye. I lost my left eyesight in 1957.

Five days after the black smoke came the old people started dying . . . [13]

The same day, Lannie Lennon was at the nearby settlement of Mintubi, 15 miles from Wallatinna. She was 20 and living with her young children:

There was a bang: it just rumbled. When the smoke drifted over us, we were walking about in it. We didn't know the danger. It was blackish, and settling all the next day on the trees. The day after, my three little kids were sick, they started vomiting. Since then, I have got a rash which comes all over me from head to toe. It breaks out in big blisters. [14]

The general contamination of Aborigines was in part due to the fact that the British and even Australian authorities were shockingly ignorant of the lifestyle of the Aborigines when the tests were initiated. The Royal Commission was told that when the British first arrived at Monte Bello their only source of information was *Encyclopaedia Britannica*. The British report on the population of the north-west of Australia, most likely to receive fallout, included exact numbers of sheep and ducks but nothing on Aborigines. White Australians simply didn't include them in their Census, and they had no vote until 1967. No attempt was made to follow up on the health of Aborigines known to have been in areas of fallout and it was assumed that radiation would have exactly the same effects on an Aboriginal

209

person as on a white person living in Britain. In fact, the Aboriginal customs of wearing few, if any, clothes, sleeping on and squatting close to the ground, of living off food found wild in their environment and cooking outside, together with the effect of the assault on their immune systems by 'imported' white people's diseases, made them much more susceptible.

David Barnes, the British health physicist who helped devise standards for radiological protection at the beginning of the tests in 1952, admitted under questioning by Andrew Collett, one of the Australian lawyers appearing for the Aborigines in the Royal Commission in January 1985, that a separate standard of exposure should have been set.

At the request of the Royal Commission a report was produced by the South Australian Health Commission in 1985 which identified 30 cases of cancer among Aborigines between 1969 and 1980, most of them north of the testing sites: 27 cancer victims had died. However, the report underlined that at this late stage it had been too difficult to draw up an epidemiologically reliable study. But the damage wreaked upon the Aborigines by the testing was not confined to radiation. Aborigines were cleared off the land to make way for the testing, for the westerners, their sites and building and equipment. Once on missions it was virtually impossible for them to continue their traditional way of life.

The report of the Royal Commission, delivered in December 1985, recommended that Britain should foot the bill to clean up the still severely contaminated test sites at an estimated cost of £100 million. By 1987, Britain and Australia had eventually agreed to share the £203 million cost of a study into a clean-up of the worst-affected site, Maralinga, where a series of 'small' tests, known as Kittens and Rats, scattered cancer-causing plutonium, with a half-life of 24,000 years, over hundreds of acres of Aboriginal land.

Australia, said the Commission, should compensate the Aborigines who were kicked off their lands and, it seems, in many cases showered with radioactive fallout. But by 1987 they had been given only £200,000 in compensation as an initial payment. Amongst the motives was the fear that compensation for Aborigines would also open the way for British and Australian veterans, many of whom later developed a range of health problems, including cancer, also to claim for damages. So far, 130 British veterans have lodged claims and are awaiting the outcome of a 'test case' to be heard in the House of Lords.

Christmas Island

> . . . after the flash – not a sound, nothing, then suddenly the air was filled with screaming birds who'd been blinded by the flash. They were crashing into the deck and the trees . . . we killed all the blind and maimed birds we could find and buried them. There were hundreds and they were beautiful but dead. I think we got drunk afterwards.[15]
>
> Barry Cotton, British veteran on Christmas Island

By the mid-1950s British public concern over the danger of atmospheric testing was growing. The Conservative government was pouring money and technological resources into developing both atomic and hydrogen bombs and was anxious to test them before the newly formed Campaign for Nuclear Disarmament and its sympathisers in the House of Commons could mount a successful challenge to the programme. Within a month three last nuclear tests were hurriedly carried out in autumn 1957 at Maralinga and then the testing site was switched.

On Christmas Island, the largest coral atoll in the Pacific, Britain detonated six hydrogen and atomic bombs in the 10 months between November 1957 and September 1958. No details have been released about their explosive yields. British veterans like Barry Cotton, quoted above, have recently started talking about the tests, but very little has been officially published. Ken McGinley, now chair of the British Nuclear Test Veterans Association, was 19 when he left Southampton for the Pacific with the Royal Engineers. At 21 he was pensioned off after suffering the first of a catalogue of illnesses he firmly believes stemmed from his presence at the tests.

Then in 1962 Christmas Island was once again the scene of testing. The US detonated 24 bombs of up to 25 megatons each over a three-month period, the most intense series of nuclear tests ever held. Christmas Island had no indigenous population at the time, but Pacific Islanders were working there on the copra. Many of them came from Kiribati. When Kiribati gained its independence its government asked the British for help in tracing the indigenous population who had been witness to the tests in order to monitor their health. The British government refused and the Kiribati government is now doing its own survey. An investigation of the long-term effects of testing on the environment and on the health of the new quite large population is also required.

Soviet and Chinese nuclear explosions

Both the Soviet Union and China have regularly detonated nuclear explosions in their own territory, but neither does so in the Pacific region.

China carries out its nuclear explosions at Lop Nor, a desert area in the north-west of its territory: by 1986 it had exploded an estimated 29 nuclear bombs, 22 above ground and 7 below.[16] It did not join with the Soviet Union, the US, Britain and France in signing the Partial Test Ban Treaty in 1963 but in 1986 Premier Zhao Ziyang finally announced that China would stop atmospheric testing. This followed demonstrations by people living downwind from the test site, mostly Moslems of Central Asia, who report cancers, genetic damage and damage to crops.

The Soviet Union conducts its nuclear explosions in Semipalatinsk, in Soviet Central Asia. Since signing the Partial Test Ban Treaty, all 412 explosions (till December 1986) have been underground. In August 1985 Mikhail Gorbachev announced a unilateral Soviet moratorium on testing: it was extended four times but eventually abandoned in January 1987 after the US continued testing.

Missile testing

During the early 1980s the US developed plans to launch longer-range MX missiles than those fired into the Kwajalein lagoon into the South Tasman Sea, between Australia and Aotearoa/New Zealand. The Australian peace movement protested and Australian Prime Minister Bob Hawke withdrew permission for the US to use Australian radar and monitoring facilities.[17] The US was forced to back down, but still plans to expand its testing facilities by firing missiles into the open ocean of the South Pacific. Sonar buoys dropped immediately beforehand will relay test results; with this new technology oceans everywhere now risk becoming target zones.

The Soviet Union, meanwhile, is also launching missiles into the Pacific. Between 1963 and 1985 it is estimated that it fired 26 missile tests there. Little is known about the tests – a result, not just of the obsessive secrecy of the Soviet authorities prior to Mikhail Gorbachev's *glasnost*, but also of the remarkable lack of publicity or protest given to the tests by western governments and media. One of the dynamics of the arms race is, ironically, mutual acceptance.

One such incident of complacent acceptance occurred in 1978, when air traffic controllers at Tokyo airport were sent into a panic by the message that the Soviet Union was about to begin a series of missile tests just as nine flights were preparing to take off towards Anchorage, Alaska, and points beyond. One of the test areas was just off Kamchatka, on the path between Tokyo and Anchorage. New flight plans had to be hurriedly worked out, skirting the danger zone. Yet Japan protested to Moscow only about the lack of warning time. Neither Japan, nor the US, which counts Alaska as its forty-ninth state, criticised the danger posed by the tests themselves.

213

Owen Wilkes, a defence researcher in Aotearoa/New Zealand, has commented:

> Each superpower needs the Pacific as a test zone, and tolerates the other doing the same. After all, there wouldn't be an arms race without the other side, would there? We have here a rather neat and unsavoury example of functioning detente between the superpowers – each side in effect says 'I won't complain about your missile tests if you don't complain about mine'. And so everyone can have a nice day at the arms races – everyone except the people who got pushed off Kwajalein to make space for the race.[18]

What is not known is whether – in parallel to displacements on Kwajalein – the Soviets have uprooted people previously living on the Kamchatka Peninsula, used as the pincushion for testing the Soviet Union's shorter-range missiles. It is thought, however, that this is highly unlikely as the peninsula is very inaccessible and probably not previously inhabited.

Uranium mining

To build nuclear weapons you first need uranium. Australia is the world's third most important producer of uranium after the USA and Namibia. It is estimated, that Australia also has more uranium than any other country – 30 per cent of the world's reserves.

Between 1944 and 1963 a handful of small Australian mines provided uranium for Britain's nuclear weapons programme.[19] Demand for uranium dropped in the late 60s but in the early 70s mines began to reopen and plans laid to quickly explore and develop new ones. However, despite the election in 1975 of an Australian conservative Liberal government sold on making profits from uranium, mining companies did not get an easy ride. Their way was barred by demonstrating Aborigines and ecology and peace groups and a strong opposition amongst trade unions. By 1981 over 70 per cent of Australia reserves remained untouched.[20] Bob Hawke, then president of the Australian Congress of Trade Unions, resigned over its opposition to uranium mining. He went on to become head of Australia's Labor government, which has not honoured promises it made to protect Aboriginal land rights from uranium mining projects.

Uranium mining is extremely hazardous to both workers in the industry and to the general public. Workers are exposed to radiation, particularly from accumulations of radon gas and its decay products. In 1975 the Australian Atomic Energy Commission reported:

> the incidence of leukemia/cancer among white Australian uranium miners has been found to be six times the expected norm; and three times the expected norm was found among mill workers.[21]

Before uranium ore can be transported to nuclear-capable countries around the world it must be made into uranium oxide, or 'yellow cake'. Known as milling, this process produces residues, called tailings, which contain at least 85 per cent of the original radioactivity of the ore. These stay radioactive for some 80,000 years, and also contain other poisonous metals such as mercury, arsenic and lead. The tailings leave the mills as slurry and are dumped into tailings ponds, which are sometimes allowed to dry out. For many thousands of years to come wet tailings ponds will give off poisonous gases, including radon gas, which can be blown as far as 1,000 miles. The wind also carries radioactive dust from dried-out tailings piles to neighbouring towns and villages. Little has been done in Australia to ensure that tailings ponds are secure and do not present a hazard to nearby communities. In 1971 a dam gave way at Rum Jungle, a disused Australian mine owned by Britain's biggest mining company, Rio Tinto Zinc (RTZ). It was Australian taxpayers and not RTZ who picked up the $A16 million bill to try and clean up the resulting contamination. Tailings ponds are clearly far from safe but no better way of dealing with the milling residue has been found.

Australian uranium is mined on sacred Aboriginal land, as Barbara Flick, an indigenous Gamalroi woman from New South Wales, told the Sizewell Inquiry in June 1984:

> The places in which uranium has been found in Australia have been places of very strict taboo. Bill Wesley, a traditional leader around Yeerlirrie where there is a potential uranium mine, said, 'We were told by our elders not to disturb the place. Not to dig, not to touch anything, not to uplift anything, because these things are pretty dangerous. They told us that when the two gods came, that is the creation of spirits, they destroyed this evil thing and put it below and said no one was allowed to touch it, but when the white men came they wanted to put their hands on it for the sake of money and it is going to destroy nearly everything on earth. I believe these things ought to be stopped.'[22]

The Northern Territory of Australia contains 18 per cent of the world's uranium but as yet it is still unmined. A land of baking sun and torrential monsoons, the extremes of nature make this an area largely unattractive to whites, and it is one of the few parts of Australia where Aboriginal people have been able to continue to live on their land. This is now under threat from mining companies. Silas Roberts, former chair of the Northern Lands Council, told the Ranger Uranium Environmental Inquiry:

> In my travels through Australia I have met many Aborigines from other parts who have lost their culture. They have always lost their land and by losing their land have lost part of themselves . . . we in the Northern Territory seem to be the only ones who have kept our culture.[23]

And yet the second Ranger Report concluded:

> There can be no compromise with the Aboriginal position; either it is treated as conclusive or it is set aside. *We are a tribunal of white men . . . In the end, we form the conclusion that their opposition should not be allowed to prevail.* (my emphasis)[24]

216

Despite a current world glut in uranium, British Petroleum and Western Mining of Australia have recently opened up a new mine on indigenous Kokotha sacred sites in Roxby Downs in South Australia. Britain's Central Electricity Generating Board and the Swedish State Power Board have reportedly signed deals for the uranium, despite Sweden's pledge to phase out its nuclear power plants. The Kokotha people, supported by white Australians, have opposed the mine by occupying a sacred site, Cane Grass Swamp, in 1983, to prevent its destruction by the building of a pipeline, which has since been rerouted. A British campaign is organising a boycott of BP because of its involvement with Roxby Downs.[25]

Dumping

The ocean is our life. It's our food. If they contaminate the ocean, we have no food to eat. We would live a nightmare, waking up wondering whether the food we ate would poison us and kill us – not only ourselves but our children and our future generations. Highly migratory fish carry nutrients long distances and are thus capable of contaminating vast ocean areas of the Pacific. Nature has its own force. They may dump (nuclear waste) in the Pacific but it may also reach the Atlantic Ocean.[26] Maria Pangelinan

In the autumn of 1985 Maria Pangelinan came to London with Jacoba Semana, secretary of the organisation for which she is treasurer, Committee Against Nuclear Waste Dumping in the Northern Marianas, in the north-west of Micronesia. The two women travelled half way round the world to attend the London Dumping Convention, a United Nations body which sets *voluntary* international agreements on the dumping of toxic wastes at sea. Nearly every adult in their country has signed a petition against dumping nuclear waste at sea. Japan would like to dump 5,000 to 10,000 barrels of low-level nuclear waste in the Marianas Trench, 600 miles north of their islands.

The voices of the Marianas people, however, cannot be heard at the Convention: the Marianas are a Commonwealth of the US and as such are allowed no independent say. Semana and Pangelinan were part of the International Friends of the Earth observers' delegation, supporting Spain's proposal for an indefinite moratorium on dumping nuclear waste at sea until it could be proven safe. The Mariana Islands are officially represented through the US, which like the other nuclear powers, wants to continue to throw the vast quantities of nuclear waste it produces into the oceans, far removed from the protests of local communities around the world who are organising against having the waste dumped in *their* backyards. Mid-ocean, therefore, seems an attractive option: no village folk barring the way of the bulldozers beneath the glare of the TV cameras, as Nirex faced in Britain in 1986.

The dumping countries admit there is no way of preventing leakage from steel and concrete drums containing the waste. Sea water decays the steel and concrete breaks up owing to rock-falls and movements of ocean currents at high pressure in deep waters. The Convention's Panel of Experts has admitted that radioactivity from existing dumps has already passed into food chains and is now present in edible fish, which migrate huge distances from the dump sites and are sold around the world. They have predicted a minimum 1,000 deaths from this contamination.

Nauru, another Pacific nation, which first co-initiated a two-year dumping ban in 1983, commissioned its own experts to examine the studies by the Convention's panel. The official panel predicted 100,000 deaths over a 500-year period if dumping were to go ahead.[27] Nauru's nuclear experts reported in 1985 that they had noted that the panel's study had not taken into account many of the risks and uncertainties outlined in its own report. With these extra factors – and no new ones – included, we could expect over the same 500-year period a staggering *four billion deaths and another three billion cases of severe hereditary harm and non-fatal cancers*. The vast majority of those casualties – greater than the entire present world population –

would be incurred in the Pacific if the Marianas Trench were opened up to dumping.[28]

Thanks to the combined efforts of the smaller, non-nuclear nations, the 1985 London Dumping Convention did indeed ratify Spain's proposal and the onus is now on the dumping nations to prove it safe. However, Japan abstained in the vote and the United States and the United Kingdom voted against. All three had hinted previously that they might flout the non-legally binding agreement, a threat which still hangs in the air.

Three nations have already dumped radioactive waste into the Pacific: between 1946–70 the US dumped 56,991 containers at 16 different sites; Japan dumped 1,661 containers about 25 miles outside Tokyo Bay; and South Korea dumped an undisclosed amount in its 'territorial waters' between 1968–73.[29]

All three, plus other nuclear states, are anxious to resume dumping waste from nuclear reactors and other sources. The US, for example, is said to be looking to scuttle three to four nuclear-powered submarines a year for the next 30 years in the Pacific. The spent fuel would be removed but 'there would still be some radioactivity contained in the reactor pressure vessels'.[30]

To get around the ban, Japan, Taiwan and South Korea are said to be hoping to construct 'above ground interim storage facilities' for high-level waste on a Pacific island: Palmyra, Wake and Midway Islands are being considered.[31] And the USA, UK and Japan are researching the potential of disposing nuclear waste *under* the sea bed. The Marianas Trench is once more a favourite target site, yet the Pacific Ocean floor is highly unstable: temperatures of 350 degrees have been measured and the trench is ringed with recently active volcanoes. Again, the long-term consequences could be disastrous. The International Transport Unions Federation is strongly behind the ban, however, and unions may play a crucial role in holding countries to it, as they did in 1983 when the British National Union of Seamen and the transport unions TGWU, NUR and ASLEF refused to handle nuclear waste and forced Britain – which has dumped 90 per cent of the radioactive waste already in the Atlantic Ocean – to respect the agreed temporary ban.

PART THREE

Alternatives

11

Pacific Initiatives

William J. Bode Jnr, US ambassador to the South Pacific from 1980–81, is reported to have warned Washington that if the nuclear powers in the Pacific weren't careful, protests against nuclear testing and dumping would turn into a comprehensive demand for a 'nuclear-free Pacific'. This, he said, would threaten American relations throughout the region.

The people of the Pacific are indeed turning to each other for support. In spite of the huge differences that divide them and the many languages and cultures of the region, people are in contact with each other from Hawai'i to Guam to Tahiti. Aotearoa/New Zealand's ban on visiting nuclear-armed or powered ships is only the most publicised part of a growing movement.

There are several levels at which the Pacific alliances are being made – with varying degrees of success. On 6 August (Hiroshima Day) 1985, countries of the South Pacific Forum signed the Treaty of Rarotonga, establishing a nuclear-free zone in the South Pacific. Australia, Tuvalu, the Cook Islands, Fiji, Kiribati, Aotearoa/New Zealand, Niue and Western Samoa signed, and were later joined by Papua New Guinea and Nauru.

Three South Pacific Forum countries declined: Tonga, because it thought a nuclear-free zone endangered US interests in the region, and Vanuatu and the Solomon Islands because they wanted the treaty to have more teeth and a guarantee to be given that nuclear weapons states – the US, USSR, Britain, France and China – would agree to its protocols. Only China readily agreed. The Soviet Union, generally supportive of nuclear-free zones, was not happy that this one allowed the continuing presence of US nuclear ships and aircraft while banning Soviet ones; Moscow later agreed to sign. France refused to allow its colonies to be included in the treaty or to stop its nuclear explosive testing. The US was relieved that the treaty was so unambitious but worried that it might be a Trojan horse, heralding a later, more radical arrangement; Britain followed the US lead.

The treaty is indeed of very limited scope. Its main achievements are to prohibit dumping nuclear waste at sea, nuclear explosions, acquisition of nuclear weapons or their basing within signatories' territorial limits. It doesn't, however, deal with missile testing, uranium mining and export, nuclear power or nuclear waste disposal on land. Even as a nuclear-*weapons* free zone it is full of gaps; it allows port calls, movement of US nuclear ships and aircraft or Command Control and Communication (C3I) facilities in Australia and Aotearoa/New Zealand. Nor does it take in the area where US presence is greatest: Micronesia. That leaves untouched not only the test base and C31 facilities at Kwajalein, but also the nuclear stockpiling site, strategic bomber base and C31 facilities in Guam and the proposed nuclear naval and air bases in Belau and the Mariana Islands.

Supporters argue that the treaty nevertheless has a political importance, because it raises the threshold of nuclear initiation, and acts as a brake on the acquisition of weapons by countries in the region (Australia would be the most likely offender) and as a confidence-building measure. It also has the effect of further isolating France as the only power breaking the 'no nuclear explosion' clause.

And it doesn't stop individual countries from taking further steps, they stress; in fact, it might provide a springboard for such initiatives. When Aotearoa/New Zealand banned nuclear-capable ships from its ports the US expelled it from ANZUS, a regional defence treaty which was never expressly nuclear-based. At the same time, France was conducting a trade war against Aotearoa/New Zealand because it dared to imprison two French secret agents for their part in blowing up the *Rainbow Warrior* in Auckland Harbour. And yet far from making the electorate run scared, the New Zealand Labour Party's anti-nuclear policy strengthened David Lange's hand. Some argue that the growing anti-nuclear consensus in a region which has a strong tradition of co-operation was one factor in this.

However, some critics suspect the treaty was designed as a sop to anti-nuclear feeling in the region while leaving the most urgent issues untouched. In its final form it embodied only the Australian government's position, all other governments favouring a more or less radical proposal; Aotearoa/New Zealand shared the analysis of Vanuatu and the Solomon Islands but settled for a pragmatic compromise in order to achieve some concrete agreement. Some Australian Democrats and sections of the peace movement argue that the treaty legitimises US nuclear involvement in the Pacific and that by masquerading as a comprehensive agreement for a nuclear-weapons-free zone it may block the drive for a more radical settlement.[1]

The countries of Micronesia sent representatives to the South Pacific Forum for the first time in 1987. It remains to be seen whether the Marshall Islands, particularly, might prove to be a restraining and conservative influence or whether the dynamic will work in reverse and RepMar will be galvanised into taking a more radical stand.

Independence

So Ambassador Bode was right to predict a surge in anti-nuclear sentiment; what he failed to grasp was that many Pacific people also link the nuclear contamination of their lands and waters with the centuries of colonial control. A coalition of non-governmental groups – indigenous movements, women's and peace groups, trade unions and churches – have been working for over a decade towards a Nuclear-Free and *Independent* Pacific (NFIP).

In the keynote speech at the NFIP conference in 1983, Barak Sope MP, from Vanuatu, captured the mood of the movement:

> It has always been my stern belief that nuclearism cannot be separated from colonialism especially in the Pacific region. For in a colonial situation there is no democracy or freedom. The people of Tahiti have no choice whether a nuclear bomb is tested in their country or not. It is the French government who makes the choice . . .
>
> Nuclearism in our region is connected with the racial question. The white powers who have and are still testing nuclear bombs in our region have no regard for the Pacific Islanders. To them we are inferior human beings and it is OK to test or dump nuclear waste in our backyard.

The indigenous peoples of the Pacific are also forming bonds around a shared identity, described by Hilda Halkyard-Harawira, a Maori activist.

> The Indigenous peoples of the Pacific observed the same laws;
> of respect for Mother Earth,
> of respect for the 'religion' of natural law,
> of respect for the wisdom of ancestors and elders,
> of respect for human life, and
> of respect for those as yet unborn
> Armed with this knowledge, this understanding, this common ancestry, the Indigenous Peoples of the Pacific have begun forging links.[2]

The reclamation of these values has been the first step towards breaking free from the most insidious effects of colonialism: self-hatred and submission. But while most indigenous groups share a wish for self-determination, there are important differences in their visions of a post-colonial society. The Kanaks, for example, are working towards a locally-grown form of socialism, while some other indigenous leaders are, in some aspects, quite conservative.

The process of cultural regeneration and decolonisation is particularly complex in countries which were used as settler states and where now the white population outnumbers the indigenous, decimated as they have been by western diseases and colonial policies: Australia and Aotearoa/New Zealand by the British; Hawai'i by the USA; Kanaky/New Caledonia and, increasingly, Tahiti by the French.

Most indigenous groups do not expect white people to leave these countries *en masse*. Léopold Jorédié, former Kanak President of the Central Region of Kanaky/New Caledonia has made this explicit: 'For us, *cohabitation* is not a problem. We want to work with Europeans. We have to make the Europeans understand that independence is not exclusive.'[3]

Indigenous groups *do*, however, expect a reversal in their systematic dispossession of land, water and forestry; constitutional guarantees of their rights; the political will to tackle both institutional and individual racism; and the opportunity to participate fully in the running of the country. Most groups would also include among their aims the reassertion of values such as co-operation between peoples and respect of the land and the sea instead of consumerism, profit and militarism. Father Walter Lini, prime minister of Vanuatu, declared that settler countries needed to acknowledge 'that our new found freedoms were fought for . . . in order that a renaissance of Melanesian values, principles and expectations could take place'.[4] Though again, while there is general agreement over what is wrong with western rule, there is diversity in proposals for alternative policies.

In none of the settler countries is change in sight; indigenous groups are engaged in a long and costly fight for their rights and their lands. It is worth examining here the situation of the Maori and the Kanaks as two such examples, and describing some developments in Fiji and in Hawai'i which illustrate the progress of conflict between western and indigenous purposes.

The Maori

Under the 1840 Treaty of Waitangi, Maori chiefs were persuaded to cede sovereignty to the British Crown. In return they received a guarantee from Queen Victoria of 'full and exclusive, undisturbed possession of their lands and estates, forests and fisheries, and other properties which they may collectively or individually possess'.[5] However, as Titewhai Harawira, who is involved with the Waitangi Action Committee and the Pacific People's Anti-nuclear Action Committee, explains:

> In 1840 the white man made a treaty between my people and Queen Victoria that guaranteed us our land, our language, our forestry and our fisheries. A treaty that in fact recognised our sovereignty. A treaty that has not been honoured . . .
>
> Three years after the treaty was signed the British began their large land wars and confiscations and my people realised that they had no intention of honouring that treaty. The whole of South Island was confiscated. Our people were killed, they raped the women . . .

In 1859 Governor Gore-Brown reported to the British Colonial Office: 'The Europeans covet these lands and are determined to enter in and possess them – rightly if possible, if not, by any means at all.'[6] Once the Europeans outnumbered the Maori and were backed by the British Army, they entered into open conflict with them. British settlers 'squatted' Maori lands, backed up by the British Army. Only a few dissenting voices were raised: the General leading the British troops was so disgusted at being expected to evict Maori from 'confiscated' lands that he resigned in 1868.[7]

To make it easier to acquire communal Maori land, a Land

Court was set up to individualise it in 1862. The following year a 'Suppression of Rebellion Act' was brought in. Based word-for-word on the Irish Act of 1799 (designed to put down Irish dissent from British rule), it suspended the right of trial before imprisonment. As in Kanaky/New Caledonia, Aotearoa/New Zealand and North America, the indigenous population were confined to reservations, though even these have been gradually reduced in size, by compulsory purchase orders.

In the 1980s Maoris are excluded from power, wealth and higher education: they make up 7 per cent of the potential labour force, but 23 per cent of the unemployed; 80 per cent of young Maori leave school with no qualification; Maori per capita income is half that of Europeans.[8]

Titewhai Harawira points out:

> From sixty-six million acres, today we have less than two million in Maori control, and most of that land is only good for growing pines and not for farming. Today we are 3.5 million people in Aotearoa and Maori people are only 10 per cent of the population.[9]

David Lange and the Labour Party have taken a courageous stand on banning visits of nuclear-armed ships, but they have done little to ensure that Maoris are accorded full civil rights. Back in 1925 the Ratana, a group representing Maori interests, officially forged links with the Labour Party: in 1932 a petition calling for the ratification of the Treaty of Waitangi was presented by Ratana MPs to the Aotearoa/New Zealand parliament. It has never been acted-on and the Maori are still campaigning for the promises made by Queen Victoria to be fulfilled, using the legal system to try and reclaim some of their land. One of the tribes is taking its land grievance to court and the tribes of Kai Tahu are having their claims heard through the Waitangi Tribunal.[10]

The Kanaks

The situation of the Kanaks is somewhat different as Kanaky/New Caledonia is still officially a French colony. The French annexed the island in 1853 for use as a penal colony. Kanak land was taken over and their numbers decimated: rebellions were quelled with ferocity. In a revolt which lasted from June to September 1878 200 French people and over 1,000 Kanaks were killed. As well as appropriating Kanak land, the French colonials segregated the indigenous population from Europeans: Kanaks were made to live on reservations, prohibited from attending French schools, needed special permission to marry whites, were obliged to do forced labour and pay heavy taxes. 'We grew up,' says one Kanak spokeswoman, Susanna Ounei, 'seeing how our parents were humiliated.'[11] The Kanak population was reduced from around 70,000 in pre-colonial days to around 26,000 in the 1980s.

From the late 1920s onwards, however, Kanak resistance took root and by the 1960s and 1970s had become a real force to be reckoned with. At this time the French government deliberately encouraged massive emigration to the colony to swamp the Kanaks by sheer weight of numbers. Former French prime minister Pierre Messmer is quoted as saying in 1973, 'Massive migration by French citizens . . . will let us avert this danger . . . The native nationalist movement will only be thwarted if the communities that are not of Pacific origin form the majority.'[12]

The Kanaks have, at different times, used the ballot box, lobbying, non-violent resistance and armed struggle to try to achieve a more equitable society. In the French presidential election of 1981 Kanaks voted overwhelmingly for François Mitterrand (and the colonials voted massively against him) on the strength of his pre-election promises. The socialists lacked the political will, however, to take on the colonials, who can rely on the support of French voters who were formerly in Algeria, Vietnam and other French colonies.

In 1984 the French government proposed a five-year transition period towards a façade of independence similar to that of Micronesia vis-à-vis the US. Elections scheduled for November that year were to serve as a referendum on the proposal: the Kanaks decided to boycott them and to disrupt the vote.

Mitterrand sent in 280 riot police and 32 people, mostly Kanaks, were killed. The proposal was abandoned.

After several months of clashes between French authorities and Kanaks, during which one Kanak leader, Eloi Machoro, was killed by French sharpshooters, a referendum on self-determination was promised. In the meantime four regional councils and a national congress were established. In the ensuing elections the Kanak Socialist National Liberation Front (FLNKS) gained control of three of the regions and the pro-colonial RPCR took control of the congress. Since then, the socialists have lost control in the French parliament and the small reforms made in Kanaky/New Caledonia have been reversed. When the promised referendum took place in 1987, French authorities secured the outcome by giving the vote to any one who had lived there for three years. Realising they were significantly outnumbered the FLNKS once again went for a boycott: 83 per cent of Kanaks responded, but the overall voter turnout was nevertheless put at 59 per cent; of them, 98 per cent voted in favour of staying with France.[13] In the wake of the plebiscite the foreign ministers of Papua New Guinea, Vanuatu and the Solomon Islands called for international pressure to end French rule. Even the governments of Australia and Aotearoa/New Zealand, not normally known for their outspoken views on decolonisation, were critical.[14]

Even in France's terms, the referendum has not solved the 'problem'. After years of Kanak lobbying, the South Pacific Forum agreed in 1986 to take their case to the UN. The Kanak case is now being taken up by the UN Decolonisation Committee. Kanaks continue to be excluded from education, from benefiting from the wealth of their country and from the political process. The economy is reported to be under the control of 50 families, most of whom transfer abroad the wealth earned in New Caledonia.

Despite UN and international pressure, France is keen to hang on to its colony for a number of reasons. It is rich in minerals, particularly nickel, but also chrome, iron, manganese and cobalt, and expected ocean-bed mineral wealth in its

200-mile exclusion zone is yet untapped. The strategic import-ance of Kanaky/New Caledonia is due to its situation 'at the junction of the South Pacific sea lanes between Australia and the US and between Asia and South America'.[15] There are now plans to build a large naval base at Noumea to accommodate nuclear submarines and the airport is being expanded for the use of fighter planes.[16]

But as former Gaullist prime minister Jacques Chaban-Delmas said at a meeting of the RPCR, the greatest value of the South Pacific island to France is in propping up its perceived image as a world power:

> If France were to vanish from New Caledonia it . . . would be followed by Polynesia – and France disappears. Your children would be poor little children with nothing left at all after the year 2000 because, if France ceases to be a nuclear power, she ceases to be a power altogether.[17]

Fiji

Not all those who have arrived in the Pacific over the last two centuries are Europeans, however. In Fiji, Indians, brought as indentured labour by British colonials, slightly outnumber the indigenous population. Recent developments in the island have highlighted the complexity of the colonial legacy in the region and the way in which political issues can be hijacked.

The two military coups in 1987, which established a military government under the leadership of Ratu Sir Kamisese Mara and Colonel Rabuka, were carried out in the name of protecting indigenous Fijians from the Indo-Fijian populations. The excuse for the first coup was the election of the Labour-Federation Coalition government – as its name suggests, a coalition between Indian and indigenous Fijians but led by an indigenous Fijian, Dr Timoci Bavadra. Bavadra's government was remarkable for several reasons: it re-established Fiji as an anti-nuclear and non-aligned force in the South Pacific (Fiji was host to the first Nuclear Free and Independent Pacific confer-ence but, wooed by Washington, the former prime minister had reversed his policy and started accepting port calls from US nuclear-capable ships); it took a strong stand in favour of anti-colonial struggles in the area; and it promised to investigate the alleged widespread corruption of the previous government.

The new military government has made a bid to appeal to anti-colonialists at home and abroad, challenging the remaining vestiges of British rule and declaring itself the voice of the indigenous population. And yet, curiously, it has again reversed Fiji's nuclear policy, once more welcoming US nuclear-armed ships and submarines; the friends it has sought to make in the Pacific feature the French colonials rather than the Kanaks and Indonesia, South Korea and Taiwan rather than the non-aligned, recently independent countries of the South Pacific Forum. The French Defence Ministry announced in Paris on 7 October 1987 that two naval patrol boats were carrying out joint exercises with the Fiji navy; according to the Fiji *Sun* (27 August 1987) France is offering $NZ 13 million towards a naval base in Fiji and may be training Fijian soldiers.[18] Even more curiously, a list of strange coincidences and circumstantial evidence point to the possibility that the CIA may have given Colonel Rabuka its blessing – if not a helping hand.[19]

Jone Dakuvula, an indigenous member of the Fijian Anti Nuclear Group, told delegates at a Nuclear Free and Independent Pacific conference: 'The fact that the Taukei and military regime in Fiji are indigenous should not blind [sic] the NFIP from seeing clearly whose interests they are actually going to serve in this part of the world.' The coups provoked some hard questions which Dakuvula put to the conference:

Is our solution to colonial racism the counter-posing of indigenous chauvinist nationalist supremacy? If indigenous nationalist movements in the Asia–Pacific region are about the development of more just, equal and democratic societies, can they achieve this by means that are unjust to other communities in the same territory in which they live?

Do we support the imposition by military force by a minority of their ideas of indigenous political control or

233

would we rather support the alternative of democratic constitution of negotiations for strong protection of indigenous rights and concerns and a system of political representation that is fair to all communities in a multiracial society?[20]

The conference, consisting mostly of indigenous groups, took a majority vote to condemn the coups and the military government's treatment of Indians and anti-nuclear activists.

Hawai'i

Other issues taken up by the NFIP illustrate the close relation between militarism and the denial of indigenous land rights. One such example is that of a group in Hawai'i, the 'Protect Kaho'olawe 'Ohana'. Every two years Hawai'i – now a state of the USA – is the scene of a military exercise, RIMPAC, which culminates in the shelling of Kaho'olawe, an island with thousands of historic sites and of deep cultural and spiritual significance for indigenous Hawaiians. RIMPAC is one of the biggest military exercises anywhere in the world and involves the US and allies pretending to capture Hawai'i from the USSR: a simulation of an attack on the Soviet bases on the Kamchatka peninsula and Kurile Islands, north of Japan.

The US, Canada, Japan and Australia have been the core participating countries since the exercise began in 1971. France joined in 1984 and Britain in 1986 – though these European powers have yet to explain what they are doing so far from any legitimate area of interest.

After protest at home, Britain agreed not to join in the bombardment. Aotearoa/New Zealand was not invited to take part in the 1986 exercise, following its own stand in 1984 forbidding nuclear-armed ships to use its ports. Apart from the US, Canada is now the only country to join in the bombing of Kaho'olawe and pressure will be put on it in 1988 to stop.

The shelling continues, but Kaho'olawe is now on the US Register of Historical Sites, as a result of Hawai'ian pressure. 'Protect Kaho'olawe 'Ohana' has won the right, through law suits and 'sail-ins', to visit the hitherto military-only island for 10 months every year, hold cultural study groups there and replant the eroded land. This action is part of indigenous Hawaiians' reclamation of their tradition of *Aloha 'Aina* which

> lays the foundation for Hawaiian religion, culture and lifestyle. *Aloha* means love and *'aina* means land. The two words together express several levels of meaning. At the deepest level the presence of our ancestors and gods of the land are acknowledged, respected and cherished, through ceremonies both public and private. This intimacy with the *'aina* is also expressed in the interdependent subsistence relationship between man [sic] and his island. Man is nurtured with taro from the land and fish from the sea, and in turn cultivates and nourishes the island.[21]

Another aspect of their work has been to challenge through the courts the commercial use of Hawai'i's biggest volcano for tourism and energy: for the indigenous Hawaiians the volcano is the home of an important goddess, Pele. The NFIP regards the fight for cultural survival as intimately linked to its other aims; its supporters argue that while the harnessing of volcanoes is a good renewable source of energy in some circumstances, in this case it is akin to the distress to Christians if an open cast coal mine were proposed on the site of St Paul's Cathedral.

Economy

The above is an example of the indigenous groups questioning western economic imperatives. Part of the long-term challenge for newly independent Pacific nations is also to change the basis of island economies. 'Development' and western aid have been widely used as bargaining chips not only in Micronesia, but also in Tahiti by the French. Migration is still happening on a massive scale in the Pacific, from smaller islands to larger ones: from the small islands of Fiji to the main one of Viti Levo; from the whole of the Tongan archipelago to the main island of

Tongatapu; from the outer Marshallese islands to Majuro and Ebeye and so on. This is part of a very general trend of migration from rural villages to urban capitals.

At the same time, skilled Europeans are still arriving in the region to dominate the white-collar and professional jobs, particularly in Kanaky/New Caledonia and in Tahiti. A Papua New Guinean report concluded, for example, that a new mining development would simply mean that 'the local people will remain second and third class citizens in their own districts while thousands of mine employees and other immigrants will bring with them an obvious affluence which will remain unattainable for the majority of people'.[22]

Landless farmers and workers from smaller islands are meanwhile obliged to seek employment away from home: Kiribati citizens frequently work on West German merchant ships; Tongans gravitate to Aotearoa/New Zealand, and there are twice as many people from American Samoa now on the US mainland as there are in the islands.[23]

Any lasting change in the Pacific, therefore, needs to include a co-operative regional economic project which can develop alternative and viable island economies, and to form a cartel to ensure that local produce such as sugar, copra and fruit are not subject to drastic fluctuations in market prices and that local countries are not competing with each other. The South Pacific Bureau for Economic Co-operation was for this reason established in 1971. A start has been made by the 16 Pacific nations who are working together to extract a better fishing deal (discussed in Chapter Eight), but Pacific inter-island economic co-operation still has a long way to go.

World-wide initiatives: radiation survivors

The NFIP puts a high priority on networking and now has links with groups in numerous countries, some of which have been formed to focus on Pacific issues, and others which include a Pacific perspective in their work (see address list on pp. 266–7).

One initiative which brings together people from around the

globe is the Radiation Survivors Network. It aims to provide a forum for radiation survivors to tell their stories and have them publicised; to exchange information on the health effects of high and low level radiation; and to focus public attention on the problems caused by nuclear bombs, tests and industries. Pacific participants include representatives of Aboriginal, Marshallese and Japanese survivors. British, Australian and US military veterans who were contaminated during testing in the Pacific are also involved. Through the network they give each other support and encouragement as they try to win recognition and compensation from their different governments.

US nuclear survivors are still involved in lengthy court battles. In a test case involving 24 'downwinders' of the Nevada site, nine were awarded compensation of between $100,000 and $625,000 in 1984 but three years later the Federal Appeals Court overturned the award on the grounds that the US Administration had inherited the powers of King George III to 'do no wrong'.[24] US veterans, represented by the National Association of Radiation Survivors, are also being forced to fight over an obscure point of law, passed in 1864 to protect Civil War soldiers and their partners from unscrupulous lawyers which dictates that legal representatives of veterans cannot charge their clients more than $10. Opposing them in court is the federally-supported Veterans' Association which was fined $145,000 in 1987 for destroying documents relevant to the case.[25]

The individual testimonies of military personnel involved – mostly enlisted – have been corroborated by recently declassified documents. Colonel Stafford Warren, head of radiation safety at Operation Crossroads, recorded that while military personnel were ordered to scrub down the target ships in the Bikini lagoon after the Baker test, 'even changing clothes and eating was dangerous since fission products were found on clothing, food and hands, in every ship in increasing amounts day by day'. Even then, the documents also reveal, US authorities were worried about claims arising out of contamination.[26]

The nuclear veterans have made some headway though; in 1979 the US government finally acknowledged a link between nuclear testing and cancers among the 220,000 veterans exposed in the Pacific, Utah and Nevada. Since 1985, 7,781 individual claims have been settled at $1,500 a month disability allowance or $300 a month death benefits.[27]

Marshallese radiation survivors hoped that as other groups around the world made painstaking progress, their own cases, initiated in 1979, would benefit from new precedents being set. But as this book goes to press in January 1988 they have lost the first round of all their cases as the judges have upheld the 'espousal' clause in Section 177 of the Compact of Free Association. They are now waiting for their cases to be heard at the Court of Appeal.

The matter of who will pay for the cost of cleaning up the contaminated atolls is also still to be finalised. Under the Compact, the Bikinians have been awarded $75 million in compensation over the next 15 years. The US Administration says they should use this to pay for cleaning up the atoll, but they argue that it is needed for medical expenses. Besides, says their lawyer, Jonathan Weisgall, it is estimated that the clean-up alone could cost $100 million. He contrasts that with the cost of the tests which, he says, by today's standards, would cost $20 billion.[28]

US experiments on Bikini point to several possibilities for cleaning up the atoll. In 1970 several families were moved back there from Kili, where they are now living, after US officials declared the danger to be over, only to be re-evacuated eight years later when health surveys showed most of the island-grown food to be contaminated. The main problem is caesium 137, with a half-life of 30 years, still present in the soil. Plants readily absorb caesium 137 because they react to it as they would potassium, which they need. Scientists suggest scraping off the topsoil to get rid of the caesium 137 but this presents three problems: it would entail sacrificing the existing vegetation; the vast amounts of contaminated topsoil would pose a major disposal problem: it would also mean losing all the nutrients needed for new plants to grow. Another possibility is to stop the plants absorbing caesium 137 by blocking it with massive doses of potassium, either in the form of fertiliser or seawater, which is potassium-rich but also lethal to many plants. Despite the problems, Bikinians say that they prefer the idea of scraping the topsoil because it will actually get rid of the radiation rather than just blocking it.[29]

As an international team of scientists prepares to carry out a study into cleaning up Rongelap, meanwhile, Rongelapese living on Mejato are waiting anxiously to find out how much longer they must remain in exile.

What next?

The obstacles facing the NFIP and the South Pacific Forum are huge. They include the entrenched interests of militarism, nuclear posturing and hunger for profit, as well as the still powerful colonial ideology.

Even between their own members there is clearly significant tension. Take the South Pacific Forum. It brings together on the one hand newly independent nations, often pushing for change in the regional power structure, supportive of indigenous rights and a non-aligned foreign policy; on the other are Australia and Aotearoa/New Zealand, the latter determinedly anti-nuclear under David Lange but both firmly in the western camp, both wary that too much change could undermine their traditional standing in the region, and both deeply ambivalent about indigenous rights. Their position is further complicated by the fact that both have colonised other Pacific islands: Papua New Guinea, for example, is now separate from Australia but still economically dependent; the Cook Islands are in 'free association' with Aotearoa/New Zealand but dependent both for finance and defence. Ironically, their present government is bitterly opposed to Lange's anti-nuclear stance.

The Pacific's predicted role as the region of the 21st century indicates, too, a heightening of tension in the area, with nations pulling in very different directions. The US has long seen the Pacific as its 'lake', but that will be increasingly challenged by the Soviet Union, China and Japan – once again a very powerful influence – as well as the newly industrialised countries of the Pacific Rim and the islands struggling to find political and economic – as well as paper – independence. France and the US, in the meantime, are digging in, increasing military co-operation by making low-profile moves in the area such as permitting the other to use respective airfields in Micronesia and French Polynesia.[30]

In the last forty-odd years 70 nations have become independent under the auspices of the UN. The patterns of history would indicate that it is only a matter of time until Tahiti and the Kanaks join them. But as France fights to keep 'the last non-independent tropical territory in the world where a developed country can settle its citizens, [the] final chance to create an extra French-speaking territory',[31] it seems that independence may take years to arrive and involve further bloodshed. It may also be that France is in the process of ensuring the Kanaks are outnumbered so that any future independence will be on the terms of the Europeans.

12

'When Will we Seize the World Around us with our Freedom?'[1]

I didn't come all the way here for you to cry for me as I can never bring [my people] back to life. I have come . . . for you to see yourself through me, as I have this experience . . . I want you to see your future, what it is going to be, through me. I'm living in contaminated land and water but what is your future going to be if this city fills with nuclear waste? . . .

There is no choice for us . . . maybe only to live in our contaminated land and die. But we don't want our friends and neighbours round the world having the same problems that we are facing . . . we have to look forward . . . [the future] is already being damaged. I do not have to look back for the damage. I have to look forwards, to reach out to my friends around the world.[2] Lijon Eknilang

In 1985 I wrote a very short piece in the *Guardian* reporting the visit to this country of two Pacific women, and a little of what they had to say of the effects of nuclear waste dumping and testing. From a small village in Yorkshire, a woman wrote to me saying it was one of the most disturbing things she had read,

241

that she couldn't stop crying whenever she thought about it. She had decided to tell her friends about it and together they had set up a small support group: they were sending me a first contribution to pass on to the NFIP.

I imagine that parts of this book may be painful to read, just as they have been to research and write. Sitting typing I would often find myself crying or raging, remembering a face or a voice of someone I'd talked to in the Marshall Islands as they recounted what radiation had done to their bodies, or what colonisation had done to their communities. Sometimes I'd stare across our small patch of garden, through the gaps in the trees and houses to the North London railway line, along which nuclear flasks are regularly transported. I'd think too of the pale, windswept sands of Druridge Bay, in Northumberland, a few miles from where I grew up, the site of a proposed nuclear power plant.

I hope, however, that the stories told by the women and men of the Marshall Islands will at the same time inform and move readers, either to take new action or to carry on with the work they are doing, aware of new links, new reasons.

Because of these many links which connect us and make us interdependent, an internationalist perspective is essential; but there can be a narrow divide between recognising these links and feeling overwhelmed by the global thirst for change. In this final chapter I'd like to discuss some of the contradictions and complexities of solidarity work – organising and lobbying in support of another community, whether in the same country or a different one. But first I want to examine a little more the feelings and emotions which, as much as thought and analysis, form a springboard for political action.

I've chosen to write here about feelings as well as political action because it felt wrong to describe lives being wrecked, people being uprooted and 'herded' (for that is how it was) onto one tiny ghetto of an island, about women giving birth to children who were so mutilated they could not survive – and not to acknowledge that this is a book not just about 'facts' but about the grief, hurt, anger and fear of the Marshallese people.

And now you've read it, what do you do with your own feelings about these events?

In many political circles – the western male left in particular – there is a dismissal of the emotional and the spiritual as apolitical. Traditional ways of organising reflect this: left political groups still operate in ways which demand that members have little time for life outside; scant attention is paid to how and why conflict arises in groups and how to deal with it; political 'lines' are constructed so that any personal truths which are seen to deviate from them are silenced. Political priorities also reflect the downgrading of the emotional and spiritual: the emphasis is on economistic analyses and low priority is given to subjects such as mental health and ecology; the arena of moral and spiritual values is abandoned to the right.

Of course, emotional and spiritual forces can be – and have been – channelled to conservative ends by religious and political leaders: both President Reagan and Mrs Thatcher have understood and manipulated the power of people's emotional response, and religious hierarchies around the world have used people's spiritual needs to consolidate their own institutionalised authority.

But the emotional and spiritual can also be a source of radicalisation and empowerment. The women's movement used 'consciousness raising', the US civil rights movement used 'tell it like it is' to reveal and describe personal experience and to uncover new possibilities and energy for political change. However, despite the women's liberation movement's emphasis on the 'personal is political', and the advances in developing feminist spirituality and psychotherapy there are broad areas of experience yet to be validated as a suitable terrain for political engagement.

At the same time, some psychoanalytical circles deny that depression can be triggered by community or global suffering, attributing all such experiences to people's need to deal with the personal problems that arise from their own history. Not all drives stem from the ego – individual needs – however, and distress over the killing, brutalisation or impoverishment of other people or fear for our common future, is equally real and well-founded. Individual experience, which forms a person's psyche, and group experience, which forms the political and social context in which they live, feed each other constantly.

Where will we go from a world of insanity?
Somewhere on the other side of despair.

T S Eliot[3]

Humankind has always lived with the knowledge of our own mortality – and our potential to kill others. But only in the last 40-odd years have we had to bear the burden of knowing that our species is now capable of exterminating all life. As if that wasn't enough, we know too that even if the final Armageddon doesn't happen, we are slowly poisoning our planet, killing off plant and animal life that is essential to the delicate ecological balance of the earth. And every day we hear news of, or experience, the terrible cruelties that one group of people is perpetrating against another: sometimes those on the receiving end also know that other cruelties are being acted out in their names – in the name of their country, their class, their race, their gender, their sexuality, their religion . . .

A frequent reaction in the face of all this is to 'not want to know'. Even people who believe in the possibility of change shy away at times, afraid of feeling powerless. Most people just don't know what to do with reactions of fear, anger and grief, and so block them: psychic numbing, as Robert Lifton calls it. He coined the term in his study of Hiroshima survivors but later used it more widely.[4] Many other psychologists, philosophers and political thinkers have observed the same phenomenon. Some, like Helen Caldicott, say it is manifested in the frenetic cult of money and consumer goods in western societies: 'manic denial', she names it.[5] Historian and diplomat George Kennan points to the western obsession with demonising the Russians: 'Our blind military rivalry . . . our government's preoccupation with nuclear war . . . are a form of illness. It is morbid in

244

the extreme. It can only be understood as some form of subconscious despair.'[6]

William G. Hyland, former Deputy Director of the National Security Council, denied the existence of such blocking 'at the top levels of government' but he went on to say: 'if you allow the emotion of nuclear war to enter the Defense Department, you'd end up totally paralysed,' confirming Lifton and Kennan's theories.[7]

Children and young people, meanwhile, who are less 'defended' than adults, pick up very quickly on what is happening in the world: but again, most societies allow little space for the expression of feelings of despair, even for children. It is hardly new for young people to feel angry with adults about the world they have grown up to find. But the American Psychiatric Association's report 'The Impact on Children and Adolescents of Nuclear Developments' talks of generations growing up with no sense of a long-term future.[8] As far as I know, no one has bothered to ask children in Vietnam how they feel about their future: the 'impact' of the US report is that on the minority of young people in the world who are not already threatened by starvation or a war being fought around them.

How do these considerations relate to this book? Many readers will live in countries with repressive governments, animated by authoritarianism, greed and bigotry. In the face of so much, it may be tempting to keep the stories in this book at arm's length, out of fear of not being able to cope with any more. And this fear keeps us immobilised, saps our strength. But when grief and hurt are allowed in, from the same place comes anger and vitality. And without them there is neither the energy nor the will for change. I am not advocating purging ourselves so we can get on with our lives unburdened, nor of wallowing in pain; but instead of calling on our reserves of wisdom, power, courage and empathy. At the indigenous caucus of the November 1987 NFIP Conference in Manila the need was voiced to re-find anger and the concomitant vitality which can get lost amongst the administrative detail of the movement.

Political action – joining with others around common objectives to change injustice – can itself be empowering, despite the conflicts which also arise in political groups. Yet in all political movements people – myself included – at some point experience 'burn-out'; chronic illness or emotional and mental collapse. One reason for this is that most people don't apply the same standards to themselves as to the world. While working for a world free of abuse, where people are treated with respect, and the earth's resources used more carefully, activists frequently treat themselves abusively. It is easy to forget that human bodies, like the world, have limited reservoirs of emotional and physical energy. We are scandalised when a multinational company pollutes our environment or a government refuses to meet the basic needs of its people – yet we do the equivalent to ourselves. I'm also slowly trying to accept that I can only do so much, can only do a few small things well; my vision has to be wide, but the territory I choose must be limited.

A second reason is that we may be involved in struggle, but still locked into despair. I have spent many years so appalled at the state we are in that sometimes I feel allergic to the man-made world. It is a state of partial numbness; of fear that if I allow myself to feel more fully I will drown in pain. But I'm learning that on the far side of fear – which drains me – is rage. I'd previously glimpsed the rage but was wary that it would consume me, before I could tap into its energy and use it for change. I've been politically active, but have been denying myself half of my own resources, mistakenly thinking that defending myself from these feelings was the only way to 'cope' and to carry on.

Thirdly, once moved to action, activists often feel we should always be strong and optimistic: but as Andrew Young, former US ambassador to the UN stated at the September 1982 Congressional Black Caucus: 'We won't allow ourselves to get into situations where we feel helpless and hopeless and somehow it's in those situations where we feel the spirit'.[9] Times of going through pain's shadow, he said, when people wept together in churches and jails, were turning points in the civil rights movement.

Which brings me back to the letter from Yorkshire, from a woman who had the courage to tell others how distressed she felt; she and they found new inner resources and the resolve to take part in a struggle which they felt was also theirs.

When Lijon Eknilang from Rongelap came to Britain to speak in 1986 she too talked of shared experience – and of why she needs our actions, not just our tears. Her challenge to British audiences, quoted at the beginning of this chapter, was twofold: to take up work in solidarity with the Marshallese – and by seeing and listening to them to learn, and to see reflections of our own lives. What she was saying is crucial to solidarity work, which often begins with people wanting to support the cause of another country or community, but in the process reaching new understandings and finding sources of inspiration. As Bunny McDiarmid, crew member on the *Rainbow Warrior* during the relocation of the Rongelapese affirmed: 'There's so much to learn from those people if only we got down from our high horses and lost our sense of superiority. It'd be like relearning our own culture.'[10]

However, solidarity work also throws up particular issues, especially for white people supporting First World struggles or middle class supporting working class. I'd like to explore here some of the tensions I've come up against in doing this work.

It is very tempting to idolise the other community of people, putting them on a pedestal and heaping expectations upon them. Sometimes this is an inversion of guilt; middle class and white people, ashamed of the advantages that society confers on them, can react by romanticising Black and working class people, assuming everything they do or say must be right. It may also be the result of disappointment at the failure of local struggles, or an idea that 'out there' the struggle is more 'real'; perhaps, because they are far away and therefore carry less personal attachment, the issues seem more basic, more clear-cut. In extreme cases this can involve a kind of macho 'violence voyeurism' – a second-hand buzz from supporting guerrillas from a safe distance. Very often, it involves yearning for a revolution: when petitions, lobbying, pressuring local authorities and so on seem an endless drip-drip on the huge store of state power, or when – as under Mrs Thatcher in Britain – the small gains made previously are swept away in a flood of repressive legislation, a distant revolution can seem a much more attractive magnet for political energy.

Whatever the cause, the effect is dehumanising to the people who have been deified, denying that they too are full human beings capable of the whole gamut of deeds and emotions. And romanticising sets up the false premise that there are no differences or conflicts within communities. In a way, it is another form of stereotyping: a 1950s newsreel shows the Marshall Islanders called 'simple savages':[11] in refuting that stereotype it is easy to fall into another – that their experience of US imperialism has made *all* Marshallese people anti-nuclear, anti-materialist, anti-militarist, in favour of non-alignment, or that their matrilineal structure means *all* women are strong incipient feminists. When I was interviewing people in the Marshalls I noticed that I *wanted* everyone to say that they were conducting their sail-ins because they hoped to reclaim their land and to halt the arms race. But of course, many people's activities are now focused on the short-term goal of making life on Ebeye bearable.

As myth, novels and films demonstrate, the need for heroes is a strong one. In real life, however, heroes are real people with real faults, who are involved in complex and possibly contradictory struggles. Their idealisation can only be maintained in the long run by pretending that everything is more clear cut, more simple, than it really is; perhaps the greatest risk of romanticisation is that when the honeymoon is over disillusionment and desertion may follow in its wake.

One example of the need to deal in complexities is the 1987 coups in Fiji (discussed in Chapter Eleven). Colonel Rabuka and Ratu Sir Kamisese Mara asserted indigenous rights but they betrayed the common vision of a just, equal, non-aligned and anti-nuclear society. Such a contradiction is painful to accept but if ignored would eat at the foundations of the movement.

But to what extent is solidarity work part of a two-way dialogue between those supporting and those being supported? And how far can we question each other's methods and aims? The relationship needs to be as equal as possible, otherwise those doing the supporting may adopt the attitude that they are simply 'helping those less fortunate than themselves'. That's another way of dehumanising people, forgetting the links which Lijon Eknilang talked of; pity creates a downward spiral of guilt and resentment; ultimately, it is a dead-end. And unless there is room for an exchange of views, those being supported may feel that solidarity literature and methods misrepresent them. Or they may think – as is the case sometimes – that their struggle is being hijacked to score points in someone else's domestic politics.

Yet many people are quite literally fighting for survival: they don't necessarily have the resources to enter into a prolonged debate. And because the relationship *is* one of supporter and supported, making it a two-way exchange involves being constantly vigilant and fluid, always open to revising the framework of the relationship.

Even the language of solidarity work is challenging, as I find while I'm writing this. If it's talked about in terms of 'them' and 'us' it sets up the construct of 'the other' – the outsider, who is not part of an assumed 'us'. (And what does 'us' mean? Does it mean the people who agree with me, live in the same place, or who fit into the same categories of identity?) Differences and similarities have to be recognised without setting up an 'us' and a 'them': a cosy, false unity will only hinder mutual recognition and respect. Ideally, the two groups are accountable to each other, without surrendering their right to be different.

The differences include political priorities: many feminists and Marshallese people may not see eye to eye about religion or contraception (and yes, there are differences among feminists and among Marshallese people over the same issues). These differences may be aired and yet tolerated as long as the two groups are linked in other ways – by a desire to end western imperialism, for example – and as long as western solidarity groups do not try to impose their culture on others.

At the end of the day the overarching principle is that people don't need to justify their wish to live with dignity and self-determination. Solidarity work, then, cannot be predicated upon imposed conditions for support; it must be a critical relationship between two groups of people and a forum for international dialogue. If it is, then the breaking-down of stereotypes and assumptions works both ways: it can also help to dent the image that the West has promoted of itself in other parts of the world – an image in which all its people are rich, white, and heterosexual.

The fear of difference is also an impetus to racism. In the words of Audre Lorde: 'Racism and homophobia are real conditions of all our lives in this place and time. *I urge each one of us here to reach down into that deep place of knowledge inside herself and touch that terror and loathing of any difference that lives there. See whose face it wears.* Then the personal as the political can begin to illuminate all our choices.'[12]

As this book demonstrates, racism underpins the policy of the US Administration towards Micronesia; racism and imperialism, are, after all, intimately connected. It is also crucial that white people working in solidarity with Black communities engage with racism – in this I include myself.

However well intentioned, however thoughtful they may be, white people will – especially if from a colonising or a settler nation – carry with them handed-down racist assumptions. Making gross generalisations about another race is not the prerogative of people with white skin, of course: the qualitative difference is that in modern history white nations have more systematically used their power to dominate and colonise others, and racism is now institutionalised in white-ruled countries.

It's very hard not to be defensive about personal shortcomings. One way of beginning to deal with racism is to accept that it is a product of political history – it doesn't mean that people are hopeless cases. There is no useful purpose in feeling guilty because of being born a particular colour, class or gender. However, it is within everyone's power to begin to change their ingrained attitudes and habitual actions and to challenge racism as it occurs in their society.

The fear of difference has also been one of the major impediments to solidarity groups working in coalitions. Coalitions are the hardest form of political organising – but they are perhaps the most essential. A great deal of work has been done in Britain and the US in recent decades on identity politics: people coming together to recognise, find, and establish a common identity which had been denied them – as Black people, as lesbians or gay men, as disabled people, as Jewish people and so on. Identity politics have been a crucial step in enabling the marginalised and disenfranchised to create a base from which to reclaim political and social power. The danger is, however, that identity becomes an end in itself and political energy is all sucked inward. Jenny Bourne has written about Jewish feminists: 'We have made finding our identity a substitute for liberation.'[13] Bernice Johnson Reagan, Black American singer and songwriter with Sweet Honey in the Rock, and June Jordan, Black American poet and essayist, have both talked and written on the need to move *beyond* identity. June Jordan:

> Every single one of us is more than whatever race we represent or embody and more than whatever gender category we fall into. We have other kinds of allegiances, other kinds of dreams that have nothing to do with whether we are white or not white . . . that is not to disparage or dismiss the necessity for what I would call issue oriented unity among different kinds of people . . . It may be enough to get started on something but I doubt very much whether it's enough to get anything finished.[14]

Coalitions only work if people are willing to recognise the differences between them as well as the ideals they share – and are clear about what they expect from a coalition and where it is going. As Bernice Johnson Reagan says so graphically:

Coalition work is not work done in your home. Coalition work has to be done in the streets. And it is some of the most dangerous work you can do . . . you shouldn't look to it for comfort. Some people will rate the success of the coalition on whether or not they feel good when they get there. They're not looking for a coalition; they're looking for a home. They're looking for a bottle with some milk in it and a nipple, which does not happen in a coalition. You don't get fed a lot in a coalition . . . you have to give . . . You can't stay there all the time. You go to the coalition for a few hours and then you go back and take your bottle wherever it is, and then you go back and you coalesce some more. [15]

Forming coalitions is one way to avoid romanticising and demonising other groups at home and perhaps a step forward in refusing to do the same to groups in other countries. And they are of essence if the aim of political activity is *change*, not just making a noise.

It is very easy for well-intentioned support work to slip into some of the patterns of colonialism: the slogan 'change not charity' is a truism, but it still holds good. Charity leaves untouched the power imbalance which imperialism depends on; in fact, it exacerbates it, with the giver feeling bountiful, the receiver forced into gratitude and the dependency deepened: US aid to Micronesia has intentionally had this effect, and the Peace Corps programme was on the face of it extending help but in reality exporting US culture and values.

At the heart of solidarity work must be the impetus for change, with those being supported setting the agenda. In the NFIP this means the Pacific groups taking the lead. But given that it involves wresting power and privileges from those currently enjoying them, deep-rooted change is the toughest nut of all; the nuclear powers have everything invested in continuing colonial practices in the Pacific.

Solidarity work also requires that connections are made with what is happening on our own doorsteps: 'think globally, act locally'. Otherwise people end up supporting a distant cause because it is too uncomfortable to face the issues that are close to home. It can be easier to talk of racism involved in US, British and French testing in the Pacific than to support local Black defence campaigns, especially when they are demonised by the press. If solidarity groups are working in broad coalitions, it is harder to ignore the issues that need to be confronted at home.

Links, moreover, are there to be made and are very real. The devastating effects of radiation are not happening only to someone else 'out there': Chernobyl brought this into sharp relief, if Three Mile Island and Sellafield hadn't already done so. As Lijon Eknilang pointed out, most people live too close to an existing or proposed nuclear power station, a railway line along which radioactive material is transported or a planned dump site, to be complacent about the dangers. And the issue of land rights and of forced relocations is not unique to Kwajalein atoll: it is part of the history of Scottish smallholders, the Aborigines of Australia, the Maori of Aotearoa/New Zealand, native American Indians and Black South Africans. Smallholders the world over have fought for land rights against absentee landlords, in Spanish Andalusia, in Ireland, in southern Italy. In Central America Guatemalans and Salvadoreans are currently forced off their land and herded into militarised 'model villages'.

The flip side of being only long-sighted – only seeing what is far away – is near-sightedness – only seeing what is near to hand. Many movements, including the British peace movement, have at times focused locally at the expense of making the global connections, in part out of fear of dissipating their own energy. The worry of losing direction and taking on too much is a real one: these balances are difficult to achieve. But if a movement is, say, trying to challenge Cold War ideology in order to lay the foundations for nuclear disarmament, it is possible to talk in very concrete, human terms about what the consequences of the Cold War are for people around the world, including the Marshall Islanders. And as June Jordan says, making inter-national links means that our roots go deep and far, so that in times of crisis, though a branch may be damaged, the tree still stands:

We cannot eliminate the problems unless we see them in their global dimensions. We should not fear the enlargement of our deliberate connections in this way. We should understand that this is a source of strength. It also makes it more difficult for anyone to destroy our movement.[16]

Today, a global and long-term perspective is crucial. For unless western movements make the connections between cruise missiles on submarines in the Atlantic and those in the Pacific, between nuclear waste sites being considered in British towns and off the coast of the Marianas, between money being diverted from health and education into defence spending and a new round of weapons being tested at Kwajalein, they are busy putting out the bonfire in their garden while behind them a forest fire rages.

In an age of global telecommunications, when corporations and defence treaties are multinational, when acid rain produced in Britain threatens the forests of Scandinavia and the deforestation of the Amazon threatens us all, when strikes for decent pay and conditions are broken because the same product can be imported from the other side of the world, when 10 per cent of the nuclear weapons now in existence could destroy each one of us, we are truly all in this together.[17]

Our main hope is that the world will get to know of what has happened here. And when you know we need your active support. Together we must stop the testing and stop the arms race: and then we will be able to begin looking at all our other problems. That's truly what we need here. I think we share the same goal. Kinoj Mawilong, Ebeye, 1986

Chronology of Testing and Displacement in the Marshall Islands

November 1945: Three months after dropping atomic bombs on Hiroshima and Nagasaki, the US military begins searching for a site for further tests.

January 1946: US Navy officials announce that Bikini atoll in the Marshall Islands will be the site for a series of nuclear tests codenamed 'Operation Crossroads'.

March 1946: The Bikinians are moved to Rongerik.

May 1946: In preparation for nuclear explosions on Bikini the people of Enewetak atoll are evacuated to Meck Island in Kwajalein atoll. The people of Rongelap atoll and Wotho atoll are moved to Lae atoll.

July 1946: 'Operation Crossroads' begins with 'Able' (1 July), an 'air drop' and 'Baker' (25 July), an underwater test; both atomic blasts are about the size of the bomb dropped on Nagasaki.

July 1947: The Marshalls, the Carolines and the Marianas become a UN Trust Territory administered by the US.

December 1947: The US Navy decides that Enewetak atoll will be used for a second series of nuclear tests and immediately moves the people to Ujelang atoll.

January 1948: The US tells about 550 Marshallese living in a labour camp on the US base at Kwajalein that they must move to Ebeye Island, four miles away; this, in turn, becomes a labour camp.

March 1948: The Bikinians, literally starving on Rongerik, are finally evacuated to a temporary Navy base on Kwajalein.

April 1948: 'Operation Sandstone' begins on Enewetak. It includes three atomic blasts ranging from 18 to 49 kilotons, detonated from towers: 'X-Ray' (15 April), 'Yoke' (1 May) and 'Zebra' (15 May).

November 1948: The Bikini people are moved once again, this time to Kili Island, which has good coconut trees but no lagoon for fishing.

April 1951: 'Operation Greenhouse' begins on Enewetak atoll. It includes four atomic tests exploded on towers: 'Dog' (9 May), 'Easy' (21 April), 'George' (9 May) and 'Item' (25 May). 'Easy' was 47 kilotons; information on the others remains classified.

November 1952: 'Operation Ivy' begins on Enewetak. 'Mike', the first thermonuclear (hydrogen) bomb, is exploded on 1 November: it is 10.4 megatons (750 times greater than the Hiroshima bomb) and vapourises Elugelap Island, leaving a vast crater. 'King' (16 November), 500 kilotons, contaminates Ujelang atoll, 150 miles away, with radioactive fallout.

1 March 1954: 'Bravo', 15 megatons, is detonated on Bikini, despite winds blowing towards Rongelap, Rongerik, Utrik and other inhabited atolls. A Japanese tuna fishing boat, the *Lucky Dragon* is also caught in the fallout. The following day radiation monitoring officers arrive on Rongelap, tell the people not to drink the water, and leave. On 3 March the Rongelap people and US weather staff on Rongerik are evacuated and the following day the Utrik people are moved.

April 1954: Rongerik, Rongelap and Ailinginae atolls are again contaminated, from the 'Union' test on Bikini.

May 1954: The above atolls plus the uninhabited Bikar atoll are showered with fallout from the 'Yankee' test at Bikini. The yield of both these bombs remains classified.

May 1954: The Rongelap people are moved to Ejit Island in Majuro atoll as Rongelap is still highly contaminated. The Utrik people, however, are told their atoll is safe and they can return.

May 1955: 'Operation Redwing' begins at Enewetak and Bikini: 17 atomic and hydrogen bombs are detonated over the next three months. 'Lacrosse' on Enewetak is 40 kilotons. Three hydrogen bombs tested on Bikini are: 'Cherokee' (21 May) described as 'several megatons'; 'Zuni' (28 May), 3.5 megatons; 'Tewa' (21 July), 5 megatons. No information on the other 13 bombs has been released.

July 1957: The Rongelap people are told their atoll is now safe for them to return home.

May 1958: 'Operation Hardtack', consisting of 32 nuclear tests, begins on Enewetak and Bikini and continues throughout August. Two hydrogen bombs are also exploded in the atmosphere above Johnston Island. The only information disclosed on the tests is the following: 'Cactus' (6 May), 18 kilotons; 'Koa' (13 May), 1.37 megatons; 'Oak' (29 June), 8.9 megatons. Ujelang atoll, now home of the displaced Enewetak people, together with the inhabited

256

Ailinginae and Wotho atolls, are contaminated with undisclosed levels of fallout during the tests, as are hundreds of US Navy personnel. In August the US announces that, after exploding 23 bombs on Bikini and 43 on Enewetak, it is concluding its atmospheric testing in the Pacific.

1959: The US Navy announces that a new use has been found for its base on Kwajalein atoll – as the site for Nike-Zeus anti-missile tests (said to be the forerunner of the current Strategic Defense Initiative).

1960: To make way for radar and tracking equipment, the inhabitants of Roi Namur Island in Kwajalein atoll are relocated to Ennubirr Island and to Ebeye (both also in Kwajalein atoll); like Ebeye, Ennubirr becomes an indigenous labour camp for the US military.

October 1961: The US Navy moves the people of Lib Island in Kwajalein atoll to Ebeye: Lib is named as the 'impact zone' for incoming Inter-Continental Ballistic Missiles fired from California.

January 1965: Marshallese living on 13 mid-corridor islands around the central two-thirds of Kwajalein lagoon – declared a new 'impact area' for missiles – are relocated to Ebeye.

June 1965: This new impact area means that Lib Island is now redundant and its residents are allowed to return after five years on Ebeye.

April 1969: A group of displaced people from Kwajalein atoll undertake the first of many 'sail-ins' back to their home islands to protest at their relocation and at the living conditions on Ebeye.

October 1972: The Atomic Energy Commission tells Bikinians that it has cleaned up the atoll sufficiently for them to return home: only three families believe that their home really is safe and set up house there again.

March 1978: Another major sail-in takes place.

September 1978: The families who had moved back to Bikini are hurriedly re-evacuated to Kili after tests showed they had absorbed large amounts of radioactive substances since their return. There was, for example, a 75 per cent increase in body levels of radioactive caesium.

July 1979: The people of Roi Namur reoccupy their island in protest at their displacement and lack of compensation.

October 1980: After fighting to have their atoll cleaned up, the people of Enewetak finally begin to return home. One island, Runit, is off-limits for ever: radioactive debris and soil from the various test sites on the atoll has been scraped up and dumped on the island, which

257

already has high levels of plutonium deposits. A vast concrete dome has been built over it, but the US Defense Nuclear Agency says it recognises that plutonium is expected to be 'released', nevertheless. Six months later, 100 people return to Ujelang, reporting that Enewetak's trees are not bearing fruit.

September 1983: The Marshall Islands vote narrowly to accept the Compact of Free Association.

June 1984: A missile fired from California is intercepted by one fired from Kwajelein: SDI is declared possible. Already the testing site for all long-range missiles (MX, Minuteman, Polaris), Kwajalein is deemed even more crucial to US military plans as the race for the militarisation of space gets under way.

1985: The Rongelap people move to Mejato, an island in Kwajalein atoll, with the help of Greenpeace, after making fruitless pleas for help to the US. Though Mejato has its own problems, the move is necessary because of continuing signs of radiation-linked ill-health.

Spring 1986: Ebeye residents organise another sail-in: this time the US asks the Marshall Islands government to send in police to remove protesters by force.

1986: President Reagan unilaterally ratifies the Compact without UN termination of the Trusteeship. Terms of the Compact mean the US is assured of use of Kwajalein virtually indefinitely; radiation survivors are given a lump sum but banned from taking their cases against the US Administration to US courts.

Source: *Marshall Islands, A Chronology 1944–81* Honolulu, Hawai'i, Micronesia Support Committee, 1981

258

The Organisation of Marshallese Society

A matrilineal society

Marshallese culture is matrilineal: land is handed down through the mother. But it has become customary for a woman who owns land to appoint a man to look after it – perhaps her brother or a grown-up son – who is known as the *alab*. So while women have a special relationship to the land and are potentially very powerful, in terms of day-to-day decision-making their power is often dormant.

Land and social relationships are also governed by a strict class system, described by Julian Riklon, a Marshallese translator and activist, as akin to feudal. Sarah Naptali, a great grandmother who owns land on Rongelap, explained:

> There are over 300 landowners on Rongelap. We have three classes of people amongst the landowners: the *iroij* (the kings), the *alab* (the nobles) and the *dri jerbal* (the workers). My mother owned the land before me. My brother is currently *alab* but before taking any major decision about the land he and the *iroij* must consult me. When my brother dies there is no one to take his place, so I will be *alab*.

Randy Thomas, mayor of the Rongelap people living on Mejato, explained how he understood the ancient law:

> If my older sister owned the land, I'd be the *alab* and she'd let me have all the power, because I'm a man; I'm more powerful and I can do everything. My sister would own it but I'm the one who'd take charge of everything. According to our custom, the woman talks to her brother and we have to listen to what she says. But in reality the woman would say – you can do whatever you want to because we've already given you the power.

259

Writing in the *Marshall Islands Guide Book*, Alik Alik talks of a dozen different types of other special land ownership. They include land given as a gift by the *iroij* to someone who had nursed or bathed them and land given by an *alab* who is the last in their family to someone who took care of them when they were too old to gather food themselves. If the recipient is a man, the land passes down through him but if he has a daughter it reverts to matrilineal descent.

These patterns of land ownership continue today but their complexity, together with the dwindling number of people who remember all the rules, has led to the establishment of a Traditional Rights Court. The system has been further complicated by westerners seizing or buying the land – which is of course outside the jurisdiction of the court.

Land is sacred to the Marshallese, both in a spiritual sense and in a very practical way – it is a scarce resource in a country made up of tiny flat islands and, along with the ocean, it is traditionally the life-support system of the people.

Electoral system

The election system now practised in the Marshall Islands is based on a combination of the British and the American models. A major concern expressed by some Marshallese, however, is that as it has been grafted onto the old structure, some people have managed to combine traditional power with elected power. (This isn't so different from other countries where many of those who enjoy elected positions are also influential in other ways – by virtue of wealth, class, positions in industry and commerce.) The President, Amata Kabua, consolidates both these forms of authority as he is also an *iroijlaplap* – a king of kings: he is regarded as fairly unshakeable.

Conflicting loyalties

One evening someone came into a Majuro bar with the news that President Kabua had just died of a heart attack. Two members of the Opposition were there: rather than thinking of any possible gain the Opposition might make, they were genuinely deeply distressed, saying that they were both distant relatives of the president. 'On a political platform I stand up and criticise him, but he is the *iroij* of my atoll and when it comes to harvest time I take him offerings.' The rumour proved to be unfounded. But as the two remarked, it highlighted their conflicting loyalties.

Glossary of Abbreviations and Nuclear Terms

ABM:	Anti-Ballistic Missile.
AEC:	Atomic Energy Commission (US).
ANZUS:	1951 South Pacific defence treaty between Australia, the US and Aotearoa/New Zealand which essentially collapsed in 1987 after the latter banned port visits by nuclear-armed ships.
DNA:	Defense Nuclear Agency (US).
DOD:	Department of Defense (US).
FLNKS:	Kanak Socialist National Liberation Front.
ICBM:	Inter-Continental Ballistic Missile.
ICRP:	International Committee on Radiological Protection.
INF:	Intermediate Nuclear Forces. Under the December 1987 INF agreement, the US and the Soviet Union agreed to destroy some 2,800 missiles (including cruise, and Soviet equivalents, Pershing 2s – but not the shorter-range Pershing 1As based in West Germany – plus Soviet SS-20s, SS-12s and SS-23s) on a three-year timetable, and to ban production of new land-based missiles between 500 and 5,000 kilometres in range. It does *not* cover sea- or air-launched weapons.
KAC:	Kwajalein Atoll Corporation, set up by the Kwajalein landowners to defend their rights and to share out fairly rent money paid by the US.
KADA:	Kwajalein Atoll Development, set up in response to one of the demands of Operation Homecoming, to handle capital-intensive development projects on Ebeye.
NFIP:	Nuclear Free and Independent Pacific movement.
RepMar:	Republic of the Marshall Islands, usually used to refer to the government thereof.
SDI:	Strategic Defense Initiative (also known as Star Wars).
USDA:	US Direct Aid

The units of radiation

The **dose of radiation** is measured in terms of the energy of the ionising radiation absorbed in tissue. The unit of dose is the **gray** (Gy). It corresponds to the absorption of 1 joule per kilogram of tissue. The old unit of dose is a **rad**, equal to one hundreth of a gray.

Radiation exposure is different. It is a measure of the ionising action of radiation on air (chosen as a standard substance because it is easy to measure). It is expressed in terms of the electric charge produced by the radiation in a given mass of air. The unit of exposure is the quantity of radiation which produces ions of a total charge of 1 coulomb in 1 kilogram of air. The old unit of exposure is a **roentgen** (R), still used on many instruments.

The relationship between the rad and the roentgen is complex. It depends on the physical properties of both the radiation and the medium through which it passes. But exposure to 1 roentgen gives rise to roughly 1 rad exposure, depending on the type of radiation and tissue exposed.

Radiation can be roughly divided into two groups, **low and high linear energy transfer** (LET). LET refers to the ionising powers of radiation. In general, for most practical purposes, the higher the LET, the greater the **relative biological effectiveness of the radiation** (RBE), also known as the **quality factor**. Alpha particles and neutrons are two examples of **high-LET** radiation, while beta rays, gamma rays and x-rays are low-LET.

The **dose equivalent** of radiation is the absorbed dose (in grays or rads) multiplied by the quality factor of the particular type of radiation. It is measured in **sieverts** (Sv). The old measurement is a rem: 1 Sv = 100 rem.

In addition to the dose itself, the **rate** at which it is delivered has an important bearing on the biological effects produced. When radiation time is short it is known as **acute** radiation; when it is over a long time it is **chronic** exposure.

Table of radiation units

Quantity	Present unit	Former Unit	Relation between them
Dose	gray (Gy)	rad	1 rad = 0.01 Gy
Dose equivalent	sievert (Sv)	rem	1 rem = 0.01 Sv
Exposure	(C kg^{-1})	roentgen (R)	1 R = 2.58 × 10^{-4}Ckg^{-1}
Activity	becquerel (Bq)	curie (Ci)	1 Ci = 3.7 × 10^{10}Bq

Information and table from SIPRI *Nuclear Radiation in Warfare* (London, Taylor & Francis Ltd., 1981) and Dr Martin Dace *Everything You Ever Wanted to Know About Radiation and Health* (London, Medical Campaign Against Nuclear Weapons, 1987).

Campaigning Guides

Books

Action Stations: The Directory of Social Action Programmes, It identifies television and radio programmes of specific interest to community groups and social welfare agencies. The Volunteer Centre UK, 29 Lower King's Road, Berkhamstead, Herts. HP4 2AB.

Making News, A readable guide to the media. Campaign for Press and Broadcasting Freedom, 9 Poland St., London W1V 3DG, 50p.

Organising Things, A guide to successful political action by Sue Ward. 1984 Pluto Press, £4.95.

Pressure: The A to Z of Campaigning in Britain, Des Wilson discusses how groups can bring effective pressure for change. 1984. Heinemann Education Books Ltd, 22 Bedford Sq., London WC1B 3HH.

Videos, tape-slides and films

General campaigning

Call for a change A guide to lobbying British MPs on foreign policy issues. 20 mins. 1985. Sale: £9.50. Hire: donation. From Audio and Visuals Unit, Oxfam, 274 Banbury Rd, Oxford OX2 7DZ. Tel: 0865-56777.

Making news Primer for working with the media. 14 mins. VHS. 1986. Sale: £9.50. Hire: donation. From Oxfam, as above.

Pacific

Nightmare in Paradise Overview of nuclear and colonial activities in the Pacific. 20 min. Video or tape-slide. Tape-slide sale: £20. From Lynda Medwell, Birchwood Hall, Storridge, near Malvern, Worcs. Cheques payable to 'Women for Life on Earth/Malvern'. Video sale: £30. From Concorde Films, 201 Felixstowe Rd, Ipswich,

Suffolk. Tel: 0274-76012. Video or tape-slide hire from Carmel Cadden, 52 Butler House, Wallwood St, London E14 7AB. Tel: 01-515-0490.

The Peacemaker, Nuclear Lagoon, Our Way, Pine Gap (assorted Pacific videos) plus videos of Pacific women's speaking tours also available from Carmel Cadden as above.

Half Life Australian film about nuclear explosions in the Marshall Islands. 1986. Video. Hire: £15 from The Other Cinema, 79 Wardour St, London W1.

Useful Addresses

Pacific Islands

Belau: Roman Bedor, Belau Pacific Centre, PO Box 58, Koror, Belau 96940; tel 745

Fiji: Fiji Anti Nuclear Group and Pacific Council of Churches, c/o Judith Denaro, PO Box 208, Suva; tel 311277

Marianas Islands: Chailang Palacios, PO Box 2025, Saipan, Commonwealth of Northern Marianas

Marshall Islands
Rongelap people
on Majuro: Senator Jeton Anjain, PO Box 1006, Majuro, Marshall Islands 96960; tel via Abacca Anjain, Majuro 3225
on Mejato: Renam Anjain, c/o PO Box 5573, Ebeye, Marshall Islands 96970
on Ebeye: Lijon Eknilang, PO Box 5813, Marshall Islands 96970
Rongelap Resettlement Fund c/o Julian Riklon, PO Box 5573, Ebeye, Marshall Islands 96970; tel Ebeye 3187
Kwajalein people c/o Julian Riklon, address above

Hawai'i
American Friends Service Committee, 2628 O'ahu Avenue, Honolulu, Hawai'i; tel 808-9886266 (Quaker-based peace movement)
Pacific Campaign Against Sea-Launched Cruise Missiles, c/o Nelson Foster, 2257 Makanani Drive, Hawai'i 96817; tel 808-8456328
Protect Kaho'olawe 'Ohana, c/o Emmett Aluli, PO Box H, Kaunakakai, Molokai, Hawai'i 96748; tel 808-5588291 (Hawaiian civil and land rights)

Pacific Rim

Aotearoa/New Zealand: Pacific Peoples Anti-Nuclear Action Committee, PO Box 61086, Otara, Auckland, Aotearoa

Australia: NFIP Co-ordinating Committee, PO Box 391, Sydney South 2000 NSW, Australia

Canada: South Pacific Peoples Foundation, 407–620 View St, Victoria, British Colombia V8W 1J6, Canada; tel 604-3814131

Hongkong: Trini Leung, Asia Monitor Centre, 444 Nathan RD 8-B, Kowloon, Hongkong; tel 3-885319

Japan: Gensuikin, 4th Floor Akimoto Building, 2–19 Tsukasa-cho, Kanda, Chiyoda-ku, Tokyo; tel 03-2943994

United States: Micronesian Coalition, 475 Riverside Drive, Room 616, New York, New York 10015; tel 212-8073202

Pacific Resource Co-ordinator, United Methodist Office for the United Nations, 777 United Nations Plaza, New York, New York 10017; tel 212-6823633

European Nuclear Free and Independent Pacific Support Groups

Britain: Rongelap Resettlement Fund, Donations to 'Pacific Fund' a/c S92846 DEL, Newbury Building Society, 17–20 Bartholomew Street, Newbury, Berkshire RG14 5LY, England

Women Working for a Nuclear Free and Independent Pacific, Bulletin and information from Diana Shanks, 10 The Drive, New Costessey, Norwich NR5 0EF, England (originally a Greenham Common peace camp initiative, now a network with speakers and groups around Britain)

Denmark: Martine Petrod, Solvgade 86 st Th, 1307 Copenhagen K, Denmark; tel 131203

Germany: Brigitt Koch, Atomwaffen Freies Europa, Goltzstr 13b, 1000 Berlin 30; tel 30-2161894

Netherlands: Madaleen Helmer, Voorstadslaan 49, 6541 AB Nymegen, Netherlands; tel 080-780-882

Sweden: Women for Peace, Pakhusgrand, S-111, 30, Stockholm, Sweden

Other Interested Groups

Aboriginal Land Rights Support Group, 19c Lancaster Road, London W11 1QL; tel 01 221 4585

Australian Council of Churches, PO Box C199, Clarence St, Sydney NSW 2000 Australia

Australian Development Assistance Bureau, PO Box 887, Canberra, ACT 2601 Australia

CIMRA (Colonialism and Indigenous Minorities Research and Action), 218 Liverpool Road, London N1; tel 01 609 1852

CND (National Office), 22–24 Underwood Street, London N1; tel 01 250 4010

Christian Aid (A Division of British Council of Churches) PO Box 100, London SE1 7RT, England; tel 01 620 4444

Evangelische Studenten Gemeinde, Annette Groth, Kniebisstrasse 29, 7000 Stuttgart 1, West Germany

Friends of the Earth, 26–28 Underwood Street, London N1; tel 01 490 1555

Greenpeace, 30 Islington Green, London N1; tel 01 354 5100

ICCO, PO Box 151, Zeist, Netherlands; tel 03404 24844

IKV, Postbus 18747, 2502 ES, The Hague, Netherlands; tel 070 469756

The Minority Rights Group, 29 Craven Street, London WC2N 5NT

NOVIB (Netherlands Organisation for International Development), Amaliastr. 7, 2514 JC, The Hague, Netherlands; tel 070 624081

X–Y, Amaliastr. 7, 2514 JC, The Hague, Netherlands; tel 070 645433

World Council of Churches, 150 Route de Ferney, 1211 Geneva 20, Switzerland

In the United States

American Friends Service Committee, 1501 Cherry Street, Philadelphia, PA 19102; 215-241-7171. Their brochure, *For a Nuclear Free and Independent Pacific,* a guide to US and Canadian organizations, costs fifty cents a copy.

Greenpeace, 1436 U Street NW, Washington, DC 20009; tel 202-462-1177

War Resisters League, 339 Lafayette Street, New York, NY 10012; tel 212-228-0450.

The People's Charter for a Nuclear Free and Independent Pacific

PREAMBLE:

1.
We, the people of the Pacific want to make our position clear. The Pacific is home to millions of people with distinct cultures, religions and ways of life, and we refuse to be abused or ignored any longer.

2.
We, the people of the Pacific, have been victimised too long by foreign powers. The western imperialistic and colonial powers invaded our defenceless region, they took over our lands and subjugated our people to their whims. This form of alien colonial political and military domination unfortunately persists as an evil cancer in some of our native territories such as Tahiti-Polynesia, Kanaky, Australia and Aotearoa. Our environment continues to be despoiled by foreign powers developing nuclear weapons for a strategy of warfare that has no winners, no liberators and imperils the survival of all humankind.

3.
We, the people of the Pacific will assert ourselves and wrest control over the destiny of our nations and our environment from foreign powers, including the Transnational Corporations.

4.
We note in particular the recent racist roots of the world's nuclear powers and we call for an immediate end to the oppression, exploitation and subordination of the indigenous people of the Pacific.

5.
Our environment is further threatened by the continuing deployment of nuclear arsenals in the so called strategic areas throughout the Pacific. Only one nuclear submarine has to be lost in the sea, or one nuclear warhead dumped in our ocean from a stricken bomber and the

threat to the fish, and our livelihood is endangered for centuries. The erection of superports, military bases, and nuclear testing stations may bring employment, but the price is destruction of our customs, our way of life, the pollution of our crystal clear waters and brings the ever present threat of disaster by radioactive poisoning into the every day life of the peoples.

6.

We, the people of the Pacific reaffirm our intention to extract only those elements of western civilisation that will be of a permanent benefit to us. We wish to control our destinies and protect our environment in our own ways. Our usage of our natural resources in the past was more than adequate to ensure the balance between nature and humankind. No form of administration should ever seek to destroy that balance for the sake of a brief commercial gain.

Suggestions for Action

Many of these suggestions came out of the 1987 Nuclear Free and Independent Pacific Conference in Manila.

Global Triple Zero
The INF deal signed by President Reagan and General Secretary Gorbachev in December 1987 was named 'Global Double Zero' because it includes the long- and short-range intermediate nuclear forces in Europe and Asia. The political climate for the deal was created in part as a result of peace movements bringing about a new public awareness of the dangers of the nuclear arms race, as well as major shifts in the Soviet outlook. It is a victory – but only a very partial one, as the agreement leaves untouched the increasing deployment of sea-launched cruise missiles (SLCMs). By 1992 the US military plans to deploy 758 nuclear SLCMs. The Soviet Union is poised to reply by deploying its counterpart, the SS-NX-21 and SS-NX-24. British Defence Secretary George Younger has admitted that NATO may consider redeploying at sea the cruise missiles scrapped under the INF deal signed in December 1987. Although almost a third of all nuclear weapons are based at sea, on ships and submarines, they are not covered by any arms agreement.

The numbers of sea-launched missiles in the Pacific will thus increase dramatically. As this book shows, militarisation of the Pacific Ocean has resulted in an intensifying of colonialism and denial of the sovereignty of the Pacific people. It also places them in the immediate firing line in the case of a nuclear war. The NFIP is emphasising the need to campaign against the arms race at sea (demanding Global *Triple* Zero) with an emphasis on the issues for the Pacific as well as the Atlantic.

Micronesia
Britain, as well as the US, is particularly caught up in Belau via IPSECO and the credit arrangements (see Chapter Nine). The UN is supposed

271

to have ensured that the US honoured its commitment to Micronesia during the Trusteeship, which plainly it hasn't. Letters of protest can be directed to all UN member countries and particularly to France and Britain which, as members of the Security Council, have consistently chosen to ignore the treatment of Micronesia. Letters to the UN *have* to be minuted, so it is well worth writing to protest that the US violated the UN guidelines in spirit and practice.

SDI/Star Wars
It has always been questionable whether President Reagan's dream of the Strategic Defense Initiative (SDI) would ever work, despite the fact that it has been through various guises, from a protective shield over the whole of the US, to a shield over the Soviet Union to stop it launching its own weapons, to some kind of defence of US missile sites only (it was soon admitted that it would be impossible to defend cities and people, given that they are not under protective silos).

If, as some observers hope, the INF deal heralds the possibility of a period of East–West detente and further arms agreements, SDI may become the subject of superpower negotiations and not simply as a ploy to block Soviet agreement. However, it has been presented to the public as a *defensive* weapons-system (even though it would be destabilising – tempting the possessor to go for first strike if they thought they could protect their missiles from retaliation) and there is less widespread public pressure to negotiate it away.

Meanwhile, General Secretary Gorbachev has said that the Soviet Union is to develop its own version of SDI. The forerunner of SDI was the anti-ballistic missile systems, (ABMs) developed in the 1960s by both superpowers (the US tested one such system, Nike-Zeus, at Kwajelein in the early 60s). ABMs were outlawed by a superpower treaty in 1972 but in the present climate the USSR will be bringing its previously developed systems out of cold storage.

Whatever the long-term prognosis, in the short term there is no doubt that SDI component research will proceed in both countries. US budget forecasts reveal the project will receive heavy funding. It is estimated that the cost of researching SDI will be something in the region of $32 billion by 1990. Projections of the cost of deployment range from $400 billion to $1 trillion and above. The cost of operating will, at conservative estimates, run at $90 billion a year. Additional air and coastal defences to cover some of the gaping holes left by SDI will cost around $5 billion a year.

Kwajalein will be involved in testing three out of six 'new technologies' being investigated for Star Wars: the ground-based surveillance and tracking system (GSATS); the space-based interceptor (SBI) and the exoatmospheric re-entry vehicle interception system; the testing of most of these systems will contravene the ABM treaty.

Other Pacific sites are also involved in the research for SDI components. At Haleakala Mountain and other places in Hawai'i, the 'mid-course' phase of missiles are observed as they head from California towards Kwajalein. And if the US goes ahead with the development of electromagnetic pulse weaponry against satellites and missiles it will require a resumption of nuclear testing in space, in violation of treaties covering nuclear tests and outer space. Johnson Islands, in the Pacific, are perhaps the most likely site for this as facilities are already maintained there – and the US would expect strong domestic dissent if it tried to use the Nevada site.

The Pentagon has conducted preliminary environmental impact assessments of SDI testing on the 15 selected sites. Its conclusion was that the only adverse damage would be to Kwajalein: the social structure of the atoll will be put under additional strain as the US population is expected to increase from 2,600 to 5,000 by 1990. Continued dredging and construction work is expected to further damage the fragile atoll ecology.

It is important that groups in countries which have agreed to collaborate on Star Wars (Britain, W. Germany, Japan, etc.) raise public awareness by making the case against it both in terms of it being destabilising (see E.P. Thompson, ed., *Star Wars*) and in terms of the everyday human cost to the Marshallese people living around Kwajalein Missile Range.

Indeed, while many people are now conscious of the environmental impact of nuclear testing, the role of missile testing in increasing the momentum of the arms race goes largely unnoticed. Testing of new missiles leads to improvements in accuracy, range, payload, reliability, manoeuvrability and invulnerability. A treaty dealing with missile testing (or unilateral pledges to stop missile testing) is needed, as well as a comprehensive Test Ban Treaty to include underground and subaqua explosions.

Australian Bicentennial

This book is being published in 1988, the year that much of white Australia celebrates Captain Cook's arrival. During the celebrations Aboriginal people will be mourning the loss of their land 200 years ago and protesting two centuries of a denial of their civil rights. They will also be demanding that the Australian government implement a uniform land rights legislation for Aboriginal people and they ask groups around the world to do likewise at the Australian embassy or consulate in their country.

Treaty of Waitangi
In 1990 the government of Aotearoa/New Zealand celebrates 150 years since the signing of the Treaty of Waitangi (see p. 228). The hosting of the Commonwealth Games there in 1990 forms part of the celebrations. Maori groups are also asking for protests outside embassies and for people to use the publicity surrounding the Games to highlight what has happened.

Rarotonga Treaty
Britain, the US and France have refused to sign the protocols of the Rarotonga Treaty for a South Pacific Nuclear Free Zone. Although this treaty is rather weak (see Chapter 11) it is nevertheless a useful lever for the island nations to assert their rights. Groups in Britain, the US and France can put pressure on their governments to sign by making public their refusal to respect the wishes of the Pacific countries.

RIMPAC
Every three years NATO and allied navies take part in RIMPAC war games around Hawai'i (see Chapter 11). Hawaiian people ask groups in these countries to campaign for an end to RIMPAC exercises and particularly for the US and Canadian armed forces to stop shelling the sacred island of Kaho'olawe and to ensure that other countries do not join them in the bombardment.

London Dumping Convention
Japan, Britain, the US and France, in particular, are working to lift the current moratorium on the dumping of nuclear waste in the ocean. Japan and the US would still like to use the Marianas Trench in the North Pacific for dumping. They are expected to stage a bid to reverse the ban at the London Dumping Convention in the autumn of 1988 – and if they don't succeed then, to try again in the future. Transport unions internationally have been a vital partner in opposing the dumping and groups can work with them to ensure the ban stays in place.

The European Community
While pro-nuclear governments are still in place in Britain, France and West Germany (Mrs Thatcher endorsed the December 1987 INF

Treaty, but has said she is not willing to negotiate away British nuclear arms) it is difficult for groups in these countries to make headway in their own parliaments. However, it is sometimes possible to bring issues to the attention of the European Parliament and put pressure in this forum on national governments. The European Greens and some socialists are trying to embarrass France into changing its policies on testing and civil rights in Polynesia. British readers can also write to or contact their local MEP about the proposed nuclear collaboration between France and Britain which would, among other things, indirectly involve Britain in the Moruroa testing.

Bibliography

Jim Albertini, Nelson Foster, Wally Inglis and Gil Roeder, *The Dark Side of Paradise: Hawaii in a Nuclear World*, Honolulu, Catholic Action of Hawaii/Peace Education Project, 1980

Asia and Pacific Review: 1987 Economic and Business Report, Saffron Walden: World of Information, 1986

Dr Rosalie Bertell, *No Immediate Danger: Prognosis for a Radioactive Earth*, London, The Women's Press, 1985

Dr Martin Dace, *Everything You Ever Wanted To Know About Radiation and Health (But Couldn't Find Anyone To Ask)*, London, Medical Campaign against Nuclear Weapons, 1987

Miriam Dornoy, *Politics in New Caledonia*, Sydney, University Press, 1984

Cynthia Enloe, *Does Khaki Become You?: The Militarisation of Women's Lives*, London, Pluto Press, 1983

Jim Falk, *Global Fission: The Battle Over Nuclear Power*, Oxford, Oxford University Press, 1982

Joseph Gerson, ed., *The Deadly Connection: Nuclear War and US Intervention*, Cambridge, Massachusetts, American Friends Service Committee, 1982

Dennis Hayes, Jim Falk and Neil Barrett, *Red Light For Yellow Cake: The Case Against Uranium Mining*, Sydney, Friends of the Earth Australia, 1977

Peter Hayes, Lyuba Zarsky and Walden Bello, *American Lake: Nuclear Peril In The Pacific*, Harmondsworth, Penguin, 1986

Francis X. Hexel, *The First Taint Of Civilization: A History Of The Caroline And Marshall Islands In Pre-Colonial Days, 1521-1885*, Hawaii, University of Hawaii Press, 1983

Kumari Jayawardena, *Feminism and the Third World*, London, Zed Press, 1986

Giff Johnson, *Collision Course at Kwajelein: Marshall Islanders In The Shadow Of The Bomb*, Honolulu, Pacific Concerns Resource Centre, 1984

Mary Kaldor, *The Disintegrating West*, London, Allen Lane, 1978

Michael King, *Death Of The Rainbow Warrior*, Harmondsworth, Penguin, 1986

Marshall Islands Guidebook, Micronitor News and Printing Company, Majuro, Marshall Islands, 1984

Donald F. McHenry, *Micronesia: Trust Beyond*, Washington, DC, Carnegie Endowment for International Peace, 1975

Malcolm McIntosh, *Arms Across the Pacific*, London, Pinter, 1987.

Micronesia Support Committee, *Marshall Islands, a Chronology 1944–81*, Honolulu, 1981

Robert Milliken, *No Conceivable Injury*, Harmondsworth, Penguin, 1986

David Pitt and Gordon Thompson eds, *Nuclear Free Zones*, London, Croom Helm, 1987

Peter Pringle and James Spiegelman, *The Nuclear Barons*, London, Michael Joseph, 1982

David Robie, *Eyes of Fire: The Last Voyage of the Rainbow Warrior*, Philadelphia, New Society Publishers, 1987

Joanna Rogers Macy, *Despair and Personal Power In The Nuclear Age*, Philadelphia, New Society Publishers, 1983

Howard L. Rosenberg, *American Victims Of Nuclear Experiments*, New York, Beacon Press, 1980

SIPRI, *Nuclear Radiation in Warfare*, London, Taylor & Francis Ltd, 1981

SIPRI Yearbook 1987, *World Armaments and Disarmament*, Oxford University Press, 1987

Joan Smith, *Clouds of Deceit: The Deadly Legacy of Britain's Bomb Tests*, London, Faber & Faber, 1985

E P Thompson, ed., *Star Wars*, Harmondsworth, Penguin, 1985

Paul Todd and 'Raven', *Arming and Disarming the Indian Ocean*, London, Campaign for the Demilitarisation of the Indian Ocean

Hiromitsu Toyasa, *Goodbye to Rongelap*, Tokyo, TsEukiji Shokan Publishing, 1986

Judy Wilks, *Field of Thunder: The Maralinga Story*, Sydney, Friends of The Earth Australia, 1981

Peter Worsley and Kofi Buenor Hadjor, eds., *On the Brink: Nuclear Proliferation and the Third World*, London, Third World Communications, 1987

Women Working for a Nuclear Free and Independent Pacific, ed., *Why Haven't You Known? Pacific Women Speak*, Oxford, Green Line, 1987

Women Working for a Nuclear Free and Independent Pacific, ed., *Pacific Paradise, Nuclear Nightmare*, London, CND, 1987

277

Notes

1 Quoted in Michael King, *Death of the Rainbow Warrior*, Harmondsworth, Penguin, 1980.
2 Quoted in Donald F. McHenry, *Micronesia: Trust Betrayed*, Washington DC, Carnegie Endowment for International Peace, 1975.

Chapter One
1 Harold Jackson, *Guardian*, 15 July 1984, 'Victims of the Nuclear Colonists'.
2 Owen Wilkes, NFIP Conference, 1983.
3 *Philadelphia Enquirer*, 4 August 1985 'US grip on Micronesia may be loosening'.
4 *Washington Times*, 26 June 1985, 'Short Leash for Micronesia Imperils "Star Wars" Defense'.
5 Richard Falk, *New Statesman* 18–25 December 1987, 'The Eclipse of Europe'.
6 June Jordan, *On Call* , London, Pluto Press, 1986.

Chapter Two
1 Women Working for an Independent and Nuclear Free Pacific, *Why Haven't You Known? Pacific Women Speak*, Green Line, 1987, p. 11.
2 From Francis X. Hezel, *The First Taint of Civilization*, University of Hawaii Press, 1983.
3 Chailang Palacios in *Why Haven't You Known?* op cit., p. 11.
4 Quoted in the introduction to Catherine Lutz, ed., *Micronesia as a Strategic Colony: the Impact of US Policy on Micronesian Health and Culture*, 1984, Cultural Survival Inc.
5 Carl Hager, *Die Marshall Inseln in Erd und Volkerkunde, Handel und Mission*, 1886.
6 Carl Heine, *Micronesia at the Crossroads*, University of Hawaii and East West Centre Publications, 1974; Glenn Alcalay, 'From

Subsistence to USDA: Strategic Economic Dependency In Micronesia', paper for the Department of Anthropology, Rutgers University, June 1986, p. 7.

7   Civil Affairs Handbooks, The Office of the Chief of Naval Operations, Navy Department, 1944.

8   Tadao Yanaihara, *Pacific Islands Under Japanese Mandate*, Boston, Harvard University Press, 1940; Alcalay, op. cit., p. 7.

9   ibid; Alcalay, op. cit., p. 10.

10 *Why Haven't You Known?* op. cit., p. 11.

11 *National Geographic*, September 1945, 'Our New Military Wards, The Marshalls: The Marshallese Are Happy Again'.

12 'The Battle of Kwajalein – a history', from BTL Public Relations Office, Kwajalein Field Station.

13 Mary M. Kearney, 'Micronesia II: History of Land Use by the United States in Kwajalein Atoll', May 1981, unpublished memorandum, p. 31.

14 'The Battle of Kwajalein', op. cit.

15 Donald F. McHenry, *Micronesia: Trust Betrayed*, Carnegie Endowment for International Peace, 1975.

16 *Why Haven't You Known?* op. cit., p. 12.

17 Quoted in Donald F. McHenry, *Micronesia: Trust Betrayed*, op. cit.

Chapter Three

1   Jonathan Weisgall, 'The Nuclear Nomads of Bikini', *Foreign Policy* no. 39, Summer 1980, p. 76.

2   ibid.

3   ibid.

4   ibid.

5   ibid., p. 78.

6   ibid., p. 79.

7   ibid., p. 80.

8   ibid.

9   ibid.

10 ibid.

11 ibid., p. 81.

12 Micronesia Support Committee, Hawai'i, *Marshall Islands: A Chronology 1944–81*, 1981, p. 11.

13 'The Effects of Nuclear Weapons', US Defense Department, 1957.

14 Glenn Alcalay, 'Cultural Impact of the US Atomic Testing

Program Marshall Islands Field Report (March 4–April 7, 1981)', Rutgers University, paper for graduate programme in anthropology, p. 21.

15 *Marshall Islands: A Chronology*, op. cit., p. 10.

16 *Marshall Islands Journal*, 1 February 1986.

17 Glenn Alcalay, 1981, op. cit., p. 117.

18 ibid., p. 8.

19 ibid., p. 8.

20 ibid., p. 4.

21 US Department of Energy, 1978 study, published 1982.

22 Alcalay, 1981, op. cit., p. 21.

23 Robert A. Conard, MD, *et al.*, 'A Twenty Year Review of Medical Findings in a Marshallese Population Accidentally Exposed to Radioactive Fallout', Brookhaven National Laboratories, 1975, p. 1.

24 Oxford biologist Irene Ridge says that the disappearance of the arrowroot is perplexing: mutation does not usually happen in such a uniform way.

25 'Three Year Report: Medical Status of Marshallese Accidentally Exposed to 1954 Bravo Fallout', Brookhaven National Laboratories.

26 Glenn Alcalay, 1981, op. cit., p. 14.

27 ibid., p. 20.

28 ibid., p. 25.

29 ibid., p. 5.

30 *Why Haven't You Known?* op. cit., p. 8.

31 Committee for the Compilation of Materials on Damage Caused by the Atomic Bombs in Hiroshima and Nagasaki, *Hiroshima and Nagasaki*, Hutchinson, 1981, p. 222.

32 ibid., p. 222.

33 United Nations Scientific Committee on the Effects of Atomic Radiation, Sources and Effects of Ionizing Radiation', UN, New York, 1977 (UNSCEAR 1977). Introduction.

34 Conard, op. cit., preface, p. vii.

35 Dr R.H. Mole, 'Radiation Effects on Pre-Natal Development and their Radiological Significance', *British Journal of Radiology*, 52 (1979), p. 614.

36 Rosalie Bertell, *No Immediate Danger*, The Women's Press, 1985, p. 47.

37 Conard, op. cit., p. 35.

38 ibid., p. 73.

39 Alcalay, 1981, op. cit., p. 21.

40 *Half Life*, film by Dennis O'Rourke, Sydney, 1984.
41 Martin Dace, *Health Care Aspects of Civil Defence*, London, Medical Campaign Against Nuclear Weapons.
42 Alcalay, op. cit., p. 17.
43 ibid., p. 5.
44 ibid., p. 5.
45 ibid., p. 18.
46 Gensuikin (Japanese Congress Against A&H Bombs), 'Report on the investigation of damage done by the Bikini hydrogen bomb test to the people of the Marshall Islands', February 1973.
47 Hansard, 9 May 1986, col. 293.
48 Gensuikin, op. cit.
49 Dr Martin Dace, *Everything you wanted to know about Radiation and Health (but couldn't find anyone to ask)*, Medical Campaign against Nuclear Weapons, 1987, p. 43.
50 Reuben Merliss, MD, 15 July 1980, unpublished paper, 'Marshall Islands Report'.
51 *The New England Journal of Medical Science*, 23 June 1966.
52 Merliss, op. cit.
53 Symposium for the American Association for the Advancement of Science (AASS), San Francisco, 7 January 1980, 'Ethno-epidemiology: The Marshall islanders, 25 years after exposure to radiation'. See also Dr John Gofman, *Radiation and Human Health*, Sierra Club Books, 1981.
54 House Interior Subcommittee on Public Lands and National Parks, 14 March 1984.
55 Alcalay, 1981, op. cit., p. 19.
56 ibid., p. 21.
57 ibid., p. 8.
58 Merliss, op. cit.
59 Konrad Kotrady, 'The Brookhaven medical program to detect radiation effects in Marshallese people: A comparison of the people's vs. the program's attitudes', 1 January 1977, unpublished paper.
60 ibid.
61 Subcommittee on Public Lands and National Parks of the House Committee on Interior and Insular Affairs.
62 Karl Z. Morgan was director of the Health Physics Division of Oak Ridge National Laboratory from 1943–73 and was then Professor in the School of Nuclear Engineering and Health Physics of the Georgia Institute of Technology until 1982. For a

quarter of a century, until 1972, he had chaired the Internal Dose Committee of both the National Council on Radiation Protection and the International Commission on Radiological Protection, which set the standards for occupational exposure to the various radio-isotopes.

63 Karl Z. Morgan, 'Consequences of radiation exposure to persons reinhabiting the northern Marshall Islands which were contaminated during the period of testing of nuclear weapons', unpublished paper.

64 Kotrady, op. cit.

65 Robert A. Conard, MD, *et al.*, 'Review of medical findings in a Marshallese population 26 years after accidental exposure to radioactive fallout', Brookhaven National Laboratory, January 1980.

66 Quoted in Glenn Alcalay, 'Nuclear Specter in the Marshalls', Newsletter of the Asian Cultural Forum on Development, July/August 1982.

67 Dace, op. cit., Table III.

68 Thomas Hamilton, 'Preliminary Report on the Rongelapese People: Health Effects from Fallout'.

69 Quoted by Jeton Anjain before the House Committee on Interior and Insular Affairs Subcommittee on Public Lands and National Parks, 8 May 1984.

70 ibid.

71 Glenn Alcalay, 'Maelstrom in the Marshall islands: the social impact of nuclear weapons testing', in Catherine Lutz, ed., *Micronesia as a Strategic Colony; the Impact of US Policy on Micronesian Health and Culture*, 1984, Cultural Survival Inc., p. 31.

72 *New York Times*, 20 September 1982.

73 DNA 6035F/Operation Castle/April 1 1982.

74 Alcalay, in Lutz, op. cit., p. 34.

75 US Department of Energy, *Radiological Survey Plan for the Northern Marshall Islands*, 1978 (released 1982).

76 'US Irradiated Humans for Nuclear War Data', *Counterspy*, September–November 1982.

Chapter Four

1 Senator Jeton Anjain to Foreign Affairs Subcommittee on East Asia and Pacific, 11 April 1985.

2 Johnsay Riklon to House Interior Subcommittee on Public Lands and National Parks, 14 March 1984.
3 Senator Anjain, April 1985, as note 1 above.
4 Hiromitsu Toyosaki, *Goodbye to Rongelap*, TsEukiji Shokan Publishing, Tokyo, 1986.

Chapter Five
1 Bell Laboratories, 'Kwajalein Field Station', report prepared for Ballistic Missile Defense Systems Command, October 1975.
2 Stanford Research Institute, 'Environmental Impact Assessment of Kwajalein Missile Range Operations', report prepared for Kwajalein Missile Range Directorate, Ballistic Missile Defense Systems Command, Huntsville Alabama, August 1975.
3 Micronesia Support Committee, *Marshall Islands: A Chronology, 1944–81*, Honolulu, 1981.
4 Kabua Kabua, *et al.*, *vs.* United States of America, US Court of Claims Petition No. 119–75, 1975, p. 9.
5 *Philadelphia Enquirer*, June 15 1979, 'Islands May Shut Missile Test Base'.
6 Statement by Senator Imada Kabua, 19 April 1982, quoted in Lee Gomes, 'Kwajelein will vote on missile test issue', *Honolulu Star-Bulletin*, 20 April 1982.
7 *Marshall Islands Journal*, 30 April 1982, 'Zeder accuses KAC of cheap shot'.
8 Konrad Kotrady MD to US House of Representatives Subcommittee on Territorial and Insular Affairs, 13 July 1976.
9 Giff Johnson, 'Occupying Kwajelein', *Pacific Islands Monthly*, 19 September 1979.
10 *Wall Street Journal*, 9 July 1982.
11 'Contradictory to our belief', in *Sojourners* magazine, 18 August 1983.
12 *Marshall Islands Journal*, 24 August 1982.
13 *Marshall Islands Journal*, 18 August 1982.
14 *Marshall Islands Journal*, 9 September 1982.
15 Giff Johnson, 'Protests at the missile range', *Islands Business Magazine*, June 1986.
16 *Marshall Islands Journal*, 25 April 1986.
17 *Marshall Islands Journal*, 8 May 1986.
18 *Marshall Islands Journal*, 8 May 1986.

Chapter Six

1   See, for example, Andrew Veitch, 'Unemployment is blamed for 3,000 deaths a year', *Guardian*, 17 September 1987: Veitch quotes Dr Richard Smith, assistant editor of the *British Medical Journal* predicting at least 3,000 deaths a year among unemployed men (no statistics for unemployed women or the families of unemployed men). According to government statistics (the Office of Population Censuses and Surveys) unemployed men are 40 per cent more likely to die of cancer and twice as likely to commit suicide as the rest of the population. Surveys showed they were generally more likely to need medical help and be referred to hospital for treatment.

2   *Gugeegue and Carlson Development – Ebeye Redevelopment*, Saipan: Trust Territory of the Pacific Islands, Office of Planning and Statistics, November 1978 (generally known as and hereafter referred to as the Ebeye Redevelopment Study); Giff Johnson, 'Protests at the missile range', *Islands Business Magazine*, June 1986, p. 20.

3   Nachsa Siren and Donna L. Scheuring, 'Murky Waters of Micronesia: A Bacteriological Water Pollution Survey of Micronesia', Trust Territory of the Pacific Islands, Department of Health Services, March 1970; Johnson, op. cit., p. 24.

4   Johnson, op. cit., p. 22.

5   Cited by Greg Dever MD, 'Ebeye, Marshall Islands: A Public Health Hazard', Micronesia Support Committee Report, July 1978; Johnson, op. cit., p. 20.

6   The Ebeye Redevelopment Study, op. cit., p. 16.

7   'Kwajelein Missile Range', a brochure 'prepared by staff of KMR headquarters, 1982'.

8   Commission of Churches on International Affairs, *Marshall Islands 37 Years After: Report of a World Council of Churches Delegation to the Marshall Islands, May 20–June 4, 1983*, #5, Geneva, World Council of Churches, p. 17; Johnson, op. cit., p. 21.

9   ibid.

10 *Marshall Islands Journal*, 1 February 1986.

11 Dr Rosalie Bertell, paper at May 1984 Stockholm Conference of Oceanologists, quoting a study by Dr Takhesi Yasumoto, Professor of Food Hygiene, Faculty of Agriculture, University of Tokyo, and reprinted in *Emergency* No. 4. Further developed in conversation between Dr Bertell and the author.

12 Michael Mecham, 'Tensions are Rising in "War of Wills" at Kwajelein', *Honolulu Star-Bulletin*, July 5 1982; Johnson, op. cit., p. 25.

13 *Marshall Islands Journal*, 27 March 1987.

14 Wellington *Evening Post*, 12 January 1988.

15 Reuben Merliss, 'Marshall Islands Report', 15 July 1980, unpublished paper.

16 *Marshall Islands Journal*, 5 September 1986.

17 Johnson, op. cit., p. 23, quoting William Alexander.

18 Paul Jacobs, 'The Natives are Forbidden to Shop on US Administered Pacific Island', *Newsday*, 13 February 1977; Johnson, op. cit., p. 23.

19 David Robie, 'Taking on the Big Guns', *NZ Listener*, 1 February 1986, p. 20.

Chapter Seven

1 Women Working for a Nuclear Free and Independent Pacific, ed., *Why Haven't You Known? Pacific Women Speak*, Green Line, Oxford, 1987, p. 12.

2 RepMar paper, 'National Measures to Improve the Socio-Economic Status of Women', 1985.

3 Vanessa Griffen, 'The Pacific Islands: All It Requires Is Ourselves', in *Sisterhood is Global*, ed. Robin Morgan, Penguin, Harmondsworth, 1985, p. 526.

Chapter Eight

1 Roger Gale, 'The Americanization of Micronesia: A Study in the Consolidation of US Rule in The Pacific', Washington, University Press of America, 1979; Glenn Alcalay, 'From Subsistence to USDA: Strategic Economic Dependency in Micronesia', paper for the Department of Anthropology, Graduate Faculty of Political and Social Science, Rutgers University, New York, June 1986.

2 Anthony Solomon, 'Report by the US government Survey Mission to the Trust Territory of the Pacific Islands', The White House, Washington DC, 9 October 1963, S–2, referring to NSAM 145.

3 Solomon, op. cit. Unless otherwise specified, all subsequent quotations are from the Solomon Report.

4 Donald F. McHenry, *Micronesia: Trust Betrayed*, Washington, Carnegie Endowment for Peace, 1975, p. 28.

5 Robert Kiste, 'American Rule In Micronesia: Where Have All The Dollars Gone?', unpublished paper, Honolulu: East West Centre, 1981; Alcalay, 1986, op. cit.

6 William Vitarelli, 'US Educational Policies in Micronesia' in Catherine Lutz, ed., *Micronesia as a Strategic Colony: the Impact of US Policy on Micronesian Health and Culture*, 1984, Cultural Survival Inc., p. 72.

7 Kiste, op. cit.; Alcalay, 1986, op. cit.

8 Women Working for A Nuclear Free and Independent Pacific, ed., *Why Haven't You Known? Pacific Women Speak*, Oxford, Green Line, 1987, p. 14.

9 Alcalay, 1986, op. cit., p. 18.

10 Kiste, op. cit.

11 Lutz, op. cit., p. 3.

12 Marshall Islands Annual Report, 1981.

13 Senator Ataji Balos in conversation with Glenn Alcalay 1985.

14 House of Representatives Interior Sub-Committee on Public Lands and National Parks, 21 May 1984, pp. 190–91.

15 Quoted in the statement of Glenn Petersen, Associate Professor of Anthropology, Bernard M. Barch College, City University of New York to the US Senate Committee on Energy and Natural Resources, 24 May 1984.

16 US Senate Committee on Energy and Natural Resources, 24 May 1984.

17 ibid.

18 ibid.

19 Alcalay, 1986, op. cit.

20 US Senate Committee on Energy and Natural Resources, 24 May 1984.

21 Sworn affidavit of Tony de Brum to US Claims Court hearing a petition to lift the espousal clause, 20 April 1987.

22 ibid.

Chapter Nine

1 See Mary Kaldor, *The Disintegrating West*, London, Allen Lane, 1978, p. 153.

2 Glenn Alcalay, 'From Subsistence to USDA: Strategic Economic Dependence in Micronesia', paper for the Department of Anthropology, Rutgers University, New York, 1986.

3 Cited by Giff Johnson in 'Paying through the nose', *Islands Business Magazine*, August 1986.

4 Statement to UN Trusteeship Council, 25 May 1983.

5 Johnson, op. cit.

6 Richard Armitage, 'The United States' Role in the Pacific', paper to National Defense University, Pacific Symposium, Honolulu, 22 February 1985, p. 3; Peter Hayes, Lyuba Zarsky and Walden Bello, *American Lake: Nuclear Peril in the Pacific*, Harmondsworth, Penguin, 1986, p. 5.

7 R. Dingman, 'American Policy and Strategy in East Asia, 1898–1950: Creation of a Commitment', in US Air Force Academy, *The American Military and the Far East*, Proceedings of the 9th Military History Symposium, US GPO Washington DC, 1980; Hayes, Zarsky and Bello, op. cit., p. 18.

8 Hayes, Zarsky and Bello, op. cit., p. 22.

9 T. Etzold and J. Gaddis, ed., *Containment: Documents on American Policy and Strategy*, Columbia University Press, New York, 1978, p. 442; Hayes, Zarsky and Bello, op. cit., p. 36.

10 Daniel Ellsberg, 'Call to Mutiny', in *The Deadly Connection: Nuclear War and US Intervention*, ed. Joseph Gerson, American Friends Service Committee, Cambridge, Massachusetts, 1982, p. 19.

11 The six cases in the Asia–Pacific region were:

● Truman's press conference during which he warned that nuclear weapons were under consideration the day after Marines were surrounded by Chinese Communist troops at the Chosin reservoir, Korea, on 30 November 1930.

● Eisenhower's secret nuclear threats against China, to force and maintain a settlement in Korea, 1953.

● Secretary of State Dulles' secret offer to Prime Minister Bidault of three tactical nuclear weapons in 1954 to relieve French troops besieged by the Indochinese at Dienbienphu.

● Eisenhower's secret directive to the Joint Chiefs of Staff in 1958 to plan to use nuclear weapons against China if the Chinese Communists should attempt to invade the island of Quemoy, occupied by Chiang's troops, a few miles offshore mainland China.

● Public discussion in newspapers and in the Senate of the (true) reports that the White House had been advised of the possible necessity of nuclear weapons to defend Marines surrounded at Khe Sanh, Vietnam, in 1968.

● Nixon's secret threats of massive escalation, including possible use of nuclear weapons, conveyed to the North Vietnamese by Henry Kissinger, 1969–72.

12 *Sunday Times*, 20 October 1985.
13 A.V. Hughes, Permanent Secretary to the Finance Minister, Solomon Islands 1979, cited in *Transnational Brief*, November 1981.
14 R. Randolph, 'The Pacific Basin, Why the Region is Getting Special Attention from US', *San Francisco Chronicle*, 17 April 1985; Hayes, Zarsky and Bello, op. cit., p. 3.
15 *Sunday Times*, op. cit.
16 Gough Whitlam, *Transnational Brief*, November 1981, p. 4.
17 Admiral William J. Crowe, *Pacific Defense Reporter*, August 1985.
18 Alva M. Bowen, cited in *Washington Pacific Report*, vol. 4, no. 11, 1 March 1986.
19 'The Potential for Soviet Penetration of the South Pacific', US State Department 1984.
20 Admiral Crowe, op. cit.
21 Hayes, Zarsky and Bello, op. cit., chap. 16.
22 William Arkin, 'The Nuclear Balancing Act in the Pacific', in the *Bulletin of Atomic Scientists*, December 1983, p. 9.

Chapter Ten
1 Dr Dorothée Piermont, MEP, 'South Sea Paradise or Nuclear Nightmare?', background paper for resolution to the European Parliament, November 1985.
2 Cited by Michael King, *Death of the Rainbow Warrior*, Auckland, Penguin, 1986, p. 233.
3 Piermont, op. cit.
4 Cited by King, op. cit., p. 231.
5 'French Nuclear Testing at Moruroa', London, Greenpeace, 1985.
6 Piermont, op. cit.
7 ibid.
8 Piermont, op. cit.
9 Oscar Temaru, cited in speech by Dr Dorothée Piermont, MEP, 'French Nuclear Testing at Mururoa', to the Medical Campaign Against Nuclear Weapons, London, 11 April 1987.
10 Cited by Peter D. Jones, 'French Polynesia', unpublished paper, February 1981.
11 Cited by Joan Smith in *Clouds of Deceit: The Deadly Legacy of Britain's Bomb Tests*, London, Faber and Faber, 1985.
12 David Leigh and Paul Lashmar, 'Britain's Forgotten A-bomb Victims', *Observer*, 3 April 1983.

13 ibid.
14 ibid.
15 Derek Robinson, *Just Testing*, London, Collins Harvill, 1985, p. 191.
16 SIPRI *1987 Yearbook: World Armaments and Disarmaments*, Oxford, Oxford University Press, 1987, p. 55.
17 Owen Wilkes in *New Zealand Monthly Review*, June 1986, p. 7.
18 ibid.
19 Jim Falk, *Global Fission: The Battle over Nuclear Power*, Melbourne, Oxford University Press, 1982, p. 261.
20 ibid., p. 257.
21 UK Anti-Nuclear Campaign, *Uranium: The Plain Facts*, n.d.
22 Women Working for a Nuclear Free and Independent Pacific, ed., *Why Haven't You Known? Pacific Women Speak*, Oxford, Green Line, 1987, p. 30.
23 Silas Roberts, 'Evidence to the Ranger Inquiry', p. 9597.
24 Ranger Uranium Inquiry Second Report, p. 9.
25 Women Working for a Nuclear Free and Independent Pacific, ed., *Pacific Paradise: Nuclear Nightmare*, London, CND, 1987, p. 30.
26 *Why Haven't You Known?* op. cit., p. 29.
27 Republic of Nauru, 'Response to the panel of Experts' Report on Scientific and Technical Aspects of Sea Dumping of Radioactive Waste', paper to the London Dumping Convention, 3–7 June 1985.
28 ibid.
29 Table 2.4 in the International Maritime Organisation's document LDC g14, 24 June 1985.
30 South Pacific Commission, 'Radioactivity in the S. Pacific', Noumea, New Caledonia, November 1983, p. 170.
31 ibid., p. 174.

Chapter 11
1 David Pitt and Gordon Thompson, eds, *Nuclear Free Zones*, London, Croom Helm, 1987, p. 56.
2 Quoted in Women Working for a Nuclear Free and Independent Pacific, ed., *Pacific Paradise: Nuclear Nightmare*, London, CND, 1987.
3 *Liberation*, 2 October 1985; Ingrid A. Kircher, *The Kanaks of New Caledonia*, London, Minority Rights Group, 1986.
4 Australian Outlook, August 1982, p. 29.

5   National Council of Churches, 'Legislation Betrays The Treaty of Waitangi', Auckland, 1984.
6   National Council of Churches, op. cit.
7   ibid.
8   ibid.
9   Women Working for a Nuclear Free and Independent Pacific, ed., *Why Haven't You Known? Pacific Women Speak*, Oxford, Green Line, 1987, p. 35.
10 Minutes of the Nuclear Free and Independent Pacific Conference, Manila, November 1987.
11 Susanna Ounei, *For Kanak Independence, The Fight Against French Rule in New Caledonia*, Auckland, Labour Publishing Co-operative Society Ltd, 1985, p. 4.
12 'Toward Kanaky' Newsletter, Auckland, November 1987.
13 *Guardian*, London, 15 September 1987.
14 ibid.
15 *Valeurs Actuelles*, 17 April 1985; Ingrid A. Kircher, op. cit.
16 Sue Rabbitt Roff, *New Caledonia: Decolonisation and Denuclearisation in the Pacific*, Third World Quarterly, London, April 1986.
17 *Le Monde*, 13 January 1985; Ingrid A. Kircher, op. cit.
18 Wellington Pacific Report, October 1987.
19 Jane Dibblin, 'Buddies in Fiji', *New Statesman*, 29 May 1987.
20 NFIP Conference, Manila, Philippines, November 1987.
21 *Protect Kaho'olawe 'Ohana*, leaflet issued in 1984.
22 'Labour in the Pacific Islands', *Transnational Brief*, November 1981.
23 ibid.
24 *Guardian* 23 April 1987, 'Court Halts Nuclear Test Compensation'.
25 *Guardian* 14 Sept. 1987, 'US Court to Hear Atom Test Claims'.
26 Glenn Alcalay, 'Let US Seek Peace Rather Than War', *Marshall Islands Journal*, 18 April 1986.
27 *Guardian* 14 Sept. 1987, 'US Court to Hear Atom Test Claims'.
28 *National Geographic Special*, 'Nuclear Exiles', shown on 25 October 1987 on WTBS (cable channel 8).
29 *San Diego Union*, 5 October 1987.
30 Ingrid A. Kircher, op. cit.
31 French PM Pierre Messmer, London, quoted in 'Toward Kanaky', op. cit.

Chapter 12

1 June Jordan, *On Call*, London, Pluto Press, 1980, p. 45.

2 Women Working for a Nuclear Free and Independent Pacific, ed., *Why Haven't You Known? Pacific Women Speak*, Oxford, Green Line, 1987.

3 Quoted in Joanna Macy, *Despair and Personal Power in the Nuclear Age*, Philadelphia, New Society Publishers, 1983, p. 24.

4 ibid., p. 13.

5 ibid., p. 13.

6 ibid., p. 15.

7 ibid., p. 13.

8 ibid., p. 51.

9 ibid., p. 23.

10 *New Zealand Women's Weekly*, 14 October 1985.

11 *Half Life*, Dennis O'Rourke, Australia, 1985.

12 Audre Lorde, *Sister Outsider*, Trumansburg, New York, The Crossing Press, 1984, p. 113.

13 Jenny Bourne, *Jewish Feminism and the Search for Identity*, London, Spare Rib, November 1987.

14 Pratibha Parmar, *Other Kinds of Dreams – Interview with June Jordan*, *Spare Rib*, November 1987.

15 Bernice Johnson Reagan, 'Coalition Politics' from *Home Girls: A Black Feminist Anthology*, ed. Barbara Smith, New York, Kitchen Table, Women of Color Press, 1983.

16 June Jordan, *Other Kinds of Dreams*, op. cit.

17 For another discussion of some of the issues in this chapter see also Teresa Thornhill, 'Other People's Revolutions: British Feminists and Northern Ireland', *Trouble and Strife*, Norwich, Summer, 1985.

Index

293